Saving London's Abandoned Babies

Saving London's Abandoned Babies

Thomas Coram's Foundling Hospital

Gudrun Limbrick

First published in Great Britain in 2025 by
Pen & Sword History
An imprint of Pen & Sword Books Limited
Yorkshire – Philadelphia

Copyright © Gudrun Limbrick 2025

ISBN 978 1 39903 547 7

The right of Gudrun Limbrick to be identified as
Author of this Work has been asserted by her in accordance
with the Copyright, Designs and Patents Act 1988.

A CIP catalogue record for this book is
available from the British Library.

All rights reserved. No part of this book may be reproduced, transmitted, downloaded, decompiled or reverse engineered in any form or by any means, electronic or mechanical including photocopying, recording or by any information storage and retrieval system, without permission from the Publisher in writing. No part of this book may be used or reproduced in any manner for the purpose of training artificial intelligence technologies or systems.

Typeset by Mac Style
Printed in the UK by CPI Group (UK) Ltd, Croydon, CR0 4YY.

MIX
Paper | Supporting responsible forestry
FSC® C013604

The Publisher's authorised representative in the EU for product safety is Authorised Rep Compliance Ltd., Ground Floor, 71 Lower Baggot Street, Dublin D02 P593, Ireland.
www.arccompliance.com

For a complete list of Pen & Sword titles please contact

PEN & SWORD BOOKS LIMITED
47 Church Street, Barnsley, South Yorkshire, S70 2AS, England
E-mail: enquiries@pen-and-sword.co.uk
Website: www.pen-and-sword.co.uk
or
PEN AND SWORD BOOKS
1950 Lawrence Road, Havertown, PA 19083, USA
E-mail: uspen-and-sword@casematepublishers.com
Website: www.penandswordbooks.com

For my husband.

Contents

About the Author   x
Acknowledgements   xi
Prelude: Elinor's Story   xii
Introduction   xvii

Part I: A City of Contrast   1
Arriving In London   1
Bills of Mortality   5
Punishing Poverty   9
Fallen Women and Their Bastards   13
Thomas's View   16

Part II: A Man to Save the Babies   19
What Made Thomas Coram?   19
A Childhood In the Old World   19
The Pull of the New World   23
Setting Up Home   24

Part III: The Quest   32
Looking Back to the New World   32
Finding Support for the Hospital   36
Ladies of Charity   46
The Darling Project   59
The General Plan   67

Part IV: The Hospital Opens   82
The First Children   82
The Early Days   88
Country Nurses   90
Foundling Hospitals in the Rest of the World   93

Part V: Great Losses   96
Losing Control   96
Keeping the Babies Alive   100

The New Building	105
A Lottery	108
Fame and Fortune	109
Thomas's Death	117
Part VI: Life in the Hospital	**125**
Thomas's Ideas for the Hospital	125
A Structured Life	128
Food	132
Clothes	135
Education	137
Work	140
Health in the Hospital	143
Part VII: Leaving the Hospital	**149**
Escape	149
Apprenticeships	150
Death	152
Reclamation	153
Part VIII: A Terrible Experiment	**160**
General Reception	160
How Many Babies?	165
The End of General Reception	171
Too Great a Price	173
Dublin Foundling Hospital	175
Taking the Strain of General Reception	177
Life in the Hospital After General Reception	179
The Hospital's Influence on Its Neighbours	185
Part IX: The Legacy of Thomas Coram	**189**
The Nineteenth Century	189
Parallels With Sir Josiah Mason's Orphanage	193
A State Response	195
Was It Just Too Soon?	197
A Personal Legacy	201
Postscript: Elinor's story	205
Notes	207
Bibliography	212
Index	214

Thomas Coram. Line engraving by A. Bannerman after W. Hogarth. (*Wellcome Collection*)

About the Author

After achieving a Master's degree in Research and Social Policy from the University of Birmingham, following on from a Bachelor's degree from the University of Oxford, Gudrun embarked on a career in researching hard-to-reach communities. She began researching people's memories of children's homes in Birmingham and after discovering the impact on individuals who knew nothing about their past spent in residential care, she established a website in 2011 to share information and memories about former orphanages, children's homes and other institutions for children. She has now written several books on memories of children's homes. She continues to work on making as much information publicly available as possible as a means of helping those who spent all or part of their childhoods in children's homes understand, come to terms with and remember what happened to them as children.

www.formerchildrenshomes.org.uk

Acknowledgements

I am indebted to many people who gave me practical assistance in creating this book, not least, the team from Pen & Sword. I am very grateful for the time and talents of Commissioning Editor, Sarah-Beth Watkins; Copy editor, Sarah Hodder; Production Editor, Laura Hirst; Marketing Handler, Lucy May; Proofreader, Frances Allenby; Book Designer, Matthew Blurton and Jacket Designer, Jon Wilkinson.

Huge thanks are also due to my family and friends whose support and patience always keep me moving forwards.

Prelude: Elinor's Story

> On Saturday, 12 March 1752, people were invited to bring children to the gates of the Foundling Hospital in London. 91 babies were brought in the hope that there would be a place for them in the hospital. Eleven boys and nine girls were admitted by lot in the presence of several of the governors. The remaining 71 babies were turned away.[1] Elinor is fictional although the scenario is real.

It was a bitterly cold Saturday afternoon. She had the baby, whom she had quietly named after her own father, John, against her skin. Her dress, shawl and a blanket covered them both. As the only water she could find was ice-cold, she hadn't managed to wash either of them properly since his birth and her dress felt crusty against her legs. John whimpered slightly. She readjusted him so that her nipple was fully in his mouth once again. He felt too cold. She could see there were already at least two dozen women in front of the hospital, each carrying a baby. There was little conversation between them – the crying of babies was too loud. Some of the women were sat on the ground. Two were lying on the ground trying to rest but sleep was next to impossible in the cold with the noise of babies crying. One woman was crouched on the floor, her baby lying next to her feet. He looked to have no life left in him.

At length, more women gathered and all shuffled to make room for each other. At 8 pm, carriages pulled up alongside them and well-dressed gentlemen and ladies stood a little apart from the women who must have numbered nearly a hundred, each holding a young baby. Most of the babies and their mothers were in distress. Many were crying. All shivered in the cold.

Onlookers, standing in the shelter of their carriages, wore fine clothes, their jewellery sparkling in the light of the torches on the walls.

For Elinor, it had not been easy to get here. She was weak with hunger and the walk with John had been very difficult. She had worked in a large house near Cavendish Square as a domestic. Sarah, the other girl there, had told her to come here. 'Stay out of the workhouse', she had warned. 'My Aggie was there. They say it is for the best but it ain't.'

As soon as the master of the house had seen that Elinor was going to have a baby, he told Elinor to leave. That was several weeks ago. Sarah had shared some food with her, handing it to Elinor at the back door. This is what had kept her from the poorhouse.

At last, a well-dressed gentleman came through the gates, and in a loud voice he welcomed the men and women of the carriages, explaining to them the proceedings they were about to witness. The women with babes in arms were instructed to arrange themselves in a more orderly fashion and a rough queue formed, although each determinedly guarded their position, refusing to allow another to step in before them.

The gentleman was handed a large bag of wooden balls. The first woman stepped forward, she put her hand in the bag, and everyone stared at the ball she pulled out. It was black. Unable to hide her despair, she wailed loudly for a number of seconds. There was muttering by the carriage that it was now another woman's turn. She must retain her dignity. She was shown a basket into which she returned the black ball and she turned away with her baby.

A second woman picked a black ball. And a third. Elinor squeezed John tightly. She had held him there, at her breast, for eight days. He had stoically and calmly clenched his tiny fists as his lips mashed at her nipple. She was astounded that she had made this little person, overjoyed when his eyes caught hers. She was so proud to be his mother. She felt it was going to break her heart to see him go, but that there was no way he could stay.

It was ten long minutes before she was near the front of the queue. The woman now at the head of the queue, Elinor noticed, was different to the rest. Her clothes were fancy, her hair neat. She was not suckling the baby but holding it awkwardly, slightly away from her body. A well-dressed man from the carriages stepped forward and whispered into the gentleman's ear. The gentleman nodded. When the woman put her hand out to pick a ball, the governor instead selected one for her and placed it into her hand. It was white. She was ushered into the gate. Elinor had heard that this was also where the wealthy society disposed of their bastard children and she was sure that this was what she had just witnessed.

Finally, it was Elinor's turn. Her hand was shaking as she reached into the bag, knocking the wooden balls against each other. Having been quiet all this time, John began to cry loudly. Perhaps he was aware that something of significance was happening in his life. Elinor grasped a ball, but it slipped out between her fingers and she fumbled for another.

She pulled it out of the bag and stared at it trying to take in what colour it was. It wasn't white but it also wasn't black. She looked up at the gentleman. 'It is red!' he shouted out to the expectant onlookers. And in a quieter voice he said to Elinor, 'You might be lucky'. He gestured that Elinor should go inside.

She stumbled slightly as her legs were trembling. The governor held her arm to steady her and took the ball from her hand. He put it in the basket. They were nearly all black balls in the basket she noticed as she glanced down – hers was the only red. But there were still many women waiting to take their turn.

She was taken into a bare room and told to sit on a bench. It was much warmer than it had been outside but still she shivered. John noticed the change, however, and quickly settled to sleep. With only the two of them in the room, it was suddenly quiet after the noise of so many women and babies. There were babies crying and people talking some way away, but she could still hear John's sleeping breaths. She didn't remember hearing it before. It was a beautiful sound and she sat, barely wanting to breathe herself, so that all she could hear was John. But her peace didn't last for long.

Another woman carrying a baby came in, and then another shortly afterwards. The third woman had news. 'You wouldn't think it was possible', she whispered. 'But this is the second time I got a red un. I was here last month and it was red then.' She explained to the other two that the red ball meant they were spares. If another baby with a white ball got sick, they'd pick again and whoever got the white ball goes in. 'We've just got to wait', she advised them.

This was news indeed. She had no idea how long she was sitting in the room. The women were left alone to wait. They could hear voices outside the room

Receiving day at the Foundling Hospital. (*Wellcome Collection*)

Prelude: Elinor's Story   xv

but could not make out what was being said. More women came in now and again and began to fill up the benches. Some were upset, some angry, most sat quietly nursing their babies hidden under the folds of their clothes and wraps. Some talked to each other in whispers. Elinor still did not know if she would be leaving with or without her son.

Elinor and the two women she sat with talked with each other as they nursed their babies. They had all been in service before they had their babies and each had no hope of getting work while they had a baby with them. Grace was the oldest, perhaps in her twenties, and it was clear that she was very sick. She had a terrible rasping cough which meant her baby was constantly shaken awake. With each cough, her baby, held tightly across her chest, scrunched up her face. Eyes tight shut and mouth open, she let out a cry, little hands squeezed into a tiny fist. Grace put her hand on the baby's bare head and the baby quietened until Grace's next coughing fit. Grace wasn't crying. She seemed too deflated to cry. Bessie was different. She talked and she cried. There was barely a time when she was silent.

She also knew a lot. A lot more than Elinor or Grace. She said each baby had to have a token – some little thing that the baby would keep with it so if Elinor went to fetch him one day, she could point him out. 'They'll change his name see', she explained. 'He'll have a new name by next week so see you can't just ask for John. They won't know him, but if you give him a keepsake, they'll know the keepsake.'

Elinor hadn't thought before that she would see John again, nor had she thought that she wouldn't. That was too hard to think about. She just knew that she couldn't keep him now. What happened to him next was something she hadn't been able to consider. She was only trying to get him safe for now. But she had no token, she had nothing to give him, and the thought that this would mean there was no hope of ever seeing him again filled her with sudden panic. She had nothing with her. Bessie said her shawl was too big and too dirty for a token and Elinor would catch her death without it. Grace had a perfectly clean handkerchief pressed into a neat little square. Bessie had an old hazelnut to give her baby.

A governor of the hospital came into the room as they were looking for another something for John to have as his keepsake. The governor asked the women to be quiet and then explained that there was one space for another baby so there was to be another lottery between them. He had a small bag. Grace picked first, another red ball. 'You wait here', the governor said. 'That is another chance for you.' Then it was Elinor's turn. She was crying now, deep tears she couldn't stop. It was a white ball. 'This way', the governor said and directed her towards the door. She stood for a second, rooted to the spot. Her legs wouldn't take her. Bessie slipped something into her hand. 'His keepsake', she said. 'Your John must have a token.'

She followed the governor into another room where a group of men stood by a table with a large book. One of the men asked her for John. She lifted her shawl, pulled her dress across, and pulled the tiny naked boy off her breast. He immediately scrunched up his face and began to cry. She handed him to the man who looked him over and then handed him to another who lay the screaming bundle onto the table next to the book and carefully examined him. He felt John with his hands and then looked at the bare skin of his belly and his legs. The second man said something to the first and took John out of the room. The first man wrote something down on the paper. 'Do you want to leave a token?' he asked Elinor.

She opened her hand to look at what Bessie had given her. It was her hazelnut. Such a tiny thing was such an enormous gift. The man took it, looked at it and shook his head. He glanced up at a clock and noted something down in the book. 'You can go', he said to Elinor. 'The baby is staying here.'

She stood for a second, unclear of what she should do. The man gestured to the door behind her.

'His name is John', she stuttered through tears. 'After my father.' 'John', she repeated. 'He's a good baby.' The man took her arm and turned her to the door.

Out in the cold night air, the tears rolled down her face. There were women and their babies still by the gate. Perhaps they did not know the lottery was over. Or maybe they just didn't have anywhere else to go. Elinor leant on the wall near them, and let the crying take over. Her sense of loss was overwhelming. The women cried together. And John? He was already fast asleep in the arms of one of the Foundling Hospital nurses.

Introduction

In Brunswick Square, in the affluent West End of London, there is an unassuming statue of a man, Thomas Coram, under which is the legend 'Pioneer of the cause of Child Welfare'. Next to the statue is a playground which permits adults only if they are accompanied by a child. The playground is called Coram Fields, dedicated to Thomas Coram, and has been there since 1936.

So who was this man who played such a significant role in child welfare? An academic? A social worker? A politician? He was, in fact, a poorly educated shipbuilder, a man who had nothing to do with children and their care.

He had a remarkable career – a life aboard ships which found him emigrating across the Atlantic, gave him hats for life, got him involved as a cause of the American Revolution and saw him shot at by a man trying to kill him. But it was a career which did not make him wealthy.

Thomas Coram's beginnings were humble at best and the passage of his life had left him poorer, not richer. He had no money to pay for the welfare of children. And he had no children of his own. He and his wife were childless despite a long marriage.

This is the remarkable story of a man who, knowing nothing about child welfare, spent more than twenty years setting up the first foundling hospital in London. His motivation for such a quest? It was the simple act of walking to work through London. Each day he saw babies abandoned on the dung heaps of the city. Some of the babies were dead, sometimes he witnessed them dying. Sadly, this was a common sight in the city in the early eighteenth century and hundreds of people had walked by without doing anything to help. For

The statue of Thomas Coram on Brunswick Square.[1] (*Source Geograph*)

Thomas, however, the terrible sight stirred something inside him and he decided that, despite his inexperience, he had to do something. This is what made Thomas stand out from everyone else. He was as flawed as anyone else – stubborn, argumentative, perhaps a little intolerant. His ordinary flaws made him human but his quest to give these babies and their mothers a chance in life was something very special indeed.

He decided that he was going to start an organisation that would take in these babies – *The Hospital for the Maintenance and Education of Exposed and Deserted Young Children* – which later became known more simply as The Foundling Hospital. He tested the tolerance of society with his plans to welcome illegitimate children in the same way as orphans or any other child. His hospital welcomed the wealthy as well as the destitute and treated them both the same. He went against the grain by making women the target of his lobbying campaign long before they had the legal equality needed to run his organisation. He withstood having doors closed in his face and persevered until princes and prime ministers willingly stood by his side. He raised the equivalent of millions of pounds armed only with a battered notebook and his personal conviction that this was the right thing to do.

The hospital opened its doors in 1741 to give London's destitute children fresh countryside air in a location that is now filled with aspirational Bloomsbury residences.

Thomas's hospital was not a hospital in the sense we know hospitals today. It was not for people who were sick. Instead, the hospital was there to provide basic care (or hospitality) – a roof over the child's head, food and preparation for a working life ahead. Effective medicine for the treatment of disease and infection was barely in existence in the early eighteenth century. Far from welcoming poorly children, in the absence of medical care, Thomas knew that he had to try and exclude any children who were sick or ailing from the hospital so that they did not infect the other children. It was thought unlikely they would have lived long enough to benefit from what the hospital had to offer.

The Foundling Hospital was effectively the first dedicated charity for children in England, paving the way for the many thousands of children's charities that have followed since. As a first foray into residential childcare for babies, it effectively provided a blueprint that, in the philanthropic era of the nineteenth century, the Victorians picked up and ran with. As a residential children's home, it functioned for two hundred years until the 1950s, with thousands of children spending their childhoods there. And the hospital's obsession with record-keeping means that we have an unrivalled archive of the entirety of the hospital's existence. No other London institution provides such an insight into institutional life in the eighteenth century.

But for Thomas the shipbuilder, it was not all plain sailing by any means. Setting up a hospital of this size and scope in a country with little experience of such a venture was fraught with problems. Many of the children taken in died before they were able to leave. But, despite this, women fought each other to get their babies taken into the hospital, such was the desperation of women who had given birth to illegitimate children or who were trapped in poverty. The Foundling Hospital, for generations, was the only place for their children to go.

About This History

A great deal has been written about the Foundling Hospital, such is the fascination with it and the man behind it. This history is an attempt to go back to the basics, to separate the man from the legend he has become and tell the story of the institution behind the headlines, through the eyes of those who knew it. The primary sources of information for this are documents and news stories which were themselves written while the institution was in London.

There are several key texts written in the eighteenth century when the work of the Foundling Hospital was still in full swing. These were written by the following men who were writing from their own perspective but had strong links with the Foundling Hospital.

Dr Richard Brocklesby
Private Virtue and publick Spirit Display'd. In a succinct Essay on the Character of Capt. Thomas Coram. 1751.
It was written for the occasion of Thomas Coram's funeral and was then reproduced in full by Brownlow in 1865. Although it was initially published anonymously, it has since been reliably attributed to Dr Brocklesby.

Written so soon after Thomas's death, it has become tantamount to an obituary and the key stand alone document in understanding Thomas's history and the Foundling Hospital's early years. Dr Brocklesby, a practising physician, was a friend of Thomas Coram but also had close links with governors of the Foundling Hospital. When Thomas needed help, it was Brocklesby along with Sampson Gideon, a governor of the hospital at the time, who arranged a pension for him. From the details in the obituary, it certainly appears that Brocklesby referred to governors for information at the time and the clear honesty in his tone and text (noting that Thomas was stubborn, poorly educated and largely unsuccessful in his career) makes this a text which carries the authority of an authentic re-telling of Thomas's history.

Jonas Hanway
A Candid Historical Account of the Hospital for the Reception of Exposed and Deserted Young Children representing the Present Plan of it as productive of many Evils, and not adapted to the Genius and Happiness of this Nation. 1759.
Jonas Hanway was a merchant who became a writer, traveller and a social reformer. He was perhaps an eccentric being the first man in London to use an umbrella (such things were for women only) and a fierce opponent of tea drinking. He blamed the problems of London's foundlings at least partly on tea drinking.[2] This, at times, critical review of the Foundling Hospital in 1759 (which was published anonymously) caused him to be pushed into resigning from his job with the *Literary Magazine*. Perhaps surprisingly, Hanway was himself a governor of the Foundling Hospital from the 1750s and rose to the position of vice-president.

Sir Thomas Bernard
An Account of the Hospital for the Maintenance and Education of exposed and deserted young Children. 1796. This was written anonymously but thought to be by Sir Bernard.

An Account of the Foundling Hospital, in London, for the maintenance and education of exposed and deserted young Children. 1799.
Sir Thomas Bernard, the son of a baronet, had an esteemed career in law. He was the treasurer of the Foundling Hospital between 1795 and 1806 and later became vice-president. Like Thomas, after he died he was buried under the chapel of the Foundling Hospital.

Nineteenth-Century Biographers

John Brownlow
Chronicles of the Foundling Hospital including Memoirs of Captain Coram. 1847.
The History and Objects of the Foundling Hospital with a memoir of the Founder. 1865.
Brownlow was himself a foundling, having been taken in by the hospital in 1800. Once there, he did not leave, taking on employment in the hospital as soon as he was old enough. He began as a clerk and rose to the roles of secretary and treasurer in the middle of the eighteenth century. It is thought that he was perhaps the inspiration behind Charles Dickens's character, also called John Brownlow, in *Oliver Twist*. The fictional Brownlow was a kindly man who helped Oliver and ultimately adopted him. As both a foundling in the hospital and an employee, there can be few people who would have known the Foundling Hospital better than Brownlow.

Hamilton Andrews Hill
Thomas Coram in Boston and Taunton. 1892.
Like Thomas, Hill migrated from England to Massachusetts, Hill leaving London in 1841. His biography is based on meticulous research of the court records relating to Thomas and his Massachusetts neighbours.

There are now many biographies and discussions of Thomas Coram and of the Foundling Hospital but the following are worthy of particular note.
   Being modern, these lack the personal connections with the London Hospital and Thomas but nonetheless have each brought, through meticulous research, new information to light.

Rev. Herbert Fuller Bright Compston
Thomas Coram: Churchman, Empire builder and Philanthropist. 1918.
Compston's biography is very much written from the standpoint of a religious man as one would expect from a member of the clergy. This is an aspect of Thomas's life downplayed by many of Thomas's earlier biographers. Compston also includes the results of his rigorous research.

Gillian Wagner
Thomas Coram, Gent. 1668–1751. The Boydell Press, 2004.
Another example of rigorous research is brought by Wagner in her incredibly detailed biography which includes comprehensive research into almost every aspect of Thomas's life, unearthing previously unknown details about Thomas.

DS Allin
The Early Years of the Foundling Hospital 1739/41 – 1773. 2010. Privately published.
Allin has analysed the data held by and about the Foundling Hospital to produce a comprehensive statistical description of every aspect of the Foundling Hospital. Allin chose not to publish the work but to distribute it to those who wanted it so that it could be freely used to add to our knowledge of the Foundling Hospital.

Eighteenth-Century Spelling

There are significant differences in how text was written in the eighteenth century to how it is written now. I have chosen to use the original spellings, punctuation and capitalisation when quoting from seventeenth-century texts.
   While the name of the hospital was officially called the Hospital for the Maintenance and Education of Exposed and Deserted Young Children, it is referred to throughout as the Foundling Hospital which was the name most commonly used for it.

Part I

A City of Contrast

'… every repulsive lineament of poverty, every loathsome indication of filth, rot, and garbage.'

Charles Dickens, 1837[1]

Arriving In London

Thomas Coram, 35 years old, moved to London in 1703 having spent the past ten years living in the New World, in the new English settlements of the east coast of North America. The majority of his earlier years he had spent at sea. He had with him his wife, Eunice, whom he had met in the New World. After marrying in 1700, they had settled in a house Thomas had built in Dighton, near Taunton in Massachusetts. Next to their house was a small shipyard that Thomas had established.

The journey from Dighton to London would have taken the couple several weeks with most of the time spent on a large, creaking wooden sailing boat. Thomas had been around boats all his life and had first gone to sea when he was 11. He had made the journey across the Atlantic from the Americas to England many times. For Eunice, born in Boston, Massachusetts as a direct descendant of those first English settlers in the New World, the journey was no doubt a first, and probably a very uncomfortable first. They would not have been able to afford what passed for luxury travel, and seasickness was rife. Food was dried, water was stale, sleep was difficult, and the flea-ridden rats were everywhere. Her life in the big family house in Boston with their domestic servants was already a world away.

While it was a relief to set foot on dry land in London after weeks at sea, the city was going to be a very big change from the wide-open spaces of Massachusetts.

In the New World, empty land was still plentiful and everywhere was sparsely populated. Boston, as the big town of the area, had a population of less than 7000 people. Dighton was only a small village and Thomas had deliberately built his house and shipyard on a side of the river where few others had settled. By contrast, London was a tightly packed city which was growing massively and already had in excess of half a million inhabitants in a built-up area of a little more than a square mile located almost entirely south of the River Thames.

London was, however, the perfect place for the couple who were looking to make money and keep busy. It was a city of genuine opportunity and a place where entrepreneurialism was actively encouraged. It was, in this sense, a city made for a man such as Thomas.

The Industrial Revolution in England was in its infancy when Thomas arrived. The next hundred years would see Britain take a central role in the global Industrial Revolution which would completely transform England's towns and cities but, already, in 1703, there had begun a move away from work on the land in many areas, with people arriving in London in pursuit of the work and the wealth they had heard would be available for them in trade and manufacturing. When Thomas was born, there were approximately 400,000 living in London; when he set up home there with Eunice, this had increased by around 200,000 people.

And the last half a century had seen much redevelopment. The city had been beset with disaster. The Great Plague of 1665 had killed close to 100,000 Londoners. The Great Fire of 1666 had wiped out an estimated 13,000 of its buildings[2] and large tracts of London had since been rebuilt. In the wake of such tragedy and disaster had come major redevelopment in the city. Areas of new buildings and wider roads were now standing alongside areas of narrow cobbled alleyways and rundown, poor housing.

Another disaster befell the city in November 1703. Thomas and Eunice, on their long journey from the New World, had been lucky to avoid being in the midst of it. The Great Storm was a cyclone of unprecedented ferociousness which brought high winds and flooding to much of the Midlands and the south of England. London was particularly affected.

The vagaries of the weather now generate thousands of media stories every year but this is a relatively new development, and certainly unheard of in Thomas's time. However, the Great Storm was so devastating that it became the first weather event to generate large-scale media interest with all the local and national newspapers of the day covering it in detail. Thousands of people died in the storm and many houses were destroyed. In London, 2000 chimneys were said to have been damaged. Hundreds of ships were crushed by the great tides or blown entirely off course by the wind and the swell. On the Thames, ships were crushed together including 300 ships of the Royal Navy which were destroyed as a result. Thomas, an experienced ship builder, no doubt relieved that he himself had not been a victim of the storm, arrived in London at a time when his skills were in high demand to help the re-building of London's shipping fleets.

Key to London's prosperity was the city's growing importance at the heart of the evolving Empire. The British Empire was about to take a central role in the world. Britain itself was created in 1706 following the Treaty of Union between Scotland and England but much of the groundwork had already been laid. European countries had been 'discovering' the Americas and Africa and were already fighting over land ownership and lucrative trading rights with many of these fights taking place at sea. Having seen the economic benefits to Europe of the natural resources in the New World and having dismissed the indigenous populations as 'uncivilised' and thus suitable for exploitation, London was taking a significant interest and already profiting from it.

The slave trade was growing hugely which had enormous impact on the wealth of London. At this stage, its cruelty had not gained anything like widespread recognition and understanding and so the plight of Africans and others who were taken from their homeland and forced to work the lands of the Caribbean and the New World was going ahead entirely untethered. And London was very much at the centre of slave-taking, both in terms of profiting from the wealth generated by the slave trade and also in terms of slave-taking itself. In the eighteenth century, more than 12,000 journeys to take slaves from West Africa were embarked on from England and British ports overseas. More than a quarter of these left from London.[3] These slave-taking expeditions did not end until 1807 when legislation outlawed them. It is impossible to imagine that most of the wealth gained by the merchants and aristocrats of London while Thomas was there was not connected to the barbaric trade in slaves, either directly or indirectly.

London was growing so quickly and amassing wealth through the rapidly developing Empire. It was, therefore, not only a benefactor of the Empire's activities but a driving force in its continued growth as the city's demand for goods increased rapidly. London was about to rival Paris, the largest city in Europe, in terms of wealth and to overtake the highly intellectual and fashionable French city in population size. These were indeed very exciting times for London.

The London that Thomas and Eunice found themselves in had some grand buildings, befitting its standing at the heart of international trade and power. Thomas would have seen buildings such as Westminster Abbey, The Tower of London, Kensington Palace and the Palace of Westminster. St Paul's Cathedral, when Thomas arrived, was in the process of being completed having been destroyed in the Great Fire of 1666. Buckingham Palace was a new-build – a large townhouse which had recently been finished. And there were aspirational areas such as Mayfair with large grand houses accommodating London's aristocrats.

Most of London, however, was not grand and spacious. Instead, it was dark, crowded and steeped in poverty.

While the wealthy lived in large townhouses in wider streets, perhaps with promenades and parkland for walking and travelling in their carriages, poor working people lived in small, crowded tenements and houses, perhaps an entire family in one room, on narrow cobbled streets. The Thames in London was crossed by just one stone bridge – the original London Bridge. A bridge which itself was crowded with houses and small traders.

Much of London was criss-crossed by rough, narrow streets packed with small wooden buildings. By contrast with modern cities, it was a place with no cars, no electricity, no concrete and no sewerage system. Piss pots were emptied out onto the streets and human and animal waste was shovelled onto dunghills. Open cess pits flowed out in heavy rain. Flies and rats were everywhere. For those new to the city, it was an assault on all their senses – it was busy, noisy and certainly smelly. There were people in front of every door, on every corner, in every space, shouting for people to buy their wares, sharpen their knives, try their milk, use their furniture. The sounds of wheels and hooves on the cobbles was constant as carriages and carts went by, and the smell of the people, the smoke from thousands of fires and the human and animal sewage was sickening.

There was no underground sewerage system – the Thames was used as both the receptacle for sewage and the source of water for drinking and washing. There were no bathrooms, only chamber pots which were emptied onto the streets where people walked, talked, plied their trades and, when times were hard, made their beds. People of wealth paid others to bring water to them for drinking, cooking and washing. This water was carried to them from the Thames.

Oil lights were yet to be common as street lighting, instead candle lanterns had to be lit with a naked flame at dusk each night. Clever travellers carried their own lanterns to light their way. But a candle is a poor source of light. The streets were at best gloomy, at worst dark and dangerous places to be at night.

It was a place where illness and infection went largely unchecked and law and order was unlawful and disordered.

With so many people crowded into a small space, London was a place of crime. Small-scale crimes such as pickpocketing and petty theft were common. The justice system, based on local magistrates, was inconsistent, unpredictable, inadequate and harsh. Public hangings were common and proved to be popular spectacles with crowds gathering to get a good view of the grisly happenings.

There was no formal police force – Westminster's Bow Street Runners, London's first formal police officers, were not in place until 1749. Night watchmen patrolled the better parts of town where the parishes could afford to pay them but they stayed well away from the poor areas where there was danger on every corner and no-one to pay their wages. Without a police service, people took matters into their own hands, joining vigilante forces and paying thief-takers to bring about order. More often than not, these created even more disorder and added to the violent crime with fighting between rival vigilante groups.

It was in 1725, during Thomas's time in London, that the notorious Jonathan Wild was executed after it was discovered that he was not only a paid thief-taker but also ran a gang of thieves, profiting both from their thefts and from handing them in as thieves. It was not, however, merely Jonathan who was corrupt, but the whole law and order system in London.

Bills of Mortality

While the Great Plague that killed thousands of Londoners happened two years before Thomas was born, the rapid spread of illness through the overcrowded streets of London remained a big problem in Thomas's time with outbreaks of diseases such as typhus, dysentery, measles, the plague, flu, smallpox and tuberculosis killing many Londoners.

There was a notable fascination in death and attempts were being made to collect data about the numbers and causes of death which were printed in the newspapers. They were often given the top news slot, such was the interest in them. These lists of deaths were called the Bills of Mortality and were compiled by parish clerks in London counting the numbers of christenings and burials and noting the causes of the deaths.

According to the Bills of Mortality of the times, the most common deaths in London were convulsions, consumption, fever, 'teeth', and smallpox.

Convulsions, the leading cause of death, were not necessarily fits as we would understand it today but it was a generic term to mean infant deaths.[4] The other common causes of death – consumption (now known as tuberculosis or TB) and smallpox were both transmitted through coughing and sneezing. Deaths reported as being caused by fever could have been caused by typhus (spread by fleas or mites) or perhaps an infected injury. 'Teeth' as a cause of death may have included infections from tooth disease or damage but also death during teething for infants.

Other causes of death reported included 'purples' (probably typhus), St Anthony's fire (believed to be a spiritual issue needing divine intervention to prevent death), planet-struck (a sudden paralysing disease thought to be caused by the influence of a planet) and worms. Execution and murder were also listed as causes, and some were simply 'found dead' or 'starv'd' or 'shipwreck'd'.

These Bills of Mortality, although inevitably flawed as medical knowledge and terminology has changed so much since they were compiled, give a great insight into London health. Infectious diseases were common which is unsurprising given the close quarters in which people lived but the big epidemics of cholera, for example, were yet to happen – the water of the Thames was not yet sufficiently polluted. Such was the extent of the lack of understanding of the link between clean water and health that the public toilets were built directly over the Thames so that, when used, human waste dropped straight into the water below, even as it was being collected for drinking water just metres downstream. The major outbreaks of tuberculosis and smallpox did not take place until the nineteenth century. London, albeit already an unhealthy place, was very much at the beginnings of its unhealth.

The Bills also demonstrate the extent of mortality with, consistently, more deaths than christenings listed in most parishes. For example, in 1725, 26,000 people were buried, while 19,000 were listed as having been christened. Christenings were far more common in the eighteenth century than they are today and people only remained unchristened in relatively unusual circumstances. However, the count of christenings was very much an underestimate, even then, of the birth rate.

Some Bills of Mortality included a record of the ages of those who died. For example, of the deaths reported in 1732, more than half were aged under 2. This brought the average life expectancy down to less than 40 years old. For those who survived childhood, around 50 or 60 is probably the age most could expect to reach.

It is certainly true to say, however, that the parish churches in London were kept busy with burials, with many being buried in unmarked pauper graves shared with their unfortunate neighbours. The graveyards were regularly full to bursting with only those who had money able to afford a burial spot of their own. The poor were often buried in mass graves, waiting until it reached full capacity before it was finally covered for good.

The lack of medical knowledge meant that the plague had been able to rip through the population of England unchecked in 1665 and, in the following decades, smaller outbreaks continued to have a terrible impact on communities.

Without adequate scientific understanding, deaths and illness were explained as God's revenge for wrongdoing; or a lack of balance between the four 'humours' of the body – blood, yellow bile, black bile and phlegm. Others put illness and death down to 'bad air'. While this in some ways mirrors what we now understand as airborne pollution, the belief was based on powers much more ephemeral than smoke particulates.

Treatments such as blood-letting, applying leeches and taking potions made of all sorts of animal parts together with mercury or other toxins were still being passed down from generation to generation and used in times of illness, despite probably doing more harm than good on most occasions. Similarly, surgery, with only alcohol to numb the pain, was brutal and often did little more than create an entry for infection.

There were hospitals in London – St Thomas's Hospital for example, not only provided care for patients but trained doctors who practised all over the country.

When Thomas was in London, the Royal Society, charged with developing science, had already been experimenting, discovering and debating for more than half a century. Understanding was on the way but it was not yet in place.

An understanding of the links between cleanliness and health and, specifically, cleanliness and the spread of disease and infection, was yet to have been developed. Anaesthetics, antibiotics and vaccinations were yet to be discovered. It would not be for another two hundred years that we would have the knowledge and medicine to tackle the sorts of diseases and infections killing Londoners in Thomas's time and another hundred years before we could eradicate the abject poverty which would enable people to be healthier.

> ### *TINCTURA AMARA SALIS BURY ANA or Salisbury's bitter Tincture*
>
> *Being an Excellent Cordial preparative for the Stomach, nothing inferiour to any other Tinctures or Elixirs commonly used, either for Virtue or Unpleasantness in Smell and Taste; and very much approven by all who have had Occasion to make use of it.*
>
> *It is composed of the best of Stomachicks, and contains in it the very Quintessence of the common bitter Draught, reduced to so small a Quantity, that 50 or 60 Drops is a sufficient Doze for Man or Woman, and a lesser Quantity for Children and others; and may be taken at any time (but best in the Morning, fasting) in White Wine, Canarie, Cydar, Beer, Ale, Spring Water, Tea, Coffee &c. and mixed in ordinary Drinking, makes one of the best of Purles.*
>
> *It strengthens the Stomach, and creates an Appetite, and helps the Digestion, and removes the Sickness and loathing of the Stomach, arising from the surfeit of Drinking. It removes the Obstructions of the Stomach, and helps the Circulation of the Blood.*
>
> *It removes all Sharp and Scorbutic Humours, it chears the dejected Spirits, it takes away all nauseous Belchings, Rectifies any offence in the Breath, and is an Excellent Preservative against Infections arising from bad Air.*
>
> *It is a noble Specifik for the Scurvy, Jaundice, or green Sickness, taking a Spoonfull thereof about 14 Mornings together…, It destroys Worms in children and is very fit to be kept in Familys.*
>
> *Price Eight Pence per Bottel. With good Allowance to those who Retail.*

8   Saving London's Abandoned Babies

Adverts for cure-all tonics and tinctures were common in the newspapers of the eighteenth century. This one professed to cure all illness – from scurvy to worms, from depression to jaundice. It was a great way for quacks to make money out of people's ill-health.[5]

The Gin Craze was in full swing in London in the early 1700s. A reduction in the taxes and licensing requirements for gin production had brought the price of it right down and its availability right up. It was possible to buy gin for pennies from all sorts of shops, even barbers, and there were many street vendors, each

William Hogarth's engraving, *Gin Lane*. A baby can be seen in the act of falling from the breast of a drunken woman.

of whom boasted that their gin was stronger than that of the next. While it may have made city life more tolerable for many Londoners living in poverty and terrible conditions, it was causing as many problems as it solved. Crime and violence and general debauchery was blamed on the over-consumption of gin. It was also blamed for sexual misdemeanours and illegitimacy. It was said to have made the streets less safe and the working poor less reliable.

In 1721 Middlesex magistrates were lamenting that gin was 'the principal cause of all the vice and debauchery committed among the inferior sort of people'.

With no formal way of policing the ill-effects of drinking gin, the Government decided that legislation was the only way to curb the negative aspects of the Gin Craze and, in 1751, the Government passed the Tippling Act which attempted to regulate the distilling of gin by not granting distillers a licence unless they paid an annual rent for their premises of at least £10 a year. This effectively put the street vendors and other small sellers out of business.

The Act stated: '… the immoderate drinking of distilled Spirituous Liquors by Persons of the meanest and lowest sort, hath of late years increased, to the great Detriment of the Health and Morals of the common People; and the same hath in measure been owing to the Number of Persons who have obtained Licenses to retail the same, under Pretence of being Distillers, and of those who have presumed to retail the same without Licence, most especially in the Cities of London and Westminster, the Borough of Southwark and other Places …'[6]

Gin has a huge impact on people's health, an impact that was not fully understood at the time and, as such, added enormously to the health problems that already existed.

The biggest problem in London, however, was not gin, or even ill-health. The biggest problem facing society was rapidly growing poverty as people moved in huge numbers away from rural areas in search of work. The idea that many had, of a city where it was possible to take advantage of its rising position in world trade and manufacturing, was simply not what they found when they arrived. What work did exist was often poorly paid and the huge numbers of people looking for work were a breeding ground for exploitation.

Punishing Poverty

London was a city with a vast population of unemployed and under-employed people who were not able to earn sufficient money to house, feed or clothe themselves or their family. There was no safety net to keep them from destitution. There have, of course, always been people in society who have struggled to make ends meet, people who, for myriad reasons are unable to work or to earn enough to look after themselves and their dependents. In English history, there were two very significant man-made shifts which created long-standing crises in terms of the number of people living in extreme poverty.

The first was that Henry VIII wanted a divorce. His first wife, Catherine of Aragon was, by all accounts, a very impressive woman. It was always in her destiny to be queen of England and she was promised to the future king of England when she was just 3 years old. This was not Henry, but his older brother, Arthur. They married when she was around 16 but he died after only a few months of marriage. After his death, she became the first woman to become a European ambassador – representing the Aragonese Crown in England.

Catherine of Aragon (1485–1536), Henry VIII's first wife. If just one of her sons had survived childhood, the history of poverty in England and Wales could have been very different.

Without Arthur, Catherine switched to his brother, Henry. When they first married, she was 22 and her young husband was in France, leaving her to sit as regent of England. According to accounts of the time, she did a great job in this important role and was instrumental in quashing a Scottish invasion. Thomas Cromwell said, 'if not for her sex, she could have defied all the heroes of history'. She also championed the rights of women, even commissioning a report of the education of girls. Despite her obvious talents, her appeal to Henry was limited.

A key problem in their marriage was the death of all but one of their children and, specifically, the death of all their sons. After three years of marriage, she miscarried their first child, a daughter, but, as she was thought to be carrying twins, the grief was twofold when the second promised child never materialised. A year later, she gave birth to a son but he died within a month. Two years later, another son but he died either at or very shortly after his birth. A year later, another son but he too did not live. Two years later Catherine had a daughter, the only child she had who survived childhood and thus the only potential heir to her father's throne.

England's people, and particularly Henry, were not ready for a woman to be queen in her own right. The pattern, for as long as anyone could remember, was that a man had taken the throne. Henry was not ready for a woman to follow him and taunted by the birth of three sons who had not lived, he was distraught.

He was also very taken with another woman – Anne Boleyn. His wife's own lady-in-waiting was the next woman he wanted to marry.

The problem was that divorce was not an option, and the Pope, despite Henry's enthusiastic lobbying, would not grant him an annulment.

Henry had to marry Anne, however, for them to produce legal, male heirs, and so he resorted to extreme measures to achieve this. In 1534, the Act of Supremacy was passed by Parliament which made Henry head of the newly created Church of England, thereby giving himself the power he needed to make a divorce legal and give his future sons a right to the throne. It also meant severing England's Roman Catholic and papal links. Famously, Henry married five more times after Catherine and took to beheading his wives rather than bothering to use the powers of divorce he had given himself.

In a fierce irony, Henry's two legitimate daughters, Mary and Elizabeth, both became queens of England in their own right after his sole legitimate son, Edward, was crowned when aged 9 and died just six years later.

The impact on poverty of Henry's actions was pronounced. The split with the Catholic Church led to the dissolution of the Catholic monasteries in the country which were powerful landowners and gave support to those in need in the communities. The removal of the monasteries (their great wealth went to the Crown) left a huge unmet need amongst England's poor and needy.

The legal response to poverty was often punishment. Vagabonds Acts in the fifteenth and sixteenth centuries punished those without work by putting them in the stocks or whipping them, with the Vagabonds Act of 1536 going so far as to say that execution was appropriate for those found without work.

1601 is generally thought to be the date marking the turning point in the legal response to poverty when Henry's daughter brought in the Poor Relief Act known as the Elizabethan Poor Law. This Act, refined by several further pieces of legislation through the seventeenth and into the eighteenth centuries, formalised and brought some form of safety net for those who were destitute, and removed the need to whip or execute people in poverty.

The basic idea was that the parish church had responsibility for the poor and needy people of that parish. This was not simply an ethical responsibility, but a financial one. Each parish funded this work through a tax, the poor rate, charged on local property owners. In effect, this is the predecessor of our rates system and Council Tax.

The relief received by the poor in each parish generally took the form of cash, food and sometimes clothing and was known as 'outdoor relief' to distinguish it from 'indoor relief' which referred to placing people in poorhouses, the early workhouses. In practice, in these times few parishes could afford to build poorhouses and the vast majority of poor relief was given as 'outdoor relief'.

Much support was also, of course, given informally on this local level with families taking care of their own, and their neighbours, when they were in need, say a family looking after a person who was disabled or infirm.

The Poor Law system provided support for many thousands of people in need while enabling them to stay in their own communities. Importantly, it also meant that those who made money from the working poor, the landowners, were forced to contribute to the upkeep of those who could no longer work. And all this had come to fruition only around fifty years after the dissolution of the monasteries.

However, for the Poor Law to work, the people in need had to be in the parish which had responsibility for them, the parish in which they were born. The first rumblings of the Industrial Revolution in the early eighteenth century were bringing vast movement from rural parishes into London where the parishes felt no responsibility for those who travelled into their area of jurisdiction rather than being born into it. Even if the Church itself had felt an ethical obligation to those dying of hunger on its doorstep, they are unlikely to have ever been able to persuade the property owners of the parish, for it was them who were obliged to pay the poor rate to fund the poor relief, to put their hands in their pockets once more.

To get poor relief, people would have needed to travel back to the parishes of their birth, an expense out of reach for those who were already in destitution.

What London's poor population was experiencing in the 1700s was this breakdown in the Poor Law and its very real human cost.

For those Londoners who were in poverty, there was another cross to bear. It was not simply the physical difficulty of surviving with no money, but also the stigma that poverty carried. With its roots in those Vagabonds Acts which decreed that poverty was punishable by law, there was a very common belief that poverty was an evil brought on by the sufferer themselves. People in poverty were accused of laziness with the poorhouses springing up in the belief that poor people had to be forced into work. Poor people were assumed to be thieves and con artists eschewing religion and common decency. Exploiting poor people was seen as fair game as they deserved nothing better.

In London society there were few groups with a lesser social standing than the workless poor, the exception being illegitimate children and their mothers. Such was the evil thought to emanate from both groups that poor people were regularly assumed to be illegitimate. When Thomas saw children abandoned on the streets, his assumption was, of course, that they were illegitimate too.

As Browning put it: 'He knew what every man who studies the human heart must know – that the motive to such a dereliction of duty must be beyond the ordinary casualties of indigence. He was not long in discovering the true source of evil. Possessing the public mind, by which an unhappy female, who fell victim to the seductions and false promises of designing men, was left to hopeless contumely, and irretrievable disgrace'.[7]

Fallen Women and Their Bastards

Illegitimacy was a topic of great interest and moral outrage in the 1700s although the actual rate of illegitimate births was probably relatively low – probably less than 2%[8] in comparison to around 51% in England and Wales now.[9] There were a number of reasons for this interest.

Legally, illegitimate babies had no rights to inherit from their fathers or to take their surnames. For wealthy families with property to pass from one generation to the next, this was a very key issue. It was not until nearly three centuries later and the 1987 Legitimacy Act that legitimate and non-legitimate births achieved parity in legal terms. However, it was also a financial hot topic amongst the poor of Thomas's London, as there was a legal requirement for men to take care of their offspring in financial terms. Without a father, the baby was the financial responsibility of the parish church and thus added to the financial burden of the property owners of the parish who paid the poor rates. In the same way as these rate-payers preferred poor people to be in the poorhouse where they could be forced to work in return for their upkeep, they preferred all babies to have a father who would take financial care of them and classed those without fathers as an evil burden.

> Illegitimate children are a yearly and great expense to parishes in general, and a disgrace to religion.[10]

There is a certain irony in this vilification of illegitimacy as it was not uncommon amongst the English aristocracy and, indeed, serving royals. George I, on the throne while Thomas and Eunice were in London, had children both within and outside his marriage. A man taking a mistress was not necessarily considered to be a problem although, perversely, a woman having a baby without a named father was considered a very significant problem indeed.

Women who had children outside marriage were characterised as having loose morals, with an inability to keep themselves pure: 'She was branded forever as a woman habitually lewd'.[11] The precise circumstances of their pregnancy were largely irrelevant, the visible evidence of their perceived fall from grace was all that was needed. By contrast a man who had fathered a child outside of marriage carried no visible evidence of it and was generally able to continue unscathed.

Rather than being seen as innocent of the sins of its parents, illegitimate babies carried the very heavy burden of their misdemeanour. The language itself gives it away. The babies were known as bastards, a word in such common usage that it remains a term of vulgar abuse which can be directed towards all men. Even if the baby's mother should marry, the baby could not lose its illegitimate status.

Single mothers faced the practical difficulty of trying to continue to work through their pregnancy and while nursing their babies as well as facing the the stigma of being an unmarried mother. Some employers did not want an employee who had childcare issues and not one who was additionally a 'fallen' woman. The Bishop of Rochester in a sermon at the Chapel of Magdalene referred to them as 'these wretched outcasts of society'.[12]

A key issue was who would pay for the child's upbringing when there was no legitimate father willing to admit to his offspring. Fathers who were named as such by the mothers were charged with paying, under the Poor Law, a sum to the parish towards the upkeep of the child. A man could take the issue to court to fight the accusation that he was the father. Without paternity testing, it was generally impossible for a mother to prove her assertion leaving a court able to throw out the claim with relative ease.

On the other side of the coin, where men were found to be the father of the illegitimate child they had to make a financial contribution and, if they could not or would not make that contribution, they could be sent to prison. Some chose not to take that chance.

Some may not have accepted their status as a father with honour. Newspapers covered cases in which the father simply ran away: 'Eloped about three years ago from the Parish of Wilton in the County of Northampton on account of two bastard children being sworn to him, the said William Rushell was about 23 years of age, stands near five feet nine inches high, stout made, has strait brown hair and has lost one of his fore teeth. He was the son of a farmer of the Parish of Wilton and was bred up to that occupation, but has since followed the employment of a porter in London'.[13]

It also seems likely that illegitimacy was on the rise or, at least, it was feared it was on the rise.[14] The growing urban population, having moved away from family and parish church, were feared to have fewer morals than they would have done if they had stayed in the country. Possibly, what should have been of greater concern was the rise of the domestic servant in urban areas. Far more women, many of whom were very young, were working as domestic servants after the rise of urbanisation. Their role as live-in subordinates made them very vulnerable to the advances of the men in the households, men who failed to resist the temptation of the women living and working amongst them but were unable to marry them without breaking the rules of society. Middle and upper class men could not marry 'the help' without very significant disapproval from their peers.

A common thread in dialogue about illegitimate births in the early eighteenth century was murder. It was a perception that women who had had an illegitimate child were capable of murdering those children. Newspapers regularly covered cases in which women were found guilty of murdering their illegitimate child and sentenced to incarceration or death. References were commonly made to 'The frequent murders of bastard children'.[15] And the 'Too common and most unnatural crime of murdering her own illegitimate infant'.[16] But was this, at least in part, a popular misconception brought about by an archaic piece of legislation?

The legislation in question was the Infanticide Act of 1624: 'An act to prevent the destroying and murthering of bastard children'. The Act stated: 'Whereas many lewd Women that have been delivered of Bastard Children, to avoid their Shame, and to escape Punishment, do secretly bury or conceal the Death of their Children, and after, if the Child be found dead, the said Woman do alledge, that the said Child was born dead; whereas it falleth out sometimes (although hardly it is to be proved) that the said Child or Children were murthered by the said Women, their lewd Mothers, or by their Assent or Procurement…That if any Woman…be delivered of any Issue of her Body, Male or Female, which being born alive, should by the Laws of this Realm be a Bastard, and that she endeavour privately, either by drowning or secret burying thereof, or any other Way, either by herself or the procuring of others, so to conceal the Death thereof, as that it may not come to Light, whether it were born alive or not, but be concealed: In every such Case the said Mother so offending shall suffer Death …, except such Mother can make proof by one Witness at the least, that the Child (whose Death was by her so intended to be concealed) was born dead'.[17]

The Act meant that any woman whose illegitimate baby was born dead or later died, was to be assumed to have murdered it. At this time, stillbirths and early infant deaths were not unusual and many women made efforts to conceal the births of their child in order to escape the shame of illegitimacy. This statute was in place until 1803, allowing the urban myth that the women of illegitimate children were 'so lost to humanity, as to become the butchers of their own infants'[18] to continue for nearly two centuries.

It is tragic to note that the mood of society was such that a woman who had a stillborn child could be hanged for it unless she could prove that it had died of natural causes. Likewise, courts berated women for naming a father without proof. The onus was on the women to provide proof where proof did not exist.

The infant mortality rate in London at the time was very high with 350–400 deaths before the age of one year out of every 1000 births.[19] This was double the national average infant death rate. This suggests that many women were experiencing infant deaths, whether or not their babies were legitimate. By comparison, the most recently recorded UK infant mortality rate is 3.7 per 1000 live births.[20]

Could courts differentiate between murder by abandonment and neglect and those deaths which were unintentional, where a mother was simply not able to keep her baby alive either because of malnutrition or illness? When Thomas was in London, women found guilty under the Act of murdering their newborn illegitimate baby were commonly executed, with little thought given to whether there was any evidence to prove it.

Gibson[21] argues that demographic evidence suggests that abandonment and infanticide were uncommon and doubts whether all the cases known about concerned illegitimate children.

Thomas's View

It is this London that Thomas and Eunice made their home. It was a city of ill-health and criminality, with huge numbers of destitute people being failed by a Poor Law system which was not keeping pace with the changes brought about by mass migration into London. But this was not a London to trouble a person such as Thomas. The issues of illegitimacy and the murder of babies were not ones to impact on his working or personal life.

London was very much a city of two halves. One was wealthy and actively exploiting London's standing in both world trade and manufacturing. The other half was poor and in the perfect position to be exploited by the wealthy to keep the vast majority firmly stuck in their situation of destitution. And Thomas was very much rooted in the well-to-do-half of city life.

He had work and very respectable dealings with the Navy Office. He was friends with wealthy merchants because of his work in world trade. And he had connections with people of good social standing through his petitions to further colonise the New World. Issues of poverty and health and infant mortality were of no concern to him. The spacious buildings of London with wide boulevards, piped water and relatively comfortable travel in horse-drawn carriages meant the occupants never had to smell the open sewers of the slums and the paid watchmen would patrol the streets keeping away those who might stray there from the slums.

People who had money did not, in London, have any cause to mix with those without money or worry about the issues of concern to them.

After some years in the city, Thomas and Eunice moved. The couple set up home near the docks of Rotherhithe, which was at that time a relatively undeveloped area on the outskirts of London with only a small population. It was the home of the first proper docks in London, built in 1700 only a few years before Thomas arrived. It was a place busy with boats, sailors, fishermen and merchants and thus a perfect place for a man of the sea such as Thomas.

He had cause to go into London for his work, but no cause to see the poverty and disorder of the poor areas.

However, it seems that Thomas was not a man to shy away from the stench and chaos. Instead of taking a carriage into the city for his work, he chose to walk there, and walk home, a route which took him through some of the worst slums of the city.

He decided to walk into the city from Rotherhithe, often in the early morning, when he could see the city coming to life. Whether he chose to walk because he wanted to see the city and take exercise or whether he wanted to save the expense of taking a carriage, we cannot now be sure but it would have taken him between ninety minutes and two hours depending on his pace and the weather and would have involved him crossing the Thames over a bustling London Bridge which itself was full of shops and traders.

These walks, by a man used to the open spaces and opportunities of the New World, took him from the relative calm of Rotherhithe docks into the chaotic bombardment on the senses. The sights, the smell, the noise – that was the heart of the city, bursting at the seams, and must have had a profound effect on Thomas.

Through his habit of walking, Thomas came to know London well. He knew the decent houses on the wider roads, and he knew the squalor of the old, overcrowded and cramped areas. He had no doubt dodged the contents of chamber pots as they were emptied out of first floor windows. He had squeezed past the horses and their carts. He had seen the beggars and the street vendors shouting for his money. He had smelt the stench of the streets. Much of what he learnt of the city, he learnt from walking through it.

It is often quoted that it is on these walks that he first saw babies dead and dying where they had been left on London streets.

> While he lived in that part of this Metropolis, which is the common Residence of Seafaring People, he used to come early into the City, and return late, according as his Business required his Presence, and both these Circumstances afforded him frequent Occasions of seeing young Children exposed, sometimes alive, sometimes dead and sometimes dying. which affected extreamly.[22]

To see babies dying now, would be a truly shocking occurrence. It is impossible to imagine what catastrophe had befallen London for anyone walking through to even come close to such a sight and yet, it is said that he saw this frequently as had, we can assume, many other passers-by. The city then was a very different place, of course, and residents were used to a much harsher existence with many sights which are not to be seen now. Violence was a much more common occurrence, along with public flogging and even executions on the streets where people lived and worked. With little effective medicine, death was a much more common occurrence and was far more likely to be witnessed on the streets and in people's homes. And most children died when very young, with most of those deaths taking place in the home. Seeing babies dying, while tragic, is not likely to have been as shocking a sight as it would be now.

And today, if a person was seen dying on the streets, there is something to be done about it. A witness could call an ambulance, a doctor or the police in the knowledge that something could be done to help the individual. At the very least, painkillers could be administered, and their family contacted. We could take instructions over the phone to administer first aid or fetch warm clothes or clean bandages. None of these were possibilities in the 1700s. Not only was there no way to help a dying baby, but there were also fears and superstitions to overcome – a knowledge that whatever evil had befallen the baby could somehow affect anyone trying to help.

Whatever the reasons, many people, perhaps hundreds of people, saw babies left on the streets and walked by without doing anything at all.

When there was so much hardship on London's streets and babies dying on dunghills, why was Thomas Coram the person who did something? Why did he spend the rest of his life attempting to provide an alternative to the dunghills?

Thomas was, arguably, not the obvious candidate. There is no evidence, for example, that he was particularly child oriented. He and his wife had no children of their own. Having lost his business in Dighton, and left his house behind, it is unlikely that he had large quantities of money. Perhaps if had been rich, he would have taken carriages into London rather that walk through the squalor. He was not particularly well-connected – he was not from a landed family, there were no titles. And he had no relevant experience – life at sea was a far cry from residential childcare. His past had been about trading, building, and the Navy. He himself must have looked back in surprise when his life became about children and women in poverty.

But perhaps the reasons why we take a particular path are not always obvious. He came from a background in which life was not easy, and tragedy was a feature. Perhaps this gave him empathy, or at least some compassion with those families also struggling. Most importantly, he had a very well-developed sense of what the newly emerging British Empire needed in terms of people and resources and he was determined to support his country in whatever way he could. The many petitions he submitted to the Government for schemes to develop links with the New World are a testament to that.

Part II

A Man to Save the Babies

'He acquired very early a sincere and warm Attachment to the true Interests of his Country, had a real Concern for them ... His Experience was his principal Guide, and from thence he learned to consider rational Liberty, active Industry and unblemished Probity, as the only Principals upon which national Prosperity could be built.'

Brocklesby, 1751

What Made Thomas Coram?

Babies had been dying on the streets for many years. Hundreds and thousands of people had walked past without doing anything. How many people lived and worked on those streets where the babies were dying? Perhaps they were so used to seeing them that they no longer even looked. What of the people paid to shovel the dirt and the filth? Did they give the little lifeless bodies a second thought? Why did Thomas not only see the babies but decide to do something about it and then devote the rest of his life to making it happen?

Why was he the one who not only decided he could do something to aid the plight of babies dying in the streets, but the one who didn't give up when it seemed like a lost cause for so many years?

Thomas's own history suggests that he most certainly lacked the relevant experience and education, and perhaps also money and contacts to do anything to help abandoned babies. But remarkably, he made up for these significant shortcomings with empathy, obstinacy and personal drive.

A Childhood In the Old World

Thomas was born in around 1668 in Lyme Regis. The town at this time was unrecognisable from the quaint seaside resort it is today and must have been an exciting place of wonder for a young boy. It is easy to see how his childhood in the town may have played a part in shaping Thomas's career and outlook as an adult.

Lyme Regis, with a population of around 400 people at the time, was at the centre of much of England's world trade. It was a very prosperous town with a cloth-making industry and a major port from which boats came and went to Europe, the Caribbean, and the Americas. The customs receipts from Lyme, despite being a small town, rivalled those of Liverpool. Young Thomas would have seen the hubbub of the port, the majesty of the large sailing ships leaving for the New World and returning with strange and exotic cargoes, and met travelled sailors and heard their tales of their times at sea. There were warehouses in large numbers along the sea front with horses traipsing back and forth to the ships taking bales of supplies and goods. This world trading role of the town was probably to determine the course the young Thomas's life was to take.

To support the maritime trading activity, Lyme also had a ship-building tradition with numerous shipyards established around the Cobb (the harbour wall). Most of the people of Lyme, if they were not involved in making or sailing ships, worked in roles related to ships and the docks in some way. Whether it was making rope, making flags, feeding the people of the shipyards or stocking ships with provisions, the narrow streets of Lyme were teeming with people talking of the boats and the adventures of the seas.

Young Thomas would have been very familiar with the noise, the people, the smells and excitement of being in a place of bustling maritime trade.

But Lyme was also a town which experienced significant conflict. Thomas, as a child, would have heard all about this and may have witnessed some of the events himself.

Sea conflicts between Holland and France were ongoing in the late seventeenth century. In 1672, when Thomas was 4 years old, there was a naval engagement between English ships and Dutch ships which was visible from Lyme. The English won on that occasion. Such a sight, and such a scene of triumph, must have been big news for many years in the town.

In 1685, when Thomas was 17, James, the Duke of Monmouth, the illegitimate son of Charles II, landed by ship at Lyme with the intention of instigating a rebellion against James II. The rebellion was not to be and he was executed on the beach along with his supporters. Three centuries later, we can still sit on Monmouth Beach, named in memory of his failed attempt at glory. For Thomas, as a young apprentice, this was an incredibly significant event to happen in a place he knew so well.

And Thomas was in Lyme Regis when the town was at its peak as a seaport. By the time the Foundling Hospital was established, Lyme was in decline. The port, no longer suitable for the larger ships of the time, was making its transition into a seaside resort.

> Lyme, although a little place,
> I think it wondrous pretty;
> If 'tis my fate to wear the crown
> I'll make of it a city.[1]

Thomas's parents were not wealthy but were comfortable, an ordinary working family. Thomas's father had work on the docks, perhaps in customs. This was a relatively safe job, being based on land rather than at sea, and would have provided stable all-year round income for the family.

When Thomas was around 4 years old, his mother gave birth to another son, William. Tragically not only did William die when only a few days old but Thomas's mother died that same year.[2]

How Thomas's father managed to bring up a child, while earning enough money to keep them both, is not certain. His father did not remarry for some years. Perhaps there was a relative to look after young Thomas while his father worked. And perhaps Thomas himself started work at a young age. Thomas as an adult was very clear that he had not received an education as a child. Aged 11, Thomas went to sea, working on the boats from the Lyme docks.

There is no doubt that this was a tragic and difficult childhood for Thomas but it was not an unusual childhood. Sadly, infant mortality rates were high with parents often having several pregnancies in the hope that one or two would survive. And giving birth carried dangers for women with many not surviving. Blood loss during childbirth was an all-too-common cause of death for mothers as was puerperal fever following infection getting into the uterus. There was no way of tackling either issue for new mothers and death was the usual outcome. As a result, growing up without a mother was common. And as for his lack of education, schooling was still very much only for those children of wealthy families. In working families, getting children to contribute to the family income was far more important. It was to be another two centuries before education for children was to become a legal right.

As an adult, Thomas was open about his lack of education: 'I cannot Wonder at my own awkwardness in such Matters when I consider I went to sea at 11½ years old and several years before King Charles ye 2d dyed & as I could never speak good English how is it possible I should write good Gramer'.[3]

Regardless of, or perhaps because of, his own lack of education, Thomas grew up to be an enthusiastic advocate not only of education for boys, but also for girls, not just within the context of the Foundling Hospital but also in the New World. It is interesting to see the parallels between Sir Josiah Mason, a famous Victorian industrialist and philanthropist who similarly became a campaigner for the education of orphans (both boys and girls) when he had received no education himself.

One thing that is clear from Thomas's early experiences is that he became both independent and practical. Going to sea as a child meant that there was really no alternative. As a young boy, newly joining a ship's crew when aged only 11, he would have been given the worst jobs on the ship as was the habit onboard. And it would have been a dangerous life. Working on boats was full of hazards – from swinging beams to monstrous waves, from scurvy to falling overboard. As a young boy, he would have had to grow strong and quick-witted to survive.

After a few years his father organised a five-year apprenticeship as a shipwright for him. It seems that Thomas's father was not a shipwright so he was not encouraging Thomas to follow in his footsteps. Perhaps Thomas himself had shown some interest or particular leaning towards shipbuilding.

Apprenticeships of this nature could have taken place on land – in a Lyme Regis shipyard, for example, or at sea, with the apprentice learning his trade as a crew member on a working, sailing boat as a carpenter's mate.

Compston tells of the conditions Thomas would have experienced while at sea: 'The bad rations came up for discussion in Parliament in 1703. Not for a century later were water-tanks in general use. The water was in casks, and within a few days of leaving port it became unwholesome to drink. The salt junk created a thirst relieved by poor beer'.

Shipbuilding was an incredibly important occupation in seventeenth- and eighteenth-century England as the status and wealth of the Empire was based entirely on its ability to win sea battles and transport people and goods long distances by boat. As such, England's coastline was littered with shipbuilding docks and ports. There were six major Royal Dockyards at Deptford, Woolwich, Sheerness and Chatham (all in Kent), Plymouth (Devon) and Portsmouth (Hampshire) and several smaller ones around the coast with merchant ports in Bristol (Gloucestershire), Harwich (Essex), London, Poole (Dorset) and Southampton (Hampshire). The key areas of shipbuilding were in Hampshire, the West Country and East Anglia.

Being a shipwright was not a straightforward occupation – every boat built had to be a team effort involving a range of people and skills. As such, a shipwright worked with a number of specialist tradesmen including: draftsmen, blockers and block makers (blocks were what the ships stood on during building); timber merchants and sawyers; caulkers (who sealed the ship's seams with oakum and pitch); mast makers, sail makers, ropemakers, riggers, and anchor smiths. Shipbuilding was not a trade that took place in isolation but involved large numbers of people who each contributed to the whole. As a shipwright, Thomas would have learnt a great deal about effective logistics to ensure that all the elements came together at the right time. Shipwrights were not always land-based, and Thomas, along with other shipwrights, may have been employed on board working boats to maintain the hull and the masts.

Five years after Thomas's apprenticeship began, Lyme avoided attack from a French galley. The boat, a wooden ship powered by around fifty oarsmen who were largely criminals and slaves, approached the town. It was on its way back from a terrible attack on Teignmouth following a triumphant battle against the Dutch and English at Beachy Head which temporarily gave control of the English Channel to the French.

The victorious fleet anchored in Torbay and some of the galleys went to Teignmouth and attacked the town. The attack is described in a contemporary report by the inhabitants: '… on the 26th day of this instant July 1690 by Foure of the clocke in the morning, your poor petitioners were invaded (by the French) to the number of 1,000 or thereabouts, who in the space of three hours tyme, burnt down to the ground the dwelling houses of 240 persons of our parish and upwards, plundered and carried away all our goods, defaced our churches, burnt ten of our ships in the harbour, besides fishing boats, netts and other fishing craft …'

One of the galleys then arrived at Lyme, presumably to carry out a similar raid. However, cannons were fired from the shore and the galley left. Lyme was saved.

Whether or not the young Thomas was physically in Lyme to see these events is not known but he would certainly have heard about them from other ships on their travels. He was fully aware of the adventures to be had in the open sea.

The Pull of the New World

After Thomas's apprenticeship there are few records of what he did during his early years. Trade with the New World was most likely what he was involved in. This would have entailed journeys lasting months at sea in what were essentially uncomfortable conditions and involved hard physical work. Crossing the Atlantic took at least six weeks in the large wooden sailing boats.

This was an unprecedented time in Britain's maritime history. Europe was establishing settlements in the Americas. The Plymouth Puritans, for example, arrived in Massachusetts in 1620. Countries like France, Holland and England were all looking to send more people to colonise land overseas. This was the start of unimaginable movement across the Atlantic. The New World was a source of materials, timber for example, which needed bringing back to Europe. And in the other direction, people and supplies were going to the new settlements, including, of course, slaves from West Africa. This movement of people and goods was to reach its peak decades later, but Thomas's time was the period when it was all new territory. Europeans were fighting over the natural resources available in the New World and the opportunity to grow crops in more preferable climates overseas, such as sugar cane in the Caribbean. They were also fighting over the source of labour in Africa, lands to settle in the New World and so on. What Thomas and his contemporaries could see was the potential of Atlantic trade – it was in its infancy and the possibilities must have seemed to them exciting and almost limitless.

England had taken New Amsterdam from the Dutch just twenty years earlier and renamed it New York. At the same time England had got a foothold in the Caribbean and was developing the sugar plantations. In 1670, the Royal African Company was set up on the West Coast. This company, very much a royal venture, had a monopoly on taking goods and people from West Africa to transport to the Americas.

Of course, what we can see from a modern-day perspective is the ugliness of all this, not least the horrors of the slave trade and the violent theft of land from indigenous people. Perhaps Thomas could see it too. When he was part of developing a new British colony in what is now Georgia, there was a vote about whether slaves could be used in the colony. The vote was against. Was that Thomas's vote too?

There were two other significant factors in Thomas's time at sea. The first was the onset of piracy. The increased trade across the Atlantic brought increased incidents of piracy where criminal pirates would board ships to steal their cargo or take over the boats themselves, often murdering all those on board. Sailors had to be watchful at all times to ensure that their boat did not fall victim to piracy.

There were also ongoing wars with France from 1688 with the British Navy and French Navy battling for supremacy at sea as the European nations vied for the best chunks of the 'empty' land of the North Americas.

These times must have provided exciting sailing challenges for the young Thomas Coram, both in terms of the logistics of planning and life on the waves.

Setting Up Home

Still a young man, aged 23, only three years after completing his apprenticeship, Thomas embarked on a complete change of pace and set up home in the New World.

The Americas is very likely to have been somewhere he had visited during the course of his time so far at sea. And Lyme Regis, his childhood home, was itself based on trade with the New World. Perhaps moving to the New World was the fulfilment of a long-held dream, or perhaps Thomas was simply capitalising on a single opportunity. As a sailor, Thomas would have heard all the news of the

New World and would have visited ports there. In those months at sea when there was little else to do but talk with the other crew members, perhaps they plotted a new life in the New World.

Whatever brought him back to the New World, he arrived in America in 1691 and settled there.

This was a relatively new place of settlement for the English. The Plymouth Puritans had arrived on the Mayflower in 1620. English settlers had first arrived in Massachusetts Bay only fifty-nine years before Thomas arrived. Their journey across the Atlantic would have taken around two and half months. In the next years, thousands of families arrived after similar sea journeys with each ship laden with livestock, provisions, and tools as well as people. This peaked in the Great Migration between 1630 and 1642 when thousands of English families arrived by boat to settle in Massachusetts, a place described 'as an almost unbroken wilderness, threaded only by Indian paths'[4] which was claimed by the new arrivals and towns of English people sprang up.

If there was a word which summed up the English colonies of America at the time, it was 'opportunity'. For the English arrivals, the colonies represented apparently limitless land ready for settlement. The Native Americans, who had lived on the land for the previous 10,000 years, would not have seen that this land was ripe for settlement. From their perspective, the land was already settled. But this was the start of the Empire that was to become the British Empire, when it seemed that all land was considered to be ripe for settlement or exploitation, unless it was already owned by Europeans.

For the English settlers, the Native Americans who lived a semi-nomadic life on the coast of the North Americas were not a huge problem. Land could be 'bought' very cheaply. Many of the native communities died out through diseases brought by the settlers, others fled to live elsewhere. Those who remained were relatively easily defeated by military action. They could then be taken and sold into the burgeoning slave trade or used as house servants. Everything was considered a resource to be utilised in the New World.

The new arrivals would have seen a land which was alive with natural resources. Forests covered much of the area providing timber for houses, fences and ships; and fruit to eat. Deer, rabbits, and ducks ran around for hunters to put meals on the table. Lakes, rivers and streams provided fresh water and also fish, as did the sea. Cash crops such as corn grew well.

It is easy to see what would have appealed about the colonies to young Thomas. As a shipbuilder, all the resources he needed were widely available, as was a market for his boats. There was a ready-made community of fellow English people, fellow English people whose entire existence there was dependent on what he knew best – boats.

It was a place where hard work would be rewarded. He would not be stopped by competition or red tape – he was free to make a success of it. The English communities in America were also still relatively free at that early stage of the old social hierarchy of England – free of the strict restrictions on social climbing by lower classes. For a man who wanted to make a life for himself as a shipwright, who was used to a practical, hard working life, this was an ideal place to establish himself.

Taunton was a very new community having only been incorporated as a town in 1639; a small town largely made up of first and second generation English people. The land had been bought from the Nemasket native population in 1637 for a pitiful two shillings an acre and it seems there was little concern for what had happened to the native communities who had been displaced in this way. Instead, the primary concern of Taunton's new inhabitants was protecting themselves from whatever the native communities would do in revenge – the communities were well supplied with guns and cannons. Many houses were built with cannons on their roofs to defend their rights as English settlers on Nemasket soil.

Once in the hands of the English settlers, however, there was a fairness about what happened to the land next. Regardless of the money and other possessions they had brought with them, the land was shared out so that families each had enough to grow a sufficiency of food for their needs and build an adequate house. Societal hierarchies were not based on inherited wealth but rather on how long a family had been in Taunton. This liberal approach seemed to appeal to Thomas.

When in Taunton, the question was considered how those who did not have a father to inherit from would get enough land for their needs. A vote of the town decided that all orphans or fatherless children should also have rights to land.[5] Did this have an impact on Thomas's thinking in London when he decided that his hospital should be open to fatherless children?

Taunton was also a very religious community, another trait shared by Thomas. However, his Anglicanism and the town's Puritanism were to prove to have differences which would be of great significance to Thomas's future in Taunton. Anglicanism had come out of the sixteenth-century reformation and was seen to have elements of both Protestantism and also Roman Catholicism. Puritanism came out of efforts to 'purify' the Church of England from any Roman Catholic influences. Puritans, during the reign of Charles I, had fled the persecution and discrimination they experienced because of their religious beliefs to reach the freedoms of the New World, the first of these famously on the Mayflower. In America, the settlers had the freedom to harbour very firm religious beliefs.

As an Anglican in a Puritan community, Thomas found himself, for the first time, in a very significant religious minority in a very staunchly religious community.

There were of course significant similarities between Thomas's beliefs and those of his Puritan neighbours and some elements must have been very appealing to him. For example, the Puritan community of Taunton had a very strong belief that everyone should read the Bible. To this end, they worked together as a community to provide free schooling to the boys in their community, with girls generally being taught to read at home. Indeed, it was the Puritans of Massachusetts who founded Harvard University as early as 1636 with the original aim of training clergy.

A stone on the entrance to the building reads:

'After God had carried us safe to New-England, and wee had builded our houses, provided necessaries for our livelihood, rear'd convenient places for Gods worship, and setled the Civill Government: One of the next things we longed for, and looked after was to advance Learning and perpetuate it to Posterity; dreading to leave an illiterate Ministery to the Churches, when our present Ministers shall lie in the Dust.'

It is dated 1643.

The importance placed on education by his Puritan neighbours was reflected in Thomas's later designs for the Foundling Hospital and for the New World.

Thomas arrived in Taunton from Boston in the late 1690s. In 1699, he chose a parcel of land, previously undeveloped by the English settlers, by the river which he described as: 'in the most commodious place on the river, with so good a depth of water, that if need were, a fourth rate frigate might be launched there'.[6] This was outside the town of Taunton, in a small settlement known as Dighton.

He started Taunton's first shipbuilding business and built a large wooden house on what is now Water Street, Dighton, on the west bank of the Taunton River. While they have been modernised over the years, the houses are still standing. Thomas's shipyard is now used by the Taunton Yacht Club. The size of the house suggests that Thomas was building for his future. The house was wooden, with many windows from which he could see his business and the water.

Life in Taunton appeared to be good for Thomas. The house he built for himself was large and grand. The shipyard which he started was busy with work. The opportunities of the area were endless. People were constantly arriving, and trade possibilities for him were extensive in the local area including the fisheries, and also with the other colonies and with England. It must have felt like business was limitless.

There are indications that Thomas also had some form of government-backing: Hamilton Hill finds he 'had the encouragement if not the direct support of the government'[7]:

Thomas was on the roster of the first Military Company of Taunton in which the men of the town joined together time to protect their town from attack or invasion. He worked with his friend, John Hathaway, in the shipbuilding business and John built a house similar to Thomas's house and next door to it.

In July 1700, Thomas married Eunice whose family were an old family; that is, Eunice had been born in Boston to English settlers and thus had the status of not being a newcomer. Thomas had come to marriage relatively late in life, aged 32, but he now had a house, his own business and now a wife. The house he had built was large with room for the children he was no doubt anticipating would arise from his marriage.

However, despite everything looking so perfect for the future of the new couple, a dark cloud was gathering over Thomas's little part of Dighton.

Thomas was not getting on with the people of Dighton and, while his business had started off successfully, it began to be impacted by disagreements. More and more, arguments were becoming a feature of his relationship with the other local people. We know that this was the case because so many of these arguments ended up as court cases which were documented at the time.

The disagreements were fundamentally about money owed by his business or to his business by customers.

The first court cases appear to have been in 1700 against local people who were supposed to be supplying materials for Thomas's shipbuilding business. The cases were relatively small but became seriously protracted as Thomas lost initial cases and then appealed and plaintiffs lodged counter-complaints against Thomas. There was a pattern of Thomas losing cases in the local courts, and then winning them on appeal but further arguments and litigation dragged the cases out for long periods.

It was an expensive process for Thomas whose new business could ill-afford to take the strain. He complained that his property was not being fairly valued by the court officials and the courts had 'the ships and all the plunder appraised by some prejudiced country fellows of their own party in no way skilled in such things'.[8]

Not only were his finances suffering from the cost of the litigation, but he was unable to run his business unhindered to bring in income. At one point he complained 'the business of my ships was holy hindered for three months or very near it'. Hamilton Andrews Hill, a researcher writing in 1893, assessed records of the cases concerning Thomas, from the Bristol County Court, and found that 'evidently there was a conspiracy in Taunton to break Coram down, to take everything from him and to drive him from the place'.[9]

Writing in 1703, Thomas showed that he felt very angry about the treatment he received from his neighbours: 'For four or five years last past I have built at Taunton in the County of Bristoll where by the barbarous treatment I have had from some of the people, I have reason to believe they are some of the very worst of creation, and to compleat and cloak their black action, have in their serpentine manner endeavoured to stigmatize my Reputation with the best of the country, and some of the Countrey Justices there abouts have been so partiall in their administrations towards me that they have violated their own oaths and given illegall Judgements against me'.[10]

Thomas put the blame for all the problems firmly on the shoulders of his neighbours, calling them 'a generation of vipers'.[11] It was a place of newcomers as everyone in the community arrived in a boat from England so it seems unlikely his recent arrival could have been the cause of such problems. But he was an outsider in terms of religion. Was it this that created such division? When he married Eunice, he married into a Boston Congregational family. As such Eunice's religious views probably had more in common with Taunton's Puritans than with her husband's. Even this, however, did not seem to have smoothed the relationship between Thomas and his neighbours.

Did Thomas think of himself as better than his neighbours? When Thomas was listed in the roster for the Military Company of Taunton in 1700,[12] it is interesting to note that he is listed as 'Mr', the only man in the roster to be given such a title. Was this a title he gave himself, or did the writer of the list call him such – a personal dig at Thomas's own self-importance? Either way, Mr Thomas Coram stands out from all the other volunteers.

What seems clear about Thomas is that he was a stubborn man. This had positive ramifications – only the most stubborn of men would have sent twenty-two years arguing that a Foundling hospital should be built when no one else would support it. But his stubbornness was also unhelpful at times. In Dighton, he refused to back down despite the barrage of litigation brought against him. He continued to stand up for himself, both inside and outside of the courts, whenever he thought a wrong had been done by him. For a relative stranger, and a religious outsider in a close community, it may have been wise to keep his head down, perhaps lose a few arguments for the sake of keeping the peace. But that was not Thomas. Again and again he returned to the courts to try to achieve what he felt was justice. Was the justice system, made up of the very locals with whom he was warring with, against him? He certainly felt so at times and was continually aggrieved that he was a victim of unfairness. Did he back down? No, he didn't. Sadly, from those cases we know about, he was generally not successful and lost more cases and appeals than he won.

The arguments and court cases were not simply aggravating and costly. Things eventually turned violent. In one case, Thomas won and he was awarded 59 acres of land. However, when he went to look at the land, he was attacked and shot at by the former landowner, Abel Burt. Thomas firmly believed he would have been murdered had not rescue come to him just in time:

> In a week or two afterwards he met me in a by Place, seized and got me down on the ground with intent to murder me and would have done it had it not been for a man coming by accidentally.[13]

In a relatively short period of time, perhaps just a few years after setting up home in Dighton, Thomas reached a point where there was no rescuing his company, his place in his community, and his life with his new wife Eunice. The court cases were an enormous drain on his resources, his reputation as a businessman was destroyed and the couple were no doubt left with very few friends in the area. Eunice had lived there all her life. How must she have felt to see such problems for her own husband?

The couple decided that the only thing they could do was to leave Dighton behind and make the move to England. The journey was one that Thomas must have been very familiar with – several weeks sailing ahead in a large wooden ship across the Atlantic.

How must it have felt to the couple to have packed up their possessions, emptied their house that he had built with his own hands, and left behind her family, his business. When they married, less than three years earlier, they had their own house, business, and were living in the wide-open spaces and limitless opportunities of the New World. Their life in London was going to be very different.

As a stubborn man, it was perhaps surprising that he gave up on his New World dream and left for London. However, it does not seem in any way that that was Thomas's permanent plan. Tellingly, he did not sell their house in Dighton but it remained ready for them for when they returned. In the years that followed he kept up correspondence with people he knew in the New World and designed several schemes for new colonies in America which presumably would have involved him and Eunice returning. When they arrived in London, it was when the Tar Act was coming into being. This turned out to be one of his greatest achievements in his life. The timing suggests that he wanted to be in London for the sake of this important piece of legislation but it also gave them a temporary break from the troubles he was having in Dighton. His intention was to return when he could.

In the meantime, he was making plans so that he would not be forgotten in Taunton and would have something to return for. The parcel of land over which Abel Burt had attempted to murder Thomas, Thomas decided to gift to fund an Anglican parish church in Taunton, so that 'if ever hereafter the inhabitants of the town of Taunton should be more civilized than they are now'.[14] He then later said that he engaged Mr Attorney General Newton of Boston to draw up the deed so that it would be 'amply strong and in due form that the crafty New Englanders might ever find a flaw in it, I knowing too well what sort of folks the major part of the inhabitants of Taunton then were'.[15] This was a double-edged sword; a gift with a heavy dose of criticism. So stubborn was Thomas, that he could not let it lie, even from 3000 miles across the Atlantic. And he was not about to let the Taunton community forget this particular annoying Anglican. In 1728, a church was indeed built in Taunton carrying the name St Thomas. He had certainly made his name in the New England.

For many people, a failed business, a failed emigration to the New World and a series of financial problems, would no doubt have caused a man to dwindle into obscurity. His chance of big success over, most people would have settled for a relatively quiet and risk-free life earning enough to keep his wife but not making so much of a splash that disaster could occur again. But this was Thomas Coram, and he had every intention of making a splash.

Part III

The Quest

'Time and Accidents could make but little Alteration in his Temper.'
Brocklesby, 1751

Looking Back to the New World

Being in London did not diminish Thomas's enthusiasm for the New World and England's settlement of it and trade with it. He was a huge proponent of maximising all that he believed was good about England's influence overseas.

Very shortly after arriving in London, the Tar Act came to fruition and was probably the reason he came to London at that time. It turned out to be by far his greatest achievement in terms of promoting England's trade with the New World. His part in it was based on the vast knowledge he had gleaned from his time in the New World, and his understanding of what England needed from trade with it. In his work, he had taken cargos of tar made in Sweden to England. Sweden had a virtual monopoly on tar which they made from their many fir and pine forests. Thomas was confident that the newly settled lands in North America had forests to rival those of Scandinavia so he petitioned for a 'reward' for English imports of tar, and other products, from America. This amounted to £4 per tun of eight barrels and was designed to reduce England's reliance on Scandinavian imports. The move ensured employment for settlers in North America while also saving importers money in England. The legislation he achieved was popularly known as the Tar Act. Thomas had not been in London for very long at all when the legislation went through.

During his life, he submitted many further petitions to the Government relating to his ideas for promoting trade with, and settlement in, the New World. Each of these must have taken considerable amounts of his time and, also, expense. He would spend time talking with people to develop his ideas and then pay someone to write them up for him as he did not trust his own writing skills to do them justice. There is no doubt that he had great knowledge and understanding of his subject but the Government often proved they did not share his thinking; more of his petitions were to be rejected than were accepted.

However, people in high places thought highly of Thomas's knowledge. Horace Walpole told his brother, Sir Robert Walpole (the prime minister of the time), that he thought Thomas was 'the honestest, the most disinterested, & the most knowing person about the plantations, I ever talked with'.[1]

Perhaps much of the plotting and drafting of these petitions took place in the long hours at sea when there was little else to be done. His work with the Navy Office and trading goods with the New World meant long sea journeys which lasted sometimes weeks, often months.

His proposals generally centred around the settlement of land on the east coast of North America, from Nova Scotia, 650 miles north of Massachusetts where he and Eunice had lived, to what is now Georgia, 1100 miles to the south. Some of this land was already settled by the English, such as in Massachusetts; some was hotly disputed, such as Nova Scotia where wars were fought between France, the original European settlers, other European hopefuls (including England) and, of course, the ever-diminishing indigenous Mi'Kmaq population while other land was largely unsettled by Europeans (and thus considered 'empty') as was the case with much of the land further south. Thomas saw it all as opportunity and the key to England's, and later, Britain's, wealth and power in the world.

This way of thinking, so firmly rooted in the England of the 1700s at the very beginnings of the British Empire, was described in his obituary – 'no other motive to that Care and Concern which he has shewn for this rising Colony, but his Affection for this Country and to whatever may contribute to strengthen her extensive Empire, and secure the Continuance of that Prosperity which she derives from Naval Power and Settlements well-placed and worthily directed'.[2]

While his motivations were no doubt based on his ambitions for the nation, he was also looking to finding a way to get him and his wife back in their home in Dighton. Thomas and Eunice had a life in London of course, a very busy one for Thomas and he certainly had contacts and friends and acquaintances, but he had very little in the way of family in the city and Eunice had left her family behind in Boston. It is nice to imagine that perhaps once or twice she was able to visit her family. After all, she had one of the few husbands who could have arranged it for her to visit Boston by joining him on one of his voyages to America. But she was known to have periods of illness and was, perhaps, too frail for such a long journey. Perhaps he was able to arrange shipment of letters and packages for her.

In this manner, for fifteen years the couple led a relatively calm life. When he was away at sea, she kept a home in a respectable area of London where she could avoid the chaos and busyness of the cobbled alleys. This is not a time Thomas's early biographers knew very much about, or perhaps they simply felt it was of little interest to their readers. However, there came an incident about which his biographers knew a great deal. Taking place in 1719, the event potentially changed the course of Thomas's life.

We know what happened at this time as his testimony, along with those of other witnesses, is a matter of public record. The event warranted an investigation shortly after it happened and, as part of this, he was asked to give a statement of his version of what happened. The following details are taken from that testimony.[3]

Thomas describes that he was on a vessel called the *Seaflower*, charged with overseeing her cargo which consisted primarily of wheat. They left Gravesend on 5 March headed for Hanover, which was, at the time, part of the dominions of George I. The aim of the trip was to sell the wheat and investigate what supplies of timber and other resources there might be there which could be of use to the Royal Navy. The thinking was that what belonged to George I, the king of England, belonged to the Royal Navy. Not all Hanoverians, as it turned out, felt the same.

On 14 March, the *Seaflower* reached the northernmost coast of Germany and the mouth of the River Elbe (which Thomas refers to as the Elve). They anchored overnight somewhere near Cuxhaven (which Thomas refers to as Coxhaven). Unfortunately, a sudden and fierce storm caused the *Seaflower* to lose her anchor and drift into shallow water where she became beached. A pilot from Hamburg (some fifty miles upriver) was onboard as he was employed to guide the boat on its journey the following day. He and Thomas left the ship's master and the rest of the crew on board and they, at low tide, walked to Coxhaven to get a new anchor and manpower to help refloat the boat. They met a group of villagers armed with axes and sacks heading towards the stricken ship but the pilot sent them away.

They had difficulty finding willing men as, being a Sunday morning, many were at church. Widening the search to nearby villages, they eventually found men who were to be paid forty dollars to bring their Evers (flat-bottomed boats) to help the *Seaflower*.

In freezing weather, however, the crew of the *Seaflower* left the boat for land so that they could warm up and dry off; some of the men were ill and needed rest.

What then ensued, according to Thomas's detailed testimony, was confusion and misinformation about whether the weather was improved enough to go back onto the *Seaflower* and, consequently, his great difficulty in arranging transport for him and the rest of the crew. Thomas, getting increasingly suspicious that he was being deliberately kept from the ship, was trapped without transport in Coxhaven; the ship's crew were elsewhere and similarly unable to get back to the ship.

The testimony recorded: 'The sudding alteration in the behaviour of those at Coxhaven, together with reflecting on the frequent barbarities report'd of those People when any English Ship happens to be drove upon their Shore caus'd a Jellousy in the said Coram that they had some Ill-Designe against the Ship. Not to assist her according to their Agreement. But to make a Wreck of her and her cargoe for their own advantage'.

Despite the protestations of the hired men that the weather was too bad to put boats in the water to attempt a rescue of the *Seaflower*, Thomas was certain that he could see activity in the water and small boats coming and going in the Elve.

After much effort, Thomas managed to find a wagon to carry him to the village where the crew were and take those who were able to travel to the *Seaflower*. As they got nearer, however, they could see that the ship was surrounded by boats and wagons who were taking her cargo of wheat and other goods. They had also broken down her cabin, cut up the decks, and were taking down the rigging and sails. Thomas noted that they had thrown overboard the *Seaflower*'s Capstand and taken away the pump gear, both of which were essential if the *Seaflower* were to be saved.

When Thomas and the ship's master went on board and attempted to stop the plundering, they were both physically thrown onto the deck by the looters.

Back on land, Thomas went to the Governor at Ritzebüttel and asked for assistance. The Governor made an order that everything that had been taken from the ship should be taken to the Admiralties Storehouse at Coxhaven where the looters would be allowed to keep one third of it, and two thirds would be returned to Thomas. At this point, although some of the wheat and other cargo was brought to the Storehouse, Thomas estimated that it amounted to only about a tenth of what had been taken. He tried to search the Evers for plundered cargo but his life was threatened by the boatmen. The *Seaflower*'s master was threatened by men with swords when he tried to make a search. Thomas paid two soldiers to guard what remained of the *Seaflower* and her cargo but he then saw them standing by while the plundering continued unabated. The Governor offered little further help.

After days of searching for the missing cargo, Thomas left Coxhaven and went to Heglioland (a group of islands to the north which Thomas refers to as Holygland) where he had heard that some of the cargo had been taken. While there, he found men who admitted that they had taken part in the thefts from the *Seaflower* but the local magistrates failed to get involved.

This incident represented a big loss financially, which Thomas is likely to have had to shoulder himself, at least partially. But it seems that the impact was not simply financial. For a proud man given valuable cargo to look after, this is likely to have been a big blow. From this point, Thomas gave up his seafaring life and instead began to focus on working in London. Whether this was due directly to the loss of the *Seaflower*, or he decided to retire from the sea simply because he was now in his fifties and wanted to spend time in London with his wife, we cannot now know. But this change in his work was extremely significant, as it appears it gave him more time for his projects.

So here we have Thomas, a man in his early fifties whose life has revolved around sailing since he was eleven years old, who is no longer sailing. He and Eunice have had no children. Petitions to the Government which could realise his dream of returning to America have not yet borne fruit. What we do know of Thomas is that he was not a man who liked to be idle. He had his job in the city with the Navy Office, a desk job which certainly lacked some of the thrills of life on the sea.

Perhaps it is of no coincidence that this is the time at which he began to think about a new project.

Finding Support for the Hospital

Living in Rotherhithe, he had a walk of up to two hours to reach the city and he would have seen a great deal of city life in that time. It is this activity that made him realise what tragedy was taking place in the city – babies were being abandoned and were dying as a result.

Thomas had many dealings with the Navy Office at this time. This was a government department responsible for the civil administration of the Navy including, of particular interest to Thomas, stores and transport. In essence, this was the procurement of items essential to the functioning of the Navy (such as timber and tar, for example) and getting them to where the Navy needed them. Famously, the Navy Office had been based on Seething Lane and was where diarist Samuel Pepys was living when he witnessed the Fire of London. A few years after this fire, however, another fire destroyed the building and it was rebuilt in the same location.

The Navy Office was very near the Tower of London, and also Trinity House which Thomas was also known to visit to present his petitions. The Customs House was also in the area. It would be a relatively quick walk from Rotherhithe today but Thomas did not have the benefit of Tower Bridge which has shortened the route. Tower Bridge was not completed until 1894 and so Thomas had to walk to London Bridge which was the only bridge across the Thames.

The walk would have taken Thomas through Southwark, which had areas of extreme poverty and destitution. One place, now known as Jacob Street and very much different to how it was then, had such notoriety for its poverty and squalor that it was described by Charles Dickens (writing in 1837) as the home

The Navy Office in 1714, to which Thomas was a frequent visitor.

of Dicken's vicious criminal, Bill Sikes, who abducted Oliver Twist and forced him into criminality.

Dickens's description of Southwark:

> Crazy wooden galleries common to the backs of half a dozen houses, with holes from which to look upon the slime beneath; windows, broken and patched, with poles thrust out, on which to dry the linen that is never there; rooms so small, so filthy, so confined, that the air would seem too tainted even for the dirt and squalor which they shelter; wooden chambers thrusting themselves out above the mud, and threatening to fall into it – as some have done; dirt-besmeared walls and decaying foundations; every repulsive lineament of poverty, every loathsome indication of filth, rot, and garbage; all these ornament the banks of Folly Ditch. The houses have no owners; they are broken open, and entered upon by those who have the courage; and there they live, and there they die. They must have powerful motives for a secret residence, or be reduced to a destitute condition indeed, who seek a refuge in Jacob's Island.[4]

It was on this walk that Thomas saw the dead and dying babies which are now famed as having given him the idea of establishing a Foundling hospital.

Had he walked past them before, but had no time to think of them? Or was he actively seeking out something to do when he realised the answer was right there on the street?

Many commentators say that the babies were not simply left on the streets but were actually thrown onto dunghills: 'He had seen the shocking spectacle of innocent children who had been murdered and thrown on the dung hills'.[5]

These dunghills cannot have been easy to ignore. Each was a mound of human and animal excrement, rotting carcasses and other waste. They would have been covered in flies in warm weather and reduced to rivers of filth in wet weather. They were home to rats and other vermin. The stench would have been unimaginable in the winter and unbearable in the summer sun. They could reach 10 metres high. To put this into perspective, one of these mounds would have been taller than a modern two storey house. Heavy rainstorms would have caused collapse and streams of foul run-off. These dunghills would have dominated any street or alley in which the grew. We would be fully aware of the health issues but the average London resident in Thomas's day may not have thought twice about their child climbing it to see what they could find that was edible or usable.

Thomas's thoughts were that he needed to do something about the babies thrown on these terrible mounds of filth. It was perhaps unexpected that a man whose career and interests were in shipping and in trade should embark on a social care project. As far as is known he held no trustee or governor positions in social care initiatives and had no personal experience of such ventures, and it is highly likely that he would have done so given his rather lowly social standing.

> Although the captain had made his fortune on the American plantations, and had seen sights in his day, he came out of it all with a tender heart; and this tender heart of Captain Coram was so affected by seeing children, dead and alive, habitually exposed by the wayside as he journeyed from Rotherhithe to the Docks and Royal Exchange that he could not bear it.[6]

There was another social care initiative in the city which was getting attention. The timing, it was completed in 1721, suggests that this might have provided Thomas with inspiration. Thomas Guy was from a background similarly humble to Thomas's but he had made a good business selling Bibles and thus found himself wealthy. He used profit from the Bibles to invest in the South Sea Company, selling at vast profit just before the bubble burst. As a governor of St Thomas's Hospital, he was aware of the issues facing the hospital's desperately ill patients and, wanting to do something to help, decided to found a Hospital for Incurables for those people discharged from St Thomas's who had no prospect of recovering from their illness. This was not an uncommon situation as there were few serious illnesses that it was possible to cure with the primitive medicines available at the time. Thomas Guy died just three years after founding the hospital, leaving a large fortune in his will to it. It was lauded as the 'largest Charity ever yet given by any such person'.[7] Thomas would have been very aware of what Thomas Guy had achieved and how it had been received.

According to a letter he wrote to Selina Hastings (née Shirley) dated 1739, he decided to do something for the abandoned and dying babies in 1722, the year after Thomas Guy's act of philanthropy and just two years after the loss of the *Seaflower*. Thomas was 54 years old, more than twenty years younger than Thomas Guy but lacking, unfortunately, his great wealth.

When Thomas saw the babies dying in the dunghills and on the streets, he decided that a hospital was what was needed for them and that, in the hospital, education would be provided. Thomas Guy's hospital may have been the inspiration for doing something, but the specific idea of the hospital, was borrowed from another source. He also made another decision; he decided that these babies who were abandoned on the dunghills were illegitimate following the general belief in society that the mothers of illegitimate babies were apt to murder their offspring.

Like Thomas Guy, Thomas decided his solution was a large hospital and, like Guy's Hospital, Thomas's would have 400 beds. His hospital was not, in the sense we use the word today, a medical facility, but a hospital in the sense of providing hospitality, or care, for those living in it.

This idea of a hospital for abandoned babies had been presented to Queen Anne who reigned in the very early 1700s. According to reports, several eminent merchants got as far as proposing a subscription and soliciting a charter. However, the idea got no further as it was thought that it would encourage vice by providing for illegitimate children. Poor Queen Anne died in 1714 having had seventeen pregnancies and no surviving children. Most died as miscarriages or were stillborn. The longest surviving lived only until he was 11.

In 1713, less than ten years before Thomas began work on his own plan, MP, essayist and founder of the *Spectator* Magazine, Joseph Addison wrote an appeal for England to have a foundling hospital: 'a provision for foundlings, or for those children who, through want of such a provision, are exposed to the barbarity of cruel and unnatural parents'. His reasoning was that there was 'scarce an assizes where some unhappy wretch is not executed for the murder of a child'. He went on to ask 'how many more of those monsters of inhumanity may we suppose to be wholly undiscovered?'[8] Sadly, Addison died in 1719 and so was unable to see Thomas begin his quest. He is likely to have been an excellent ally should he have lived. Addison's description of what he saw as the situation and how it should be resolved is so closely mirrored in what Thomas's plan became that it is impossible not to imagine that Thomas was not in some way aware of, and persuaded by, Addison's ideas.

Even when Addison penned his solution to the problem of foundlings, it was by no means a new idea. Addison looked to what he termed the 'great cities of Europe' and said he felt we should be following their example in providing foundling hospitals.

There were foundling hospitals in many cities in Europe and beyond. In Venice and Rome, foundling hospitals had been in existence since the fourteenth and fifteenth centuries. In Paris, there had been a foundling hospital since 1640. The Dublin Foundling Hospital was founded in 1704, eighteen years before Thomas started his quest. There were foundling hospitals in many cities of Europe, particularly those where the Catholic Church was strong. Thomas's plan would bring London in line with the rest of Europe.

Without the money to fund such a project, Thomas came up with a simple plan. He had been advised that he would need to evidence support for his project, and specifically financial support, before the Government would take it seriously. Thomas decided he would present his idea to people he knew through the Navy Office, Trinity House and other merchants, and he would ask them either to pledge money and support or to suggest someone else who would pledge money and support. The numbers of people putting their name to his project would persuade the Government that the facility was necessary while also providing start-up funds to make it happen.

So, he had motivation, he had time and he had a tried and tested idea – a foundling hospital – which already had had some public interest, albeit not enough interest to make it come to fruition yet. All he had to do was to persuade individuals to back his petition. But this is where things became much more difficult than he could have imagined.

His plan was to rely on his own powers of persuasion. He would meet with people, tell them of the great need, describe the foundling hospital he envisaged and suggest that this would bring London into line with other European nations. He had no photographs to appeal to his potential donors, for the camera had yet to be invented, he had no statistics to make his case as data was not collected, and he had no expert opinions, as there were few practitioners in the field. He had a petition, which he had paid to have written out and copied, and a notebook for his own use, but that was about all.

The idea was so clear, had such lineage and was so necessary, that Thomas must have been completely shocked to find that many doors closed to him. In fact, for the first six years of his quest, he had very little success at all. Precisely how many times he was turned away, we don't know. But each day he went out, he returned, presumably passing each time more infants left for dead on the dunghills, with the hospital no further forward.

In his obituary, Brocklesby, Thomas's close friend, wrote of this quest, 'an abler hand might have easily undertaken the task, but none could perform it with a better will' casting doubt on Thomas's abilities. Did Brocklesby think perhaps that Thomas did not have the skills to explain his project and persuade people to support it? Did he not have sufficiently good connections? He did, however, have the will to continue, and as his quest for support stretched out from days to months to years, he certainly needed this will.

Looking at other projects of the time, Thomas's struggle was unusual. For example, the founding of Westminster Hospital appeared to take only four years. Initially, there were parallels. Westminster Hospital began as a meeting of four people who ostensibly had nothing to do with the caring professions – they were a banker, a religious writer, a wine merchant and a reverend. They had recognised the need for care for London's poor and began the process of raising money. It is unclear what happened in the intervening three years but, in 1719, they met again with others they had encouraged to join and titled themselves 'the Trustees and Managers of Charity for Relieving the Sick and Needy'. They then rented a small house in Pimlico that same year and the following year opened their doors to the first patients, becoming the first voluntary hospital in the world funded entirely by public subscriptions and gifts. The following year, they published their Charitable Proposal for relieving the sick and needy.

> And by the blessing of God upon this undertaking, such sums of money have been advanced and subscribed by several of the nobility and gentry of both sexes and by some of the clergy, as have enabled the managers of this charity (who are as many of the subscribers as please to be present at their weekly meetings), to carry on in some measure what was then proposed: – for the satisfaction of the subscribers and benefactors, and for animating others to promote and encourage this pious and Christian work.[9]

What could Thomas have changed to replicate the quick success of the Westminster Hospital? Could he have worked in partnership with others rather than going it alone?

It is possible that this is a way forward that Thomas did indeed try. A newspaper of July 1721[10] announced that on 18 July in London 'a Number of young Gentlemen, have formed themselves into a society, for maintaining illegitimate children; And have erected an Office for that purpose in Gray's Inn'.

Was this a different attempt to form a foundling hospital? Or was Thomas involved but then decided to go solo? Unfortunately events in Dighton and in Thomas's later life suggest that this perhaps would not have been the way forward for him. He did not always function well when working with others.

Should Thomas have considered a greater role for the Church? Thomas was certainly a religious man himself but did not have formal connections to the Church and seemed convinced that the way forward for the foundling hospital was to be independent from the Church.

Thomas's main problem was that he wanted control over the project and yet did not have a large sum of money to invest in it; similarly, he did not attract anyone willing to donate that single lump sum which could have got the project off the ground, even on a smaller scale. As he continued to knock on doors to find support, he must have maintained a belief throughout that he would eventually be successful. Perhaps this confidence played a part in stopping him just rethinking the whole endeavour and setting about it via a different route.

There were undoubtedly other ways forward which need much less money and thus far less time to set up. For example, John Pounds was another individual, like Thomas, who had no money but wanted to do something for the children he saw living on the streets where he lived in Portsmouth. Rather than come with a grand plan he had no funds for, he took in individual children he found and taught them basic skills such as reading and writing. He is credited with starting, in this way, the ragged school movement which gave a free basic education to thousands of poor and homeless children in the nineteenth century. Interestingly, like Thomas, he also began life as an apprentice on ships – although he was unable to continue work as a shipwright after an accident on the docks which left him with disabilities.

A few decades later, in 1868, Dr Barnardo was also starting small. He set up a small ragged school for homeless boys in London. Before he died, this small school had led to him setting up more than hundred homes for children with an estimated 8500 children going through their doors. His name remains synonymous today with children's homes.

But Thomas did not have the benefit of knowing what these men could achieve later from starting small. He had his sights set on a much larger vision.

It is very likely that this idea of a very large institution which could accommodate, at any one time, children numbering in their hundreds came from the foundling hospitals of Europe and beyond. Some of these hospitals had been functioning for centuries before Thomas began his quest. Their very longevity must have been a great reassurance to him that this was a good model to follow. The Catholic Church in Europe had long had a tradition where babies left at church doors were taken in by the Church and given out to foster families. It is this long tradition which resulted in the successful foundation of many Catholic founding hospitals throughout Europe.

Christ's Hospital was established in 1555. Interestingly, it was set up by Royal Charter, which is the model that Thomas decided to take. It was based in Newgate, a little to the north of St Paul's Cathedral. It is likely that Thomas passed the school on his walks around London and was very familiar with its work, particularly as it had a role in training naval officers and merchant seafarers. Perhaps Thomas's colleagues had spent time there. Crucially, however, while taking in children and giving them an education, the school specifically excluded children who were illegitimate.

The charity school movement was also in full swing in London. The schools were set up, generally but by no means exclusively, by local churches. They were everything that Thomas's foundling hospital was not, in terms of scale. They took children in locally, to teach them as a free service, during the day. So, making them small-scale, low investment. But, together, they took in hundreds of children across London. Again, Thomas must have been very aware of this movement and would have seen the children in their uniforms going in and out of their schools.

One route that Thomas could feasibly have considered was setting up an Anglican version of a charity school. However, the schools did not solve the problem of homelessness, nor that of care for young infants. The charity school movement did not take the pressure off parents who had no money to house or feed their children, nor did it remove the burden of crushing social stigma felt by unmarried mothers. While providing an excellent free education to help children in their futures, the charity schools did nothing for those babies left dying on the city's heaps of dung. The charity school movement also proved to be relatively short-lived and was all but over in London by the mid-1720s.[11]

The route that Thomas chose was expensive and ambitious. It is possible that Thomas knew that people would not fund something small, a project had to be significant for people to stand behind it. It had to stand alongside projects such as Christ's Hospital and not look second best. Who would want to put their name to something which looked inadequate? As London was rapidly heading towards becoming Europe's largest city, and, as Thomas always had an eye on where Britain stood in the world, there was also a clear need for whatever was provided in London, to rival those foundling hospitals which already existed in Europe, and specifically, that which existed in Paris. This was not simply a matter of providing for the city's poor, it was about London and England's status in the world. For Thomas, there was no alternative, this had to be a project with scale and grandeur.

He did perhaps waiver at least once and considered toning down his idea. Jonas Hanway, who was a governor of the Foundling Hospital from 1758, and wrote an account of the hospital in 1759, said that Thomas once proposed 'that tents might be set up on Lamb's Conduit Fields, that people might bring in their children as foundlings from all parts'.[12]

It is a wonder that at some point he didn't pick up an abandoned baby and take it home with him. Would Eunice have cared for it? Did either of them want children themselves? It is an interesting idea that a man could spend twenty years of his life, and giving what money he had, to rescue babies of the future but never pick up and rescue one. He always walked by. Perhaps the fear of catching the baby's disease was too great. Or he knew that such an infant would have no hope of a future adopted in such a way. Perhaps he thought that becoming a parent to a deserted baby would end his own credibility in the kind of circles he needed to impress to make the project happen.

One issue which no doubt meant that doors were closed in Thomas's face was the issue of illegitimacy. There was a great abhorrence of illegitimate babies. They, and their mothers, were frequently termed 'evil' and not deserving of rescue or support. Our perspective now in the modern age is that babies cannot be evil, they begin with innocence. That was not a view commonly shared in the early eighteenth century.

It is interesting that Thomas decided that the babies he saw abandoned and dying on the streets were illegitimate. There was no evidence or data to this effect and it certainly wasn't an idea that made his quest popular.

It is also interesting to note that Thomas may have consciously taken some steps to distance himself and his project from the issue of illegitimacy in these days when he was trying to impress the aristocracy. His later petitions did not mention the word illegitimate. In the Royal Charter that founded the hospital in 1739 the text did not mention illegitimacy but instead referred to 'poor miserable infants'.

It is possible that timing was another of the issues that meant his quest was so drawn out. At this time, conflicts over land and thrones in both Europe and overseas were relatively common. Britain was involved in two significant wars – the War of the Spanish Succession with France which ran on from 1701 until 1714, and the Great Northern War, which started in 1700 but was not to end until 1721.

The War of the Spanish Succession was fundamentally a war to decide who should take control of the Spanish Empire after the Spanish king died without leaving an heir. Much of Europe got involved simply because of the size of the Spanish Empire which included swathes of Europe, taking in the Low Countries and Italy but also the Philippines and the Americas. Whoever gained the throne would be both powerful and wealthy, and Britain was determined not to let France gain that power. For this reason, Great Britain ploughed money and men into the conflict at great expense to the country. The Great Northern

War was a conflict between The Tsardom of Russia and the Swedish Empire. Britain initially joined to protect George I's Hanover.

There was also the issue of the South Sea Company. The company was in part private initiative and partly a public enterprise. It was set up in 1711 to trade in people who were stolen from Africa to be used as slaves in the South Sea islands and South America. The Government effectively sold the trading 'rights' of this slave market to the company in return for the profits which would fund the extensive national debt built up by the wars. The profitability of the slave trade together with the idea of doing something for the newly created Great Britain meant that there was a frenzy to buy stocks in the company. Such investment seems abhorrent now but people from all walks of life put their money into the shares confident of a good return. The shares initially increased in value very significantly.

Thousands invested thinking that they would get rich, but many lost all their wealth when the share price first peaked and then, when the bubble burst in 1720, plummeted.

The impact of the loss was so great that the entire country's economy struggled following the collapse. Investigations following the burst bubble found the project was plagued by corruption, insider trading, bribery and over-inflated claims designed to encourage the public to invest. The price of the stock had been artificially inflated by the company which was, in effect, lending money to its investors so that they could invest more.

It is estimated that around 34,000 people were taken from their homes in Africa and traded as slaves by the company. Many died while being transported. It has been argued that such were the horrors in the plantations awaiting many of the survivors that they wished they had died too.

It was during this time that Thomas began his campaign to get investments into the hospital. Many of those he was hoping to attract were still reeling from their own personal losses and an economy which had taken a battering.

Some people, of course, did not lose everything but instead sold their shares before the collapse and potentially made enormous profits. Robert Walpole who was prime minister when the hospital was granted its charter, was one such lucky investor. He is said to have made a 1000% profit. And Thomas Guy founded and funded his hospital using the fortune he had made by speculating in the South Sea Bubble with his earnings from selling Bibles.

In the main, however, Thomas was asking for funds at a time when there was extreme unease about individual and public finances.

Ladies of Charity

Thomas found himself trying to raise support for a very ambitious and deeply unpopular cause – that of illegitimate babies and their murderous mothers – at a time of deep financial troubles for many. It is perhaps not surprising that he spent the first seven years trying and failing to garner sufficient support for his project.

This is not to say that he had achieved nothing before this time; he had made some progress. The newspapers had already reported that a proposal would soon be presented to the Government for a foundling hospital in London where children would be nursed and educated. Thomas was achieving attention for his project, albeit a little over-optimistic in tone.

Newspapers reported in early 1729,[13] for example, that at an assizes (court hearings of criminal and civil cases) in Surrey, 'after dinner, on a Proposal from a great Man, 1,600 pounds was agreed to be raised by Subscription, as a beginning, towards erecting an Hospital for Foundling, or Bastard children'. Those present had heard several indictments that day relating to what was judged to be the murder of newborn children. Interestingly the meeting decided that these murders, and other similar cases which they felt probably never came to light, 'have sprung as well from Indigence and Poverty as the Sense of Shame' thus linking poverty as much as illegitimacy, to the cruel treatment of babies. The Honourable Mr Onslow, the Speaker of the House of Commons, was present at the event. In the same month, one of the gentlemen of the king's privy chamber died and left his entire estate to the forthcoming hospital. Some newspapers even reported that a piece of land had been identified for the hospital. Thomas's quest was undoubtedly making progress, although not as much progress as was needed.

Various men of standing refused to sign Thomas's petition to support the hospital idea despite Thomas spending years asking. A different man may well have given up after so many refusals and doors closed in his face. This endeavour was not free. While costs were low, Thomas was still having to pay to have his petitions written up and there were costs involved in travelling to prospective supporters who lived beyond walking distance. He needed a stubborn attitude and deep pockets to continue. Thomas, however, had dogged determination and obstinately stuck both to his cause and to his way of working, asking for support from influential individuals.

That Thomas was stubborn appears as a constant theme from his biographers. Hill, quoting a peer of Thomas's in 1720, says he 'is a man of that obstinate, persevering temper as never to desist from his first enterprise, whatever obstacles lie in his way'.[14]

What followed these first years of Thomas's quest is known about in some detail as Thomas's notebook from the time still survives. His biographers in the eighteenth and nineteenth centuries referred to what was in his notebook as much as researchers and commentators do today.

In 1729 there was a breakthrough – his cause was recognised by what he termed in his notebook 'Ladies of Charity' and who, in later petitions, he referred to as ladies of quality and distinction. They were women who were born into, or married into, wealth and political power in England. March 1729 saw the first of such women sign his petition.

Appealing to women makes good sense from where we are sat today. But it made no sense at all in Thomas's time. Women were in no way equal members of society to the men of the day, even women of wealth and heritage. Women belonged to their fathers and then to their husbands. Titles passed to sons, not daughters, and generally the wealth did too. Women could not legally be a director of a company, or a charity. It is worth remembering that women did not get the vote until 1918, two hundred years after Thomas's petition. This was a society that was not used to listening to the views of women; it was men who had the ideas and did the talking, held the power and controlled the wealth.

The 1751 memorial written to Thomas on the occasion of his funeral, describes that Thomas approached women not least because they would be easily persuaded: 'They did not listen much to his arguments; for the sweetness of their own Tempers supplied a Tenderness that rendered Arguments unnecessary'. While this condescending tone was probably typical of the time, we do not know that this mirrors Thomas's feelings about women, or if this is why he decided to approach women.

It seems likely that, in contrast to popular thinking of the time, Thomas appreciated the worth of women in society. Not only did he appreciate the potential value of female signatories on his petition but he proved himself to be a keen supporter of the education of girls. Spending ten years in the New World, living within the much more equal social structure of the new colonies, may well have been a factor in this as would the continuing influence of Eunice, his Boston wife.

It is also possible that he was inspired by the role of women in Vincent de Paul's Foundling Hospital in Paris where women played a formal and significant role in the hospital, providing the funding for it. It is perhaps of no coincidence that Thomas gave his female signatories the title 'Ladies of Charity' in his notebook, as the female supporters in the Parisian Foundling Hospital were called *les dames de charité*, the Ladies of Charity.

What is clear from Thomas's Ladies of Charity is that they were very well-connected and these links to each other and to those in power, was probably

48   Saving London's Abandoned Babies

key to Thomas's Foundling Hospital idea becoming a reality. Their connections helped the Foundling Hospital develop right through the eighteenth century, perhaps making them more influential than even Thomas could have imagined.

In his battered notebook, which is now looked after by the Foundling Hospital Museum in London, under the heading 'An exact account of when each Lady of Charity signed their Declaration', Thomas wrote the following list of names:

Signed in 1729:
Charlotte Seymour, Duchess of Somerset
Ann Vaughan, Duchess of Bolton
Henrietta Needham, Dowager Duchess of Bolton
Sarah Lennox, Duchess of Richmond

Signed in 1730:
Isabella Montagu, Duchess of Manchester
Ann Russell, Duchess of Bedford
Elizabeth Knight, Baroness Onslow
Anne Pierrepoint, Dowager Baroness Torrington
Frances Byron, Baroness Byron
Selina Shirley, Countess of Huntingdon
Juliana Hele, Duchess of Leeds
Frances Finch, Countess of Winchilsea (now spelt Winchelsea) and
    Nottingham
Frances Hales, Countess of Lichfield
Dorothy Boyle, Countess of Burlington
Elizabeth Brudenell, Countess of Cardigan
Frances Thynne, Countess of Hertford

Signed 1733:
Mary Tufton, Countess of Harold

Signed 1734:
Anne Lennox, Countess of Albemarle
Anne Weldon Barnard, Baroness Trevor

Signed 1735:
Anne King, Dowager Baroness Ockham
Margaret Cavendish Harley, Duchess of Portland

These signatories became known as the Ladies of Quality and Distinction as they were all from Britain's aristocracy either by birth or marriage or, more usually, both. The twenty-one women included eight duchesses, eight countesses and five baronesses. Several of the women were ladies of the bedchamber for Queen Caroline in the last years of her life. These women were the queen's personal attendants and would have spent time with her, accompanying her to engagements and attending to her personal needs. For Thomas, this was an excellent link between him and the royal family which turned out to be a critical factor in his ultimate success.

Aside from their aristocratic status, there were few other things that the ladies had in common. All were married or recently widowed. Their number included a poet, an artist and a woman who was prominent in the Methodist movement. Whether any of them had particular reason to support the Foundling Hospital, it is not easy to tell. One was herself illegitimate; two had fathers who were illegitimate. Two had brothers who had died in their infancy, one had four children who had died as babies. One was the executor of her father's trust for poor children. Four had no children, the remainder had children of their own and some had stepchildren as well. Were any of these experiences factors in deciding to support the cause or did it have more to do with the fact that they had friends and relatives amongst the other signatories? Or perhaps Thomas simply made a convincing case that the hospital needed their support.

Charlotte Seymour, the Duchess of Somerset, was the first woman to sign Thomas's petition. She signed in 1729. She met with Thomas and signed the document where she lived in Petworth, West Sussex, which must have been quite a journey by horse and cart for Thomas. No doubt the excitement of getting her signature made the journey worthwhile. She was 35 when she signed and had been married for three years to Charles Seymour, the 6th Duke of Somerset. A duke is the highest non-royal title which could be bestowed. Charlotte's husband was around thirty years older than she was and his children were grown up. Their daughter was less than a year old when she signed that March so the fate of babies of a similar age may well have struck a chord with her. One of Charlotte's stepsons was Algernon Seymour, who was 45 at the time.

After the excitement of that first signature, it was six long weeks before the next woman agreed to sign the petition. She was Ann Vaughan, the Duchess of Bolton. Her father was the 3rd Earl of Carbery. She was 40 when she signed and had been married to her husband Charles Paulet, the 3rd Duke of Bolton, for sixteen years but they had had no children. He was an MP and also had royal connections as he had been a gentleman of the bedchamber of the Prince of Wales. She did have stepchildren, one of whom was married to Henrietta Needham who also signed the petition just three days later.

At 47, Henrietta, the Dowager Duchess of Bolton, was older than her step-mother-in-law, Ann. She was very well connected, with Charles II as her paternal grandfather although Henrietta herself was illegitimate and used her mother's surname, Needham. She married the 2nd Duke of Bolton when she was around 15 years old. He was an MP and had been Lord Chamberlain of the Household, the most senior office in the royal household. They had a son, Nassau Powlett, a year later. When she signed the petition, her son was 31 years old, an MP and had been knighted, and Henrietta had been a widow for seven years. Lord Nassau married Isabella Tufton in 1731. Her sister, Mary, signed the petition two years after the marriage. Henrietta died in 1730, five years before the petition was presented to the king.

It was another eight months before Thomas achieved his fourth signature of support. Sarah Lennox signed in December of 1729. Not only was it great for Thomas to get another signature, Sarah also had particularly useful connections as she was one of Queen Caroline's ladies of the bedchamber, a post she had held for five years when she signed the document. This was to prove to be a key link for the success of Thomas's plan for a hospital. Henrietta had been one of the ladies of the bedchamber some years earlier but, for Sarah, the role was current. Sarah was just 24 when she gave her signature but had already been married (to Charles Lennox, the 1st Duke of Richmond) for ten years, a marriage arranged to clear debts incurred by Sarah's father, Lord Cadogan. Sadly, up to the point when Sarah signed the petition, married life had been engulfed by tragedy. The couple had had three daughters and two sons, but all had died.

The next twelve months proved very successful in terms of signatures, as Thomas managed to persuade another twelve aristocratic women to support his project.

In January, Lady Isabella, the Duchess of Manchester signed. Like Sarah, she was no stranger to the pain of infant deaths. She was 23 when she signed and her brother had died two years before at the age of 2. He was the third of her brothers to die in infancy. Isabella had been married to William Montagu, 2nd Duke of Manchester for seven years but they had no children. Lady Isabella was the first of Thomas's signatories known to be a talented artist.

The day after Lady Isabella signed the petition, Ann Russell joined her. Ann was 24 when she signed and had been married for five years. When Ann was 20, she married Wriothesley Russell, the 3rd Duke of Bedford, who happened to be the younger brother of Lady Rachel Russell who her father (1st Duke of Bridgwater) had married in 1722 following the death of Ann's mother. Ann and Wriothesley had no children.

Thomas waited three months for the next signature. She was Elizabeth, Baroness Onslow who was 37. She was the daughter of a merchant who had

London: the river Thames and the buildings of the City, looking northwards beside London Bridge. Coloured engraving, 1730, after J. Kip. Wellcome Collection. (*Wellcome Collection*)

made the family fortune on the back of the slave trade. She married Thomas Onslow, the 2nd Baron Onslow, in 1708 when she was 16. They had one surviving son, Richard, who was 17 when Elizabeth signed the petition. Elizabeth died in 1731 before the petition was even presented to the king.

The following week, Anne Pierrepoint signed. She was aged about 30 and was widowed; her husband, Thomas Newport, 1st Baron Torrington, having died in 1719 after eleven years of marriage. Not only did they not have any children but he had none from either of his two previous marriages. Anne died in 1735.

The next was Baroness Frances Byron who was to become the great grandmother of the poet, Lord Byron. At the time of the signature, however, she was only 20 and thus the youngest of Ladies of Charity. Well-connected in her own family's right, she was the daughter of the 4th Baron Berkeley of Stratton, a judge and politician and the son of an Admiral. She married William Baron, the 4th Baron Byron in 1720; she was 17 and he was 51. Between them, they had six children. William Byron was a politician but also had been gentleman of the bedchamber to Prince George of Denmark, Queen Anne's husband.

Selina Shirley, Countess of Huntingdon was the tenth signature on the petition. She was 22 when she signed. Shirley, the daughter of the 2nd Earl Ferrers, was a very significant player in the development of the Methodist Church in England at the time and much of her personal fortune was given to the cause. Just two years before she signed the petition, she married Theophilus Hastings, 9th Earl of Huntingdon. When she signed, her first child, Francis, was around a year old. Selina is very significant to the story of Thomas Coram as it is only through a letter that he wrote to her, as Selina Hastings, which still survives, that we know that his quest began in 1722.

Selina's aunt, Frances Finch, Countess of Winchilsea and Nottingham, signed just a few days after Selina. She was 39 and had been married to Daniel Finch, the 8th Earl of Winchelsea for a year. She was probably pregnant with her daughter, Charlotte, when she signed the petition. Frances died in 1734.

Juliana Hele was 23 when she signed the petition. She had been married to Peregrine Osborne, Marquess of Carmarthen, for five years. He died in 1731.

Like Henrietta Needham, Thomas's third signatory, Frances Hales, Countess of Lichfield, had links to Charles II. Frances's mother-in-law was his illegitimate daughter. Frances married her husband, George Lee, 2nd Earl of Lichfield, in 1718. In 1730, when she signed the petition, she had at least three children under ten and was probably in the midst of her ninth pregnancy. Her daughter, Frances, had died seven years earlier aged 3.

The fourteenth signature was that of Dorothy Boyle, the Countess of Burlington, who was aged 30. She was related to the very first signatory, Charlotte Seymour, through Charlotte's father, Daniel Finch, who was also Dorothy's grandfather. Dorothy married Richard Boyle, the 3rd Earl of Burlington, in 1721 and they had two daughters; the second, born in 1727, died in 1730. Dorothy was a talented artist and a great patron of the arts. She was a patron of Handel's. Was this how Handel became interested in the Foundling Hospital himself? Charlotte was also one of Queen Caroline's ladies of the bedchamber, along with Sarah Lennox, Anne Lennox, and Frances Thynne.

Elizabeth Brudenell was aged 40 when she signed the petition in May 1730. Her mother was Lady Elizabeth Seymour and her father was Thomas Bruce, the 2nd Earl of Ailesbury (now Aylesbury). She married George Brudenell, the 2nd Earl of Cardigan, in 1707. By 1730 the couple had four sons.

Frances Thynne, the Countess of Hertford, was the last aristocrat to sign in the busy April and May of 1730. She was 31 when she signed and had been married to Algernon Seymour (the Earl of Hertford and also stepson to Thomas's first signatory, Charlotte) for fifteen years. They had married when he was 30 and she was 16 and they had two children. Their youngest, a son, was 5 when she signed the petition. She was a published poet and a patron of literature and was also one of the ladies of the bedchamber of Queen Caroline.

Frances was the last of the twelve women who had signed the petition in 1730. This was a remarkable upturn in Thomas's work and he must surely have felt that his Darling Project was on the way to success by the end of the year.

However, it was still to be three and a half years until Thomas found another signatory. The is because he was distracted during this time by another cause that warranted his attention.

Hats were a very significant part of the outfits worn in the early eighteenth century. Tricorne hats were three-cornered hats worn by men, particularly those associated with the Navy and mobcaps, a flimsy bonnet, or flat straw hats were worn by women. Initially, hats were worn because they protected the wearer from the rain and the sun but, as they were not cheap to make, they became an ostentatious symbol of the wealth of the wearer. Thomas, however, was not known to be a particular fan of hats but he became closely involved with them.

While he was a great supporter of the colonisation of North America and the utilisation of the natural resources there, he also had an appreciation of the negative impact that opening up this huge source of imports could have on British businesses. He was approached by British hat manufacturers to help them in their concerns about the manufacture of hats in North America impacting on sales of British hats. He took their case on and was influential in the adoption of the 1732 Hat Act which restricted the ability of North American hatters to export to England.

It was a particularly harsh act as it not only prevented North American hat manufacturers from entering the British market, but it also sought to restrict their ability to make hats for their own North American market by limiting the number of apprenticeships that could exist. Thus, North American hat-buyers were forced to look at expensive imports from Britain. This seems perhaps out of character for Thomas as his endeavours were usually based on a spirit of fairness and the promotion, rather than the suppression of enterprise in the New World.

Such was the gratitude of British hat makers for protecting their livelihoods that they ensured Thomas had free hats for the rest of his life. Most of the few portraits of Thomas depict him hatless with his long, curly white hair hanging freely. In 1741, however, he was painted by the artist Balthazar Nebot wearing a long black coat and a tricorne hat, presumably one gifted to him by the Hatters' Company.

Thomas Jefferson, prior to the American Revolution, made mention of Thomas's Hat Act and the anger towards it which remained: 'By an act passed in the 5th Year of the reign of his late Majesty King George II, an American subject is forbidden to make a hat for himself of the fur which he has taken perhaps on his own soil; an instance of despotism to which no parallel can be produced in the most arbitrary ages of British history'.[15]

Commentators have gone so far as to say that the Hat Act was a significant contributing factor to the American Revolution.[16]

Thomas Coram; in the foreground is an infant in a basket, in the background the Foundling Hospital. Line engraving by J. Brooke, 1751, after B. Nebot, 1741. (*Wellcome Collection*)

In this 'break' from soliciting support for the Foundling Hospital, Thomas was also soliciting support for another project. Back to what he knew best, Thomas had become involved with a group of men who were petitioning for a new colony in the New World. The area in question was again on the east coast of the Americas but this time a thousand miles south of Massachusetts where he made his home with Eunice. The area was southern South Carolina and was to become Georgia. The project was granted a charter in April 1732 as the last of the thirteen British colonies in America. It was unique in that it was the only colony to be ruled by a board of trustees and Thomas was appointed as one of those trustees. After his long campaign of petitioning for settlement of the east coast of America, this must have felt like a huge triumph for him. As a trustee, he was specifically charged with soliciting donations and he set about the task with relish once more visiting prospective donors and persuading them to part with their money just as he had been doing for his foundling hospital. He was there in Gravesend in November 1732 as the first settlers set sail for their new home. As he watched the laden ships leave England with the excited settlers waving goodbye to England, was he wishing that he and Eunice were on board too?

Soon after the triumphant departure of the first Georgia settlers from England however, cracks began to show between him and the other trustees and a row about the rights of women to inherit land appears to have diminished his enthusiasm relatively early in the process. He finally left the board of trustees less than ten years after the Charter had been granted.

Whether Thomas was flush with the success of his Hat Act or despondent over his disappointment with the Georgia trustees, Thomas returned to the issue of his hospital and began seeking out signatures of his Ladies of Charity once more.

The sixteenth name on his petition was that of Mary Tufton, the Countess of Harold, who signed in July 1733. She was the daughter of Thomas Tufton, the 6th Earl of Thanet who had died in 1729 and she took on the responsibility for his charitable endeavours including a school for poor children. She had married Anthony Grey, the Earl of Harold when she was 17 but he had died just five years later from an incident in which he choked on an ear of barley.

A year later came the eighteenth signature, Anne Lennox, Countess of Albemarle, who, like Mary Tufton, was one of the ladies of the bedchamber of Queen Caroline. She was the daughter of Charles Lennox, 1st Duke of Richmond, who was himself an illegitimate son of Charles II, making Anne the third close relative of Charles II to become a signatory. She had on the date of signing the petition, four sons and a daughter who was only a matter of months old.

Anne Weldon Barnard was, unlike the other signatories, not born into aristocracy but was the daughter of a textile trader in Fleet Street. She was the oldest of the signatories being around 67 when she signed. Her first husband was Sir Robert Barnard, and the second was Thomas Trevor, 1st Baron Trevor who was Attorney General and later Lord Privy Seal. She had eight children.

Baroness Ockham Anne King was part of the Welsh aristocracy and was married to Peter King, 1st Baron King, with whom she had six children. She was 45 when she signed the petition and all her children were grown up.

The final signatory was Margaret Cavendish Harley, the Duchess of Portland, who signed on 7 May 1735 when she was just 20, making her one of the youngest signatories. She had married William Bentinck, the Duke of Portland, the year before and gave birth to her first child just a month after signing.

The process of gathering the twenty-one signatures took Thomas six years. The painstaking nature of collecting these signatures is hinted at by the dates of the signatures. At no stage was Thomas able to talk to more than one person at a time. Each person was visited on a separate day and an individual appeal made to them by Thomas. The task involved significant travelling which he paid for out of his own funds, an expense he had to make whether the person he visited deigned to sign his petition or not.

With the twenty-first signature on the list, Thomas decided that the petition was complete. Whether he ran out of potential further signatories or he became aware that the list had sufficient gravitas with twenty-one Ladies of Charity that he need labour on it no more, we cannot know. He certainly was now well-equipped for the next stage of his quest.

The most immediate benefit to Thomas was the clear link between his Ladies of Charity and the queen. Queen Caroline had become queen consort two years earlier when her husband, George II, took the throne of Britain. Queen Caroline was 46 when the first of her ladies of the bedchamber signed Thomas's petition. Several other ladies of Caroline's bedchamber also signed. Whether Caroline heard of Thomas's foundling hospital from her ladies of the bedchamber, or whether they learnt of it from her, is unknown, but she certainly became one of the project's biggest supporters and news of Thomas's progress was certainly shared between the women. Queen Caroline used her own influence to ensure that the hospital came to be, although she died before without knowing that her husband had finally granted a Royal Charter to the hospital. Before she died in 1737, she commissioned a report into the workings of the Paris Foundling Hospital which became an important part of the shared knowledge about foundling hospitals. This was published in 1739 as 'an account of the foundation and government of the Hospital for Foundlings in Paris drawn up at the command of her last majesty Queen Caroline and now published for the information of those who may be concerned in carrying on a like design in this city'. The document reads like a blueprint of the foundling hospital Thomas established.

Caroline herself was no stranger to tragedy. He father died of smallpox when she was 3 and her stepfather also died of smallpox. Caroline's mother then died

Queen Caroline, wife of King George IV, head and shoulders in profile. Stipple print by T. Woolnoth after T. Wageman, 1820. Wellcome Collection. (*Wellcome Collection*)

when Caroline was just 13. Caroline gave birth to her first child, Frederick, in 1707 when she was 24. After the birth she herself contracted smallpox and so was kept away from her new son until she had recovered. In all, she had eight children, one of whom died in infancy. The others were grown up by the time George became king and she became his consort.

The text of Thomas's petition which was signed by the Ladies of Charity:

Whereas among the many excellent designs and institutions of Charity, which this nation, and especially the city of London, has hitherto encouraged and established, no expedient has yet been found out, for preventing the frequent murders of poor miserable children at their birth; or for supressing the inhuman custom of exposing new born infants to perish in the streets; or the putting out such unhappy Foundlings to wicked and barbarous nurses who undertaking to bring them up for a small and trifling sum of money, do often suffer them to starve for want of due sustenance or care; or, if permitted to live, either turn them into the Streets to beg or steal, or hire them out to loose persons by whom they are trained up in that infamous way of living; and sometimes are blinded, or maimed and distorted in their limbs, in order to move pity and compassion, and thereby become fitter instruments of gain to those vile merciless wretches.

For a beginning to redress so deplorable a grievance, and to prevent as well the effusion of so much innocent blood, as the fatal consequences of that idleness, beggary or stealing, in which such poor Foundlings are generally bred up; and to enable them, by an early and effectual care of their education, to become useful members of the commonwealth, We whose names are underwritten being deeply touched with compassion for the sufferings and lamentable condition of such poor abuses and mischiefs to which they are exposed, and in order to supply the government plentifully with useful hands on many occasions; and for the better producing of good and faithful servants from amongst the poor and miserable cast off children or Foundlings now a pest to the public and a chargeable nuisance within the bills of Mortality; and for settling a yearly income for their maintenance and proper education, til they come to a fit age for service; are desirous to encourage, and willing to contribute towards erecting an Hospital for infants, whom their parents are not able to maintain, and who have no right to any parish; which we conceive will not only prevent many horrid murders, cruelties and other mischiefs, and be greatly beneficial to the publick; but will also be acceptable to God Almighty, as being the only remedy of such great evils, which have been so long neglected, tho' always complained of; provided due and proper care be taken for setting on foot so necessary an establishment, and a Royal Charter be granted by the King to such persons, as his Majesty shall approve of, who shall be willing to become benefactors for the erecting and endowing such an Hospital, and for the receiving the voluntary contributions and well-disposed persons, and for directing and managing the affairs thereof gratis, to the best advantage; under such regulations as his Majesty in his great wisdom shall judge most proper for attaining the desired effect of our good Intentions.[17]

The petition written by Thomas, and signed by his Ladies of Charity, was eloquently and flamboyantly written. However, it only briefly mentioned what the root cause of the problem might be. The hospital was described as being able to save babies who might otherwise have been murdered by their parents, abandoned on the streets, or put out to beg perhaps after having been maimed. We know from both earlier documents from Thomas and later biographies, that Thomas was keen that the hospital should be open for illegitimate babies as they were particularly at risk of being murdered by their mothers (although we also know that mothers of illegitimate babies were particularly at risk of being charged with murdering their babies whether or not they had). He does not, however, mention illegitimacy. Towards the end of the petition, he mentions that the hospital would be for babies whose parents could not afford to maintain them and who did not have the option of poor relief from their parish as they did not have a parish, presumably because they had moved away from their place of birth.

The element of the hospital that Thomas does not mention, and that is never a primary focus in the later hospital documents, is that the hospital was not simply going to benefit the babies who were left there, it would also benefit the parents. Having a baby out of wedlock was so shameful that a woman would lose her job, be thrown out of the family home and be shunned by neighbours and the Church. By leaving her baby in the care of the hospital, she would have a chance of being able to return to her normal life, or at least find a job elsewhere. The parents who had no money to feed another mouth, could leave their baby with the hospital, and, by so doing, be able to afford to feed themselves and the rest of their family.

The assumption that society so often made in the eighteenth century, that all unmarried parents would have killed or abandoned their babies to save themselves, is no doubt over-simplistic or simply wrong. Not all parents would have killed or abandoned their babies, most would have done their best to make the most of the situation, possibly endangering their own health and lives and the wellbeing of the rest of their family.

The Darling Project

While the twenty-one signatures Thomas gained between 1729 and 1735 and the support from Queen Caroline that he enjoyed as a result no doubt represented a real turning point in the fortunes of his hospital idea, this was not the end of his quest.

Following the petition signed by the Ladies of Charity, Thomas put together a second petition signed by Lord Derby and '51 other important men' in 1735 which referred to the first petition. A further petition was signed by Justices of the Peace and other 'persons of distinction'. This petition, presented in 1737, also lent very heavily on the importance of the Ladies of Charity having put their names to the idea: 'That many Noblemen and Gentlemen highly approving the said Ladys Charitable Inclinations Have by Another Instrument in Writing declared their hearty Concurrence for advancing to the utmost of their power so Human and Christian an Undertaking promising each for himself that whenever Your Majesty may be Graciously pleased to Grant Letters Patent for the more effectual carrying on so useful a Designe they will readily employ their Interests in Recommending and Contributions in Supporting an Hospital in or near London for the reception Virtuous Education & usefull Training up of all such helpless Infants as may be brought to it'.[18]

During this time, Thomas was also petitioning for another project. This time it was the colonisation of Nova Scotia. With his interest in the Georgia project waning, and the foundling hospital project stalled in a cycle of petitions, Thomas turned his attention once more to New England. This time Thomas's plan was that the area of Nova Scotia should be settled by 'a competent number of Industrious Protestant Families' who could establish a government similar to that in England and take advantage of cod fishing and raising hemp and other resources for Naval Stores. This would also have the advantage of pushing out the French inhabitants there. To try to gain support for the plan he busied himself drawing up petitions, writing letters and talking to others about the plans.

However, the Nova Scotia plans took a back seat to the foundling hospital project when, five years after the last of the Ladies of Charity signed Thomas's petition, and seventeen years after Thomas is understood to have first begun seeking support for the project, a Charter of Incorporation was granted for the *Hospital for the Maintenance and Education of Exposed and Deserted Children*. The latest petitions, leaning heavily on the precedent set by Thomas's Ladies of Charity, had finally given the Foundling Hospital enough gravitas to be accepted. On 17 October 1739 the king of Great Britain and Ireland, George II, signed the Charter document.

Thomas's campaign had begun when George II's father was on the throne. George I had a relatively busy reign leaving him with more on his mind than foundlings; the bursting of the South Sea Bubble, for example, and the significant amount of time he spent in his birth place of Hanover.

By contrast his son George II reigned over a relatively peaceful and economically stable Britain. With Robert Walpole still the Chancellor of the Exchequer, effectively taking the role of prime minister, Britain was experiencing a long period of peace largely because Walpole was very set on avoiding conflict in Europe. This peace was giving the country time to recover from the South Sea Company losses without having to fund expensive wars. The economic and political stability probably meant that the conditions were ideal for a project such as the hospital. But maybe boredom also played a part: George II was very much moulded in the tradition of the military king. This long period of peace may have left him hoping for something else to make his name and occupy his time.

Another key influence on George II of course, was his wife Caroline. She had been very keen on the idea of the foundling hospital, had discussed it with several of her ladies of the bedchamber, and no doubt with her husband as well. Although she died in 1737, her husband may still have been swayed by her. It was known that theirs was a loving relationship. When he died, he left instructions for his coffin to be laid next to hers with the side panels removed so they could lie together. Perhaps in some way he felt that the hospital would serve as a memorial to her and the fulfilment of her wishes.

The Royal Charter signed by King George II on 17 October 1739 set out the constitution, the legal rules for how the Corporation was to be run and it was accompanied by the first list of governors, those people who were responsible for ensuring that the constitution was followed.

Even at this time, Thomas felt that his cause, with the evil of illegitimacy at its core, was treated without the generosity which would have been afforded other causes. He is quoted as complaining 'The fees will be more than two hundred guineas to prepare and pass the charter through all the offices and officers notwithstanding it is so compassionate a case, but I am told, and do believe, if it was to prevent the abolishing of Christianity out of the World no lawyer or office man would abate of his fees.'[19]

The Charter text referred to the importance of the role of the women as signatories of one of the petitions. There was no need to mention that people of both sexes were involved unless Thomas wanted to use the opportunity to give his particular thanks to them.

> The Royal Charter, establishing an Hospital for the Maintenance and Education of Exposed and Deserted Young Children…. Our Trusty and well-beloved Subject Thomas Coram, Gentleman, in behalf of great Numbers of helpless Infants daily exposed to destruction, has by his Petition humbly represented unto Us, that many persons of Quality and Distinction, as well as others of both Sexes (being sensible of the frequent Murders committed by their parents to hide their shame, and the inhuman Custom of exposing new-born children to perish in the Streets, or training them up in Idleness, Beggary, and Theft) have, by Instruments in Writing, declared

their Intentions to contribute liberally towards the erecting an Hospital, after the Example of other Christian Countries…(*sic*)

The original Charter was signed by 351 governors which increased to 376 by June of 1740 when a second version was printed. Each year following, more governors were added. At one point, the number of men signed up as governors was nearing a thousand.

Modern charities are run by trustees, say a dozen or fewer would be usual. Having 376 governors, and more, involved in the running of an organisation is an incredible feat. Of course, some governors were more proactively involved with the hospital than others. Some were not active at all but were appointed as governors in return for a donation. Others were signed up more in the hope that they might make a donation, or other contribution, in the future.

The 1739 Charter list of governors appears to uphold the idea that most governors were appointed for their wealth and connections rather than for their useful skills. The list includes seventeen dukes, twenty-nine earls, six viscounts, and a large number of lords together with the Attorney General and Solicitor General. The list included of course, Lord Robert Walpole, as the leader of Parliament, and the king's son was added in the following year. The Speaker of the House of Commons, Arthur Onslow, was also listed.

To have men of such power and influence was an impressive feat, largely due to Thomas's dogged determination. Walpole was known to be a close friend of Queen Caroline – whose ladies of the bedchamber were represented in some number on Thomas's petition.

At the foot of the list of governors was a stationer, a druggist and a bookseller, men who were perhaps wealthy or otherwise useful in their own right but found themselves dwarfed within a list of such aristocracy and power.

The most significant things about the governors was, however, that they were all men. Women, despite them taking such a key role in the setting up of the hospital, could not themselves be involved in Thomas's hospital on any management level. As women, they could not become governors. There were women involved in the hospital, of course, primarily as nurses, but the governors were all men. However, despite not having power, the women again proved their influence. While four of the women had died before the Charter came into being, most of the other signatories remained loyal to the project despite it being, in some cases, ten years since they had given their names to it. Of the twenty-one women who signed Thomas's petition, only six did not have one or more close relatives sign the 1739 Charter – husbands, sons, fathers signed where the women could not. For example, a son of Baroness Byron signed the Charter as a 17 year old. The Duchess of Leeds had lost her husband since she

The House of Commons: the Speaker, Arthur Onslow (seated, centre), calling upon Sir Robert Walpole (left) to speak. Stipple engraving by R. Page after W. Hogarth and J. Thornhill. (*Wellcome Collection*)

signed the petition in 1730. However, her second husband signed the Charter. Both the husband and the father of the Duchess of Portland became governors as did the Countess of Winchelsea and Nottingham's husband, although she had died five years earlier.

And, of course, Queen Caroline's son, Frederick, Prince of Wales was listed on the 1740 update of the Charter document.

The Charter not only listed governors but included those who had been given specific offices to hold – the president, his six vice-presidents and the treasurer. These men were successful in their own right but were not necessarily the wealthiest or the most powerful amongst the governors. Instead they were selected for their allegiances to the project, Thomas or the king. It is interesting to note that Thomas himself did not take one of these roles. It is likely that he was aware that he did not have the standing amongst such a group of men to assume leadership over them, but probably what was of equal importance to a man such as Thomas was that he wanted to be in the midst of things. He wanted to be the person out getting things done rather than someone who had a more restrictive, or honorary role.

The Duke of Bedford was appointed the first President of the Hospital, a post he maintained until his death some thirty years later. He was John, 4th Duke of Bedford, a title he had inherited in 1732. Born in Streatham he was a prominent Whig politician. Horace Walpole described him as 'a man of inflexible honesty and good will towards his country'. Lord Charlemont said he was 'a man of excellent parts, though deficient in common sense'. Perhaps it was fortunate that he had six vice-presidents to support him in his role at the hospital.

His sister-in-law, Ann Russell, Duchess of Bedford, had been one of Thomas's twenty-one Ladies of Charity having signed the petition nine years earlier. When he was made president, he was 29 and at the beginnings of his political career. He was to go on to become the First Lord of the Admiralty, the Lord Privy Seal and the Lord Lieutenant of Ireland but the presidency of the hospital was the first of such appointments. He went on to negotiate peace with France in 1763 which brought to an end the Seven Years' War.

Perhaps his own personal life had some part to play in his interest in the Foundling Hospital. His first child, John Russell, died at birth seven years earlier. And his death was followed shortly afterwards by his first wife's death in 1735. When the Charter was signed on 17 October 1739, his second child (from his second wife, whom he married in 1737) was less than a month old.

John Russell was also very connected to the locality of the hospital, his family owning the Bedford Estate which incorporated Bloomsbury.

The president was supported by six vice-presidents who also almost all came from the world of politics, primarily Whigs. The Whigs, as a party, were against absolute monarchy and, in a sense, this was the first heyday for politicians. Robert Walpole was appointed Chancellor of the Exchequer in 1721 and had not only managed to guide the country through the crisis of the South Sea Company debacle but had managed to do so with minimal damage to the reputation of the Government, a remarkable feat considering that many in government were involved in the scandal both in official and personal capacities. His time

Martin Folkes. Engraving by T. Cook after W. Hogarth. (Wellcome Collection)

in government had also seen the taming of the power of the monarchy, with politicians taking the helm. Although he did not hold the title officially, the role he took was that of Britain's first prime minister. Since this time, the prime minister has held the power in parliament and has controlled the relationship with the monarch.

While it seems unhelpful in this day and age to see an organisation such as a foundling hospital headed by politicians, it makes more sense in the context of the power shift in government. The close link between Britain's aristocracy and its politicians is also brought into sharp focus when looking at the duke's first vice-presidents.

Lord Vere Beauclerk was a politician (taking his seat in 1726) and a Royal Naval Officer. Like his president he was rooted in aristocracy as was one of the grandsons of Charles II (through his illegitimate son). Lord Vere Beauclerk had very young children, making him one of the few men heading up the Foundling Hospital who may have had relevant practical experience of childcare although it is likely that servants did all the hands-on caring. Similarly, Sir Joseph Eyles was a Whig member of parliament and also the son of a baronet. He was not in post for long as he died in February 1740 before the hospital was functioning.

Micajah Perry was another politician but, unlike Lord Vere Beauclerk and Sir Jospeh Eyles, he was not born into aristocracy. He was, however, born into enormous wealth as the grandson of a very successful London-based tobacco merchant and he inherited the family business in 1721. At the time of his appointment as vice-president of the Foundling Hospital, he was Lord Mayor of London. Having the Mayor of London involved was certainly a great coup for the new hospital but, unfortunately, his usefulness turned out to be short-lived. Soon after his appointment, the family tobacco business went into sharp decline leaving him with significant financial woes; he lost his parliamentary seat in the general election of 1741. His health deteriorated sharply and he died within a few years.

The fourth politician was Peter Burrell. He had made his money as a merchant and had been a sub-governor of the South Sea Company during the time after the bubble burst. He had had children who were largely grown by the time of his appointment.

Not all the vice-presidents were politicians, however. Martin Folkes was an academic. He was also a father. Interestingly, he was a known atheist which must have given him an interesting perspective on what was essentially a Christian endeavour founded by a Christian man. James Cook, the last of the six vice-presidents listed, was described as a merchant.

The first Treasurer of the Foundling Hospital had what we would arguably consider to be the most useful career of all of those listed as officers. Lewis Way was a barrister and legal advice is always useful in setting up an organisation of this scale. He was also closely linked with Guy's Hospital becoming president of Guy's for a time which, as another very new social care venture in London, may have provided very useful learning for the Foundling Hospital. Such direct experience of social care was rare amongst the governors.

The Charter specified how the hospital would be managed. Each year, in May, a General Court would be held at which governors could be elected to join the Corporation. There would be a president and six vice-presidents and, from their number the governors would elect fifty, including the president, vice-presidents and treasurer, to form the General Committee which would then appoint a secretary to carry out the administration of the General Committee. The General Committee of fifty men effectively undertook the main role of governing the Corporation and held monthly meetings between the annual General Courts.

Many of the governors had political experiences, others had knowledge of business or trade, some had children of their own (although it is unlikely that they, as men, would have hands on experience of childcare) and one or two had links to London's hospitals. The governors had not been signed up for their particular skills and talents in infant welfare. By and large, this was a very sizeable group of men who were all learning on the job.

The General Plan

Once the Charter was signed, after nearly two decades of movement at a snail's pace, everything began moving very quickly for the Foundling Hospital.

Thomas was a 71-year-old man at this time, which was a great age for a man of humble beginnings in the eighteenth century. Additionally, in the months leading up to the granting of the Charter, both Thomas and Eunice had been very ill warranting a prolonged period of recuperation. Thomas, however, was not going to let either his age or his recent illness hold him back.

On 20 November, just a month after the Charter was granted, the governors held a public reading of the Charter at Somerset House, a very grand building which had been refurbished by Christopher Wren and had long been used as an occasional residence of the consorts of the kings of England. Sited on the Strand, on the north bank of the Thames, it was an illustrious place to hold a first meeting.

Before the 170 governors present, Thomas read out the Charter. What a moment! A man who had spent his career in the filth and hardships of sea travel; who had worked tirelessly to build boats; who had been beaten and threatened; who had no illusions about the shortcomings of his education and he was standing before the very wealthiest, most successful, most academic, aristocratic and royal men of society.

Was he intimidated? It seems that he wasn't. He spoke eloquently and at length. Was he obsequious in the face of the status of the 170 aristocrats before him? It seems not. He was certainly grateful and humbled but he was not afraid to say what he thought. He had qualms about the project, not complete confidence in what might happen next and he included a warning for those very men who had got him to where he was. He said that the project could only be successful 'provided due and proper care be taken for setting on foot so necessary an establishment.'[20] Wiser men might simply have been grateful at such an occasion, but not Thomas. It was an audacious act, certainly, but was it a sign that Thomas was already concerned about how things were progressing?

As a governor, Thomas stood for election onto the General Committee at the first meeting and he was elected with 49 of the other governors. They began having their monthly meetings immediately and the work started in earnest. Suddenly, Thomas's solo venture was a team effort with meetings involving many men, each of whom brought their own ideas, their own interests and their own egos. Having worked alone for so many years on this project, this was an incredible change for the entrepreneur. Thomas was a very active member of the General Committee, taking a great interest, if not a leading role, in every aspect of the committee's work and its sub-groups.

Compston, writing about Thomas's life in 1918, remarks at the speed with which the project was shaped at this stage. He makes a comparison with how Thomas used to make ships in his yard in Dighton. He was known for having the ships rigged before they were launched when, ordinarily, this was completed after they were on the water. Compston makes the case that this was also how Thomas dealt with the Foundling Hospital – he already had the plans in place – the ship was rigged before the Charter was granted so that the governors could simply get on with making it happen.

At the December meeting the General Committee agreed the Corporation Seal. The design was straight out of the Old Testament depicting Pharoah's daughter and her maids finding Moses in his basket in the bullrushes of the Nile. Underneath were the words *Sigillum Hospitii Infantum Expositorum Londinensis* – Seal of the London Hospital for Exposed Children.

Thomas is quoted as giving the reason for choosing Moses as 'an Impression of the Common Seal of the Corporation which I chose out of the affair mentioned in the 2^d of Exodus of Pharoah's Daughter and her Maid's finding Moses in the Ark of Bulrushes which I thought would be very appropo for an hospital for Foundlings Moses being the first Foundling we read of'.[21]

After finding him, the Pharoah's daughter raised him as her own son.

The General Committee decided to write to other foundling hospitals in Europe, including Dublin and Paris, to ask for their advice and guidance to support London's endeavour. They already had the review of how the Paris Foundling Hospital worked which Queen Caroline had commissioned before she died.

The first forays into the purchase of land from the Earl of Salisbury to build a purpose-built hospital happened within weeks of the Charter being granted. In the meantime, the Committee agreed that the first foundlings would be taken into a building rented for the purpose in Hatton Garden. By December, this was in place and the process of fitting it out with beds had begun.

The governors sent out a circular letter distributed 'about the Kingdom' asking for local information which would help with issues such as the availability of wet nurses.

Most of this early activity took place in one of the coldest winters the country has ever experienced – in fact, since records began in the seventeenth century only one winter has been colder than that of early 1740. The frost was so severe in January and February that the potato crop in much of Ireland failed and hundreds of thousands of people died. In London, the population was certainly not so devastated as in Ireland but the fierce frost killed many and must have given the General Committee a tremendous sense of urgency to prevent future children from being abandoned on the streets where they too would surely have frozen to death.

In May 1740, legislation was passed which 'confirmed and enlarged' the powers of the governors. This was thought necessary to make the hospital function. The act relating to this, being passed only seven months after the Charter was granted and while the General Plan was being written, would have been a little embarrassing for those responsible for the original Charter wording. The matter was underplayed publicly to avoid losing general support for the project and was greatly aided by the speed with which the legislation was drawn up and passed through parliament. Could this have been what Thomas was making reference to when he announced in the first meeting of the hospital that 'proper care' was needed 'for setting on foot so necessary an establishment'?

Fundraising was a key endeavour for the governors. They not only had to fund the costs of renting and fitting out temporary accommodation for the hospital but also funds were going to be needed to start the building of the new premises. The active people in fundraising included, unsurprisingly, Thomas Coram who was joined by Martin Folkes (an academic and one of the vice-presidents), Taylor White (a barrister and naturalist) and Alexander Hume Campbell (a lawyer and MP). Although these men were themselves well-connected and by no means poor, they were not members of the aristocracy as many other governors were. Perhaps their role was, at least in part, to solicit donations from some of their titled peers.

There were also large-scale funding proposals being put forward for the hospital. This was not too far-fetched an idea, as the Dublin Foundling Hospital was already receiving much of its income from a tax on imported coal. And the Cork Foundling Hospital was to be founded on very similar lines within the next decade. The funding ideas for the Foundling Hospital were, however, not based on coal but on ideas as disparate and unlikely as dogs, convicts and New England settlers.

In 1736 the idea hit the newspapers of taxing dog owners with the proceeds going to fund the hospital. 'For as much as some dogs are kept for Profit, others for Pleasure, and others for Use, Defence, and Safeguard and many are kept by persons in mean Circumstances and others, that are of no use or benefit to the Owner, but oftentimes do much Mischief to their Neighbours, by killing of Sheep and Lambs and running mad; now as well to prevent these Mischiefs in some measure, as to raise a Fund for erecting Hospitals for, and maintaining of the Poor therein, let there be an Act Pass'd for taxing the owner of all Dogs and Bitches'.[22] Not all dogs were to be taxed to the same level – a lap dog, for example, would bring the owner an annual tax bill of eight shillings. Farmers, on the other hand, would only have to pay a bill of three shillings for each of their working dogs.

The dog tax did not make it through to becoming law, however there remained speculation in the newspapers[23] that a way of providing long-term funding for the hospital had been found. It was reported that the governors had hit on an idea which meant the hospital would be able to fund itself. Was this perhaps a reference to Thomas's scheme to establish another British colony in America and use the profits from what the settlers cut, grew or caught to fund the hospital?

Another news story suggested that convicts, instead of being transported, were to be put to work for the good of foundling infants. The idea was that convicts 'would earn their own Bread and raise a considerable yearly Fund towards supporting an Hospital for Foundlings which, to the burden of several Parishes, the pampering of some Parish Officers, the Murder of many Poor Infants, and consequently to the high Disgrace of this Nation, has been but too, too long neglected'.[24]

However, the main source of funds was not to come from schemes such as this but in small, largely unpredictable subscriptions from individuals and through gifts left in people's wills.

One of the governors of the hospital was William Hogarth, already a famed artist by this time. There is a connection between him and one of the Ladies of Charity as he painted Baroness Frances Byron's portrait in 1736. It may have been in conversations that took place while she was sitting for the portrait that Hogarth became aware of the Foundling Hospital and Thomas Coram. However he found him, Hogarth became a friend of Thomas and a very active governor. He designed the seal of the hospital and its coat of arms and then turned his art towards helping the fundraising sub-committee. He designed a very intricate letterhead which described visually Thomas's ideas for the hospital and was used for the fundraising letters sent out by the governors.

Hogarth was an astute observer of human nature and his art frequently exposed the harsh, cruel or tragic realities of human life. The image he designed for the hospital's letter paper, however, appears an idealised depiction of what Thomas hoped the hospital would be. Thomas himself is shown with the Charter document under his arm. Angelic children surround him, with learning tools – books, papers and tools – indicating the education side of what the hospital was intended to achieve. There is a building but all the children are outside surrounded by countryside. A woman is distraught on her knees in front of a

Coram and several children carrying implements of work; a church and ships are in the distance. This artwork was used as a letterhead for the initial fundraising appeal. Engraving by T. Cook, 1809, after W. Hogarth, 1739. (*Wellcome Collection*)

baby being carried away by a man with a mace, perhaps indicating his high status. In the background, a woman is leaving a baby in a basket while another baby lies abandoned in the undergrowth. In the background are ships which several of the young boys are looking towards as a clear reference to the future Thomas envisaged for the boys in the hospital's care.

The fundraising letter, on the paper designed by Hogarth, was sent from the governors as far and wide to as many people as they could think of. As such it was probably the country's first direct mail fundraising campaign and the start of a lifetime of soliciting donations for the hospital.

Early in 1740, however, Hogarth turned his attention to focus fully on Thomas himself.

The portrait is considered one of Hogarth's masterpieces. Hogarth depicted his friend wearing a long red coat and a kindly expression. Around him are references to travel and ships, a globe at his feet, maps on the table, ships in the background. In his right hand is the seal of the 1739 Charter, at his feet a battered notebook. Thomas did not pay for this portrait, nor did Hogarth gift it to him. Instead, in May of that year, he presented it to the hospital. While Thomas would never know it, this one portrait became the first of many paintings which were to be exhibited in the hospital in years to come, giving the whole project another dimension.

Lord Tenterden, a barrister, was a governor of the Foundling Hospital's verse. Somewhat unexpectedly, he wrote a few lines of verse[25] having become used to seeing Hogarth's portrait of Thomas Coram hanging in the hospital:

Captain Coram by William Hogarth, 1740.

> Lo, old Captain Coram, so round in the face,
> And a pair of good chops plump'd up in good case,
> His amiable locks hanging grey on each side,
> To his double-breast coat o'er his shoulder so wide.

What a time of excitement it must have been for Thomas. It was not just the culmination of the work of the past seventeen years in soliciting support for the project but also a validation of the other areas of his career where he had worked so hard, come so close to great triumph but ultimately suffered disappointment after disappointment. This no doubt made up for the collapse of his shipbuilding yard in Massachusetts; the end of his sailing career by the *Seaflower* episode; the end of his Navy Office career in relative obscurity; and his failure to return to live in America. The king granting a Royal Charter to Thomas's Darling Project was a genuine dream come true.

To make the Foundling Hospital a reality, he was sitting in regular meetings on an equal footing with many aristocrats and great men. He had an equal voice and a chance to utilise all that he had learnt about setting up a foundling hospital and share the many contacts he had made. Donations arrived in great numbers from people he had personally met and whom he had persuaded to sign his petitions.

But there was also a terrible cloud. Eunice, his wife of forty years, died shortly before the autumn of 1740, a terrible loss in the midst of all the excitement about the Foundling Hospital. He and Eunice had never had any children but had remained a strong unit through all the changes in their lives.

In a letter to Dr Colman, a friend in Boston, he told him of her death and described her as a 'virtuous, kind and prudent wife, without a fault'.[26] Brocklesby, writing in 1751, described the loss of Eunice for Thomas as 'the only Loss for which he ever shewed much Regret'.[27]

She had left her family home in Boston to be with him in Taunton and had then fled Taunton with him to arrive in London, thousands of miles from her family and the community she knew. In those first years in London, he was no doubt away at sea for long periods of time, leaving her in a foreign city to make her own way and then, when he retired from the sea, she was in poor health for several years. Life had not always been easy for her.

And now, when his great plans were coming to fruition, she was no longer by his side to share in the great experience. It was indeed a terrible loss for Thomas but perhaps he took some comfort from knowing that she had lived long enough to see the Charter granted.

In July, newspapers reported that three children were 'dropped' (the term used for 'abandoned' in the eighteenth century), in Middle Temple, a few minutes' walk away from Hatton Garden. It was speculated that they may have been left by someone who assumed that that was where the hospital was sited.

A number of governors were appointed by the rest of the committee to write down what the project would look like and, a year after the Charter was received, all agreed on this written plan. It was not a long document, only around 4000 words long. This was the first public account of the ideas that Thomas had been holding in his head for so long.

The plan described a 'proper' house with a walled courtyard (walls being at least six feet high) with a porter's lodge.

Children, two months old or younger. could be brought to the hospital and, as long as they passed an initial examination for any outward signs of illness or disease, the infant would be given into the care of a nurse in the hospital. On the first Sunday after the child was taken in, it would be baptised and a new name given to it.

If a child needed to be given breast milk, it would be sent out to a wet nurse in the country until it was 3 years old and then it would return to the hospital where it would be taught to read and given lessons in Christianity. The child would be given work to do fitting their age.

When they were old enough the children would be apprenticed out; the boys in husbandry or the Sea Service while the girls would be put into domestic service either in the hospital or elsewhere. The hospital would supply the children with clothes and whatever else they needed and would have contracts drawn up to ensure that the children were kept safe by their apprentice masters.

This was the first time that the public, including the donors and governors, were given written details of what *The Hospital for the Maintenance and Education of Exposed and Deserted Young Children* would actually be.

The details of what happens to the children and what they could expect from life in the hospital are actually very sparse and only covered in the first chapter of the report. The remaining ten chapters cover record-keeping, staff and the procedures of the governors.

In this respect, the plan very much mirrors the report that Queen Caroline commissioned from the Paris Foundling Hospital.

The Paris Foundling Hospital had been set up by Vincent de Paul after he was said to have seen someone injuring a child in an effort to elicit more sympathy and so make them more effective as a beggar. Vincent de Paul wanted to take these children off the streets so that they could not be exploited in this way. In this sense, the Paris plan was arguably more solidly grounded than Thomas's aim to prevent women murdering their illegitimate babies. Queen Caroline's commissioned review of the Paris Foundling Hospital described an open door policy with no questions asked of the person bringing the baby. It was stated that the babies were to be from Paris and its suburbs but, as no questions were asked, it is not clear how this was policed. If the babies were found to be diseased, they were sent to the hospital for treatment before they could be admitted. Once admitted they were immediately given to a nurse to be suckled and they were baptised the following day. If they had a name of their own, that was used; if not, they were given a new name.

The babies were sent to foster families in the countryside as soon as possible and did not return to the hospital until they were 5 years old, at which point they were educated in reading and writing. They were employed in making stockings and caps for the younger children. Some were housed in the hospital building. Others went into houses in the suburbs which had been acquired for this. When aged 15 or 16 the boys were apprenticed out to trades and the girls were 'disposed of to charitable persons' or given an allowance if they were getting married. If the parents, at any point during the baby's time with the hospital, wanted to claim their child, they were charged a search fee and the board of directors made a decision about whether the child was theirs and if it could be returned to them 'without any inconveniency'.

The report that Caroline commissioned was 35 pages long. More than 25 of these pages were dedicated to paperwork and accounting rather than the functionality of the organisation and childcare. Evidently, the hospital was very strict about detailed record-keeping. Each child wore a leather patch carrying their identity details on a necklace. By this means, careful record was kept of each child's whereabouts throughout their time under the care of the hospital in a comprehensive series of registers. This was a practice very much reflected in the plans for the London hospital.

In the General Plan[28] for the London Foundling Hospital, not only were the details about childcare limited – the basics of taking care of the babies had to be learnt through trial and error – but there was also very little in terms of financial planning, other than a statement that frugality would be needed 'as your Revenue at present amounts to only about Six hundred Pounds a Year, it will require the greatest Frugality to maintain even Sixty Children'. 600 pounds would be worth around £70,000 today, or £1,100 per child.

While the General Plan may have given scant detail to childcare and finances, it did make very clear some basic principles which would guide the hospital, its staff and its governors.

The General Plan focused on six key areas:

1. **General admittance, limited only by finance**

   'No Child shall be returned who is not above the age of two Months except such as has the French Pox, Evil, Leprosy, or Disease of the like Nature.'

The General Plan made no restrictions on the children who could be admitted to the hospital other than that they should be less than two months old. There were no geographical limits such as, say, children coming only from a specific distance from the hospital and no limitations based on the circumstances of the family. However, each child had to be subject to an inspection by the chief nurse and the apothecary in case there was any sign of disease. While the inspection was being carried out, it was the porter's job to ensure that the person who brought the baby did not leave. If the baby was found to be diseased the baby was to be handed back to the person who brought him or her in or it was to be 'otherwise disposed of'. It was not detailed what this might mean. In the Paris Foundling Hospital, those who were found to be ill were taken to a medical hospital.

2. **A clean slate for each foundling**

   'They [the staff] shall not presume to ask the Person who brings the Child any Question whatsoever, or by any Means endeavour to discover who the Person is, on pain of their being dismissed.'

A form would be completed for each child accepted into the hospital which would note the time and date the baby arrived at the hospital and details such as its gender and assumed age. If there were any birth marks or such on the baby, that would be noted too along with any clothes or anything else the baby had with it. Crucially, no record would be taken of the person who left the baby or any other details of the baby's circumstances and family before being admitted to the hospital.

By this means, a completely clean slate had been designed for each baby. What had gone before was not recorded and could be forgotten and each was given a new identity and baptism. This was to have the effect of equalising all the babies; no matter what their background they were all as one in the hospital.

3. **Usefulness to the country**

   'As the Children who shall be brought up by this Hospital owe their Preservation to Charity, we have proposed that they may be educated and disposed of, as shall make them most useful to the Publick.'

Thomas always had a focus on what was happening with trade and British colonies overseas. The General Plan included a reference to boys being sent to sea. For Thomas, producing children who were useful to the country was an important role of the hospital. Girls could not be sent to sea but would be trained as domestic servants. Servants were in great demand in the ever-growing number of important households in the city.

> *'As soon as they attain proper Ages, the boys shall be put out to Husbandry, other Labour, or to the Sea Service; and the Girls be employed in the House or place out at Service; the General Committee taking care that they are furnished with Cloaths and Necessaries; and that proper Contracts be made with their Masters and Mistresses to prevent any Abuse.'*

To train them for these positions, the General Plan made provision for the children to be given work in the hospital itself or outside the hospital and for apprenticeships to be arranged for them when they were old enough. Each child was to be given clothes when sent out and proper contracts were be made with their employers 'to prevent any abuse' and a register kept of which child was where.

When a child was old enough to no longer be the responsibility of the hospital, they were to be given clothes of the value of ten pounds or less. A girl could be married before this time and would be given money or clothes to the same value. The Charter had already stipulated that the hospital would be responsible for the girls until they were 21 or until they were married, (which ever came sooner) and the boys until they were 24. As children were regularly working from the ages of 5 upwards, it is incredible to think that they were to be part of the hospital until they were in their twenties. The hospital was very keen that the children leaving would be old enough, and sufficiently well-trained so that they would be useful citizens immediately.

At this early stage, the General Committee were already thinking about children being claimed and taken out of the hospital by their parents. The General Plan stipulated that the family looking to reclaim a child left in the hospital would have to go to the Daily Committee who would question them about their right to have the child and whether their current circumstances meant they could take care of the child. They would also be asked to pay for the time the child had already spent in the hospital. The registers would then be searched to see if the child was still alive.

4. Governance

'Nothing being so necessary to execute this Charity as a constant Visitation and Inspection into the Behaviour of all the Persons employed in it, to prevent Abuses, preserve the Children, and keep up the charitable Disposition of Mankind. There should be at least two Governors appointed daily to visit and inspect the Hospital. To make this Duty more easy to the Governors, we propose that the whole Number be divided into twelve Classes, each Class to have the Inspection of the Hospital during one Month, and two Governors of it to visit the Hospital every Day.'

The primary focus of the General Plan, in terms of the number of words spent on the topic, was governance – how the hundreds of governors would be made useful and accountable and the plan laid out how the governors (numbering in their hundreds) would be organised, how many meetings there would be and their responsibilities in terms of inspecting the workings of the hospital. The Plan also provided for specific roles to support the governors, such as the treasurer and the secretary.

A General Court of all governors was to be held annually on the second Wednesday of May. This court would elect the president, vice-presidents, a treasurer and a secretary. They would also elect the General Committee of forty-two other governors. Three other General Courts would be held each year at which such matters as signing leases and adopting by-laws could take place.

The General Committee had responsibility for matters such as staff and the general running of the hospital and met regularly, generally monthly.

A Daily Committee, formed of at least two governors for the day, would visit the hospital and deal with any matters arising that day including staffing issues, the reception of babies and such like.

The General Committee set up sub-committees for particular tasks. These included a building committee, for example, to look at a location and plan for a new hospital building; and a fundraising committee.

The governors did recognise the omission of the women in the General Plan: 'we hope we may receive the assistance of the Fair Sex who, although excluded by Custom from the Management of Publick Business, are by their natural Tenderness and Compassion particularly enabled to advise in the Care and management of Children'. The role given to the women was as volunteer inspectors of the wet nurses in the country, generally some miles away. Women were not only excluded from the meetings, but they were also kept at a physical distance from the hospital.

5. Providing care

> *'The nurses shall keep themselves and the Children neat and clean, and dress and undress them at proper Times, and be accountable for the Children's Cloaths delivered to them, and give the Children only the Food appointed for them, prepared in such Manner as shall be directed by the Daily Committee from time to time. If the Nurse shall dare to give any strong Liquors or Opiates to any Child, or shall be found to have any such in her Custody, she shall be immediately discharged.'*

The General Plan described nurses as being the primary or sole carers of the foundlings, employing both wet (those who would breastfeed) and dry nurses. However, the details of how this care was to be provided was very limited. Direct reference to childcare amounted only to very broad statements such as each nurse having to state that they had had smallpox, to avoid catching it and passing it onto others.

The General Committee noted that, having consulted the College of Physicians, the babies did not need to be breastfed unless they 'cannot be brought up by hand'. Those babies who did need to be breastfed were to be sent out to nurses in the country until they were 3 years old. The babies were wrapped in flannels and swathes to keep them warm.

It was very much up to the nurses to work out how best to provide care for the babies. While none were expected to have ever cared for such a large number of babies before, it also has to be said that the governors didn't expect any of them to have had experience of caring for even one baby themselves as the General Plan stipulated that they should each be unmarried.

However, to encourage their good work, the Daily Committee could award a nurse a bonus of up to ten shillings if the child in her care was found to be healthy and thriving after two years or more.

6. Keeping records

> *'Immediately on the Reception of each Child, the Steward shall enter on a Sheet of Paper, its Sex, supposed Age, the Year, Day, and Hour when brought, Description of the Child, the Marks (if any) on its body, and the Child's Dress; and particularly Mention is to be made of any Writing or other Thing brought with the Child.'*

The General Plan, very much in line with the Paris Foundling Hospital report, spent much time on the subject of record-keeping. From the moment the child was accepted into the hospital, details of it were to be kept in the hospital's registers with some details affixed to the child itself on a label so that the child could be traced in the registers.

The Books to be kept by him [the Steward] are,

A General Inventory Book

A General Register Book of the hospital, divided into proper Columns, to contain, 1. the Time of Reception, 2. Reference to the Paper of Marks, 3. Reference to the Baptism, 4. The Name and Number of the Child, 5. Reference to the Nurse's Book, 6. Reference to the Book how disposed of, 7. Reference to Placing out, and, 8. Times of Death, or Reference to Discharge.

A Register of Baptism to contain 1. The Number of the Child, and Reference to the General Register, 2. The Name and Surname, and Number of Baptism, 3. Days when christened And, 4. by whom christened.

The Nurse's Book to contain 1. Name of the Nurse and Abode, 2. Reference to the General Register, and Agreement made with her, 3. Name of the Child delivered to her, and Time when, 4. The Name of the Person to Inspect And, 5. Time when the Child is returned.

A Disposal Book to contain 1. Name of the Child, 2. Where the Children are, 3. Reference to placing out And, 4. Reference to the General Register.

A Placing out, Death and Discharge Book to contain 1. Name of the Person, and Place of Abode, with whom, 2. Reference to Agreement, 3. Name of the Child, 4. When returned, 5. Death, when, 6. Where buried, 7. Reference to Certificate thereof, 8. Discharge, when, and how And, 9. Reference to the General Register.

A Servant's Book, to contain, 1. Names, 2. When taken in, 3. Agreements with them, 4. When discharged, 5. Cause of Discharge.

A minute Book of Nurses and Servants retained, which shall contain, 1. Their Names, 2. Places of Abode, 3. Terms on which they are to come And, 4. Reference to the Servants and Nurses Book respectively.

A Day Book of small Expences

A Book of the Steward's Receipts and Payments

A Book to contain the Receipts and Issues of Provisions; and

A Book for entering the Money, Bills or Effects received from charitable Persons.

Each of these registers listed was handwritten and had to be kept up to date and safe for any governors wishing to refer to them.

The General Plan was very detailed about such matters as what records should be kept and by whom, when meetings should take place, the characters of employees, who had responsibility for issuing clothes and so on, but had little of what we might consider important today such as training for staff, how many hours of education a child should receive, what recreation was provided for them, how their wellbeing would be monitored, how their progress would be tracked and so on. It is difficult to look at the long list of registers and the fact that the 4000 word General Plan document devoted only a few hundred words to childcare and not see these foundlings, with their numbered tags, as being treated as a form of commodity rather than someone's child. However, the foundling hospitals of continental Europe had been taking in foundlings for centuries and had developed these efficient ways of monitoring the children out of necessity, without the sensitivities we now have. After all, what they were doing was fighting fire and removing children from near-certain death on the streets with no time, or money, to spend time worrying about wellbeing and welfare issues.

Part IV

The Hospital Opens

'The mothers of illegitimate children should have other means within their reach of hiding their shame than the destruction of their miserable offspring, and thus they say they seek to hide the shame of the mother as well as preserve the life of the child.'

Brownlow, 1865

The First Children

The General Plan stressed that the idea was to begin receiving children immediately. The governors had wasted no time and had already located and agreed a suitable house to use as a temporary hospital while the building of the new hospital was underway. A house was selected in Hatton Garden which the governors could use as a temporary base for the Foundling Hospital.

The house they chose belonged to an aristocratic member of parliament, Sir Francis Tench, and had been standing empty for a while. While now known as a centre for jewellery and gems, Hatton Garden was a then relatively well-to-do residential area of large houses, approximately a twenty minute walk north from the Thames.

In January of 1741, just fourteen months after receiving the Royal

The first temporary base for the hospital was a large house very similar in design to, and over the road from the building pictured. This one still stands while the original hospital building no longer does. The two figures are representing Charity School children from the time when the St Andrew's Charity School used the building.[1]

Charter, the governors were able to hold their General Committee meeting in the Hatton Garden house.

Weeks later, the house was furnished and staff were appointed. The house was not ready for sixty children as those writing the General Plan had hoped, but it was agreed that thirty children could be accommodated as a first step. It was clear that this was only a temporary move as the site of a purpose-built hospital had already been found and agreed by the General Committee.

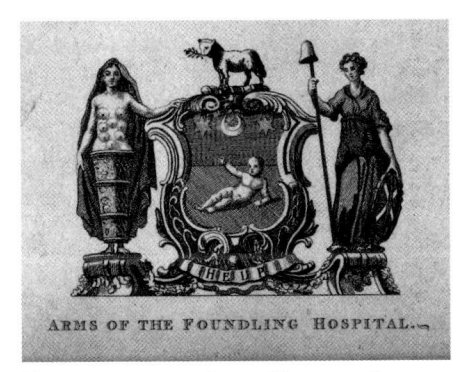

The achievement of arms. Engraving by T. Cook, 1809, after W. Hogarth, 1739. (*Wellcome Collection*)

The Foundling Hospital's coat of arms, designed by Hogarth, was hung over the door. It depicted a baby with the word 'help' written under him, who is gesturing to a woman with eight breasts, perhaps Diana of Ephesus, representing nurture. Above the baby is a lamb carrying a sprig of thyme and, on the baby's left side, stands Britannia. It is certainly a striking image.

The governors issued the following advertisement:

To-morrow, at eight o'clock in the evening, this house will be opened for the reception of twenty children, under the following regulations:–

No children exceeding the age of two months will be taken in, nor such as have the evil, leprosy, or disease of any like nature, whereby the health of the other children may be endangered; for the discovery whereof, every child is to be inspected as soon as it is brought, and the person who brings it is to come in at the outward door and ring a bell at the inward door, and not to go away until the child is returned or notice given of its reception; but no questions whatever will be asked of any person who brings a child, nor shall any servant of the house presume to endeavour to discover who such person is, on pain of being discharged.

All persons who bring children are requested to affix on each child some particular writing, or other distinguishing mark or token, so that the children may be known hereafter if necessary.[2]

The children Thomas had seen dying on the dunghills were, it was assumed, those of people living in the slums of London nearby. Estimates of national literacy levels vary from 30% to 60% but it is safe to assume that rates were lower amongst the poorest of the country. How many would have been able to read a notice such as that written by the governors. It is perhaps much more likely that word of mouth was the way in which most of those who arrived at the house bringing their babies heard about the hospital.

The following day, Wednesday 25 March 1741, was an auspicious day as the hospital prepared to open its doors. For the governors, this was taking place just five months after they had agreed the General Plan which is a very impressive feat in itself. For Thomas, however, this was the culmination of a quest that had taken the best part of two decades and would be the first time that talk would be replaced with real-life babies.

There were many questions for the anxious governors. How many babies would be presented? How would the mothers react? Would there be a crowd of spectators? Or protestors? Would they be able to feed the babies? They walked around the house, checking that all was in place. The nurses were sitting ready. The cots were lined up, with blankets on each. Milk was standing ready for the infants. The fires were lit downstairs. As darkness fell, candles on the walls of the reception room and the hallway were lit. The porter was reminded again of what was expected of him.

More governors arrived to witness this first evening of reception. As each came to the door, they brought news of yet greater numbers of women waiting outside. They chatted excitedly and sipped on brandy in celebration of their great achievement. As eight o'clock approached, everyone was quiet as the reality of what was about to happen hit home. Governors checked their pocket watches, nurses straightened neat piles of bedding.

At 8.00 pm, the clock in the hallway chimed and a governor nodded at the porter. He opened the door of the Hospital for the Education and Maintenance of Deserted and Exposed Young Children to the very first children. The expectant silence of the house was about to be broken by the screams of thirty cold and hungry babies.

The minutes of the Daily Committee of that first day of admitting children on 25 March 1741 give a detailed picture of what happened that evening.

The Daily Committee (the governors whose turn it was on the rota to inspect and visit the hospital together with the steward and the matron) met that evening at the Hatton Garden premises at 7.00 pm. At this time there was already a crowd of people gathered in the street outside the building. Some had babies with them, others did not. Presumably those without babies were there simply out of curiosity, to see what was going to happen that evening having seen the notices about it in the local newspapers or having heard about it from their friends and neighbours.

When movement and activity was seen inside the building, some women tried to hand over their babies early but the Daily Committee decided that, as the General Committee had set the time at 8.00 pm, they would stick to it and have everyone wait until then. That was felt to be the fairest way forward.

At 8.00 pm, the porter opened the outer door and immediately a woman rang the bell. The porter opened the inner door and the messenger took the baby she was holding from her. He asked for her to go into a room on the right of the door where she was to wait. The messenger then took the baby into the steward's room. Already waiting in the room were governors and Dr Robert Nesbitt (who was one of the initial governors and also a qualified doctor). They took the baby and examined it for visible signs of sickness or disease. Having no signs of either, this was to be the first baby to be admitted into London's new Foundling Hospital, the first of around 25,000 to be admitted in the next two hundred years.

The baby was assigned a number and this, together with a description of the baby and what he was wearing, were written in the register along with the time and date of his or her admittance. Three of those present took responsibility for writing these details in the register and checking them, such was the importance given to the task of record-keeping.

The baby was then taken away by a nurse and the messenger was sent to tell the woman that the baby had been taken into the hospital. She was then shown out of the building. At no point was she asked anything about herself or about the baby or the circumstances in which the baby was being given to the Foundling Hospital.

Once she was outside, the next woman with a baby entered the hospital. In all, the governors saw 32 babies that evening. Two were given back to the women who brought them, one because the baby appeared older than two months and the second because the baby was seen to have what they called the Itch; perhaps this was scabies or a rash caused by something else. The rest of the babies, nineteen boys and eleven girls, were admitted into the Foundling Hospital.

The children were described as being 'dressed very clean' with the exception of three who were not so presentable. The governors took the clean clothes of the majority as a reassurance that the babies were not in the care of parish officers and thus the parents were not already in receipt of poor relief. However, the governors also observed that many of the babies brought that evening seemed stupefied as if they had been given opiates. Some looked as if they were in a state of starvation and the governors felt some were close to death despite the care that the nurses were able to give them.

The General Committee had decided that thirty children was the maximum number they could accept on this first day and so, once these thirty had been admitted, that was the end of their business of the day. The whole process had taken four hours and so it was at midnight that the porter was sent outside to announce to the waiting people that no more babies would be received that night.

The Daily Committee minutes say that some of the crowd, hearing that no more babies would be accepted, were 'a little troublesome' and one of the governors had to go outside to reassure them that another day for accepting children would be announced soon but there was nothing that could be done until then as the hospital was now full. The women who had not been able to give their children into the care of the hospital were described as being just as upset as those who had given up their babies. The scene was depicted as being unimaginably moving.

The governors remained concerned that some of the women carrying babies were going to leave them on the street outside the hospital and simply walk away. Fearful that these babies would die if they were abandoned, they again reassured the women that they would have an opportunity very soon of bringing their children back and so must look after them until that point. The crowd was told that they must now leave the area. This they now did leaving the street empty, although the hospital watchman remained outside the building in case of problems.

The governors left the hospital when they felt reassured that all that could be done for their new charges was being done by the nurses, although they expressed fears that some of the babies were going to die despite this.

With the exception of Dr Nesbitt, that evening was probably the first time the governors had held or inspected a baby or written a description of one. These were men of some social standing; handling squirming, crying babies was simply not something that such men did.

The key role of these governors at receptions was to assess the age and health of the baby and to make an accurate record of each baby in the register. This was by no means an easy task, even for someone used to being around babies. On that first evening, they spotted that one baby had a rash which they diagnosed as the Itch. They were also attempting to spot signs of smallpox and typhus, both of which were common and caused skin rashes. Both were highly contagious and so needed to be kept out of the hospital. Diseases like the plague and cholera may have been trickier for the governors to spot in such small babies.

The fact that the governors suspected many of the babies they saw that evening to have been given opiates is interesting. Opiates, particularly in the form of laudanum, were becoming a relatively common way of treating pain. Opiates were derived from a species of poppy and were being imported primarily from India at this time. They are likely to have made the babies very sleepy and limp and it was often given to them to make them stop crying. For mothers who were attempting to hide their newborn babies, so that her shame wouldn't be found out, or simply so that she could get on with work, this may have been a common thing to do.

The General Plan made provision for nurses, but only two were to be wet nurses who could breastfeed the babies. The General Committee had consulted with doctors and had been advised the babies could be fed by hand – perhaps cow's milk – and so the nurses were mainly 'dry nurses' who could not breastfeed the babies. It was certainly possible to source cow's milk in London, and no doubt easier than it is now to buy farm fresh milk when in central London. However, without refrigeration it would go off very quickly which left it potentially more harmful than helpful for vulnerable infants.

Nurses and a matron had already been appointed and were in the house ready to receive the babies and take care of them on that first night. For the staff, it was probably a nervous time with thirty babies to watch, feed, soothe and encourage to sleep.

> Last Wednesday Night the Governors and Guardians of the Hospital for the Maintenance and Education of exposed and deserted young Children, began to receive such Children into their House in Hatton Garden: Those above the Age of two Months were rejected, as were those that had any infectious distemper on them. There were 19 males and 11 females, being all that could be receiv'd at present. They are to be Baptiz'd, after Evening Service, at the said House, on Sunday next by the Rev. Mr. Smith. Rector of All-Hallows by London Wall, when some of the first Rank of Nobility will be there to stand Godfathers and Godmothers to the said Children. The General Committee have determin'd, that the first baptiz'd of the Males shall be named Thomas Coram, after the Name of the first Promoter of the said Establishment; and the first baptiz'd female to be Eunice Coram after the Name of his Wife, deceas'd who was a wife, virtuous woman &c. The most robust Boys are design'd for the British Sea service. 'Tis said, that amongst those to be baptiz'd some will be named after our great Men in former Times, as Drake, Norris, Blake, and other fam'd Admirals, of the greatest Renown for their Virtue, Honour, &c. which may greatly inspire those happy Foundlings in another Age.[3]

Four days later, Sunday evening Divine Service was performed in the Hatton Garden hospital itself at 5.00 pm. The Duke of Bedford, as President of the Hospital, was there, as were the Duke and Duchess of Richmond, Lady Carolina Lennox, the Countess of Pembroke and 'several other Persons of Distinction'.

Newspaper reports of the time say that twenty-eight of the children first received into the hospital were baptised that evening, the other two babies having already died. The first boy was christened Thomas Coram and the first girl Eunice Coram after Thomas's late wife. A collection was made to sponsor the children and more than thirty pounds was raised. This must have been a remarkably moving occasion for Thomas for so many reasons. It was the first time he was able to publicly thank God for the hospital, the first children were christened and he was honoured for his work by giving his name to a baby. His wife, Eunice, whom he had lost so recently was also a part of the ceremony with a child given her name.

The move to christen the foundlings (even though some may already have been baptised), and thus completely remove their history was a very bold one. The hospital kept no record at all of the child's original name or whether he or she had been baptised before and so the past was entirely removed by this move. It is unthinkable now that a child would be so separated from their identity, heritage, culture and birth family but there was no outcry in the newspapers, merely a celebration of such a great move by the hospital. The advantage of this clean slate was that all the children would be treated equally, regardless of who they were, the circumstances of their birth, or whether they were rich or poor. Further, the absence of any possible link to the mother, father or wider birth family meant people were encouraged to bring their children to the hospital as they could not be shamed for it – neither for the act of abandoning their child to charity or for the child's illegitimacy. For the hospital, this was a powerful message to send out to the public and the first time that this was done in such an open and forthright way.

The Early Days

The Hatton Garden house was large for a house, but very small as a hospital. Thirty babies were brought in on that first evening. There were also a number of staff to accommodate.

The governors had taken care that they had sufficient staff employed from the outset to care for the children and run the hospital.

The staff listed in the General Plan were as follows:

The Steward: his responsibility was to oversee the reception of children and maintain all the records of the hospital and to manage the men servants.
The Matron / Chief Nurse: her responsibility is to oversee the nurses and maid servants.
Nurses: two wet nurses and four dry nurses.
Maid servants.
Laundry woman.

Cook.

Men servants.

Porter and watchman: the porter's responsibility was to take in children and ensure the people bringing the children stayed until the process of receiving their baby was completed.

Messenger: the messenger would run errands and take messages between the governors and the staff.

The General Plan suggested that an apothecary might be appointed in the future and that, for any medical issues arising, 'the General Committee shall, as they think fit, apply to such Physicians and Surgeons who are willing to attend without Fee or reward'. It was not thought that the budget could stretch to medical care. Dr Nesbitt, on that first reception of babies, worked without being paid for his services.

The General Plan suggests that there were at least seventeen members of staff working with the intake of thirty babies, and that most of these lived in the building with the children. Shift-working and weekends are things of the modern age. Staff in the hospital would have worked around the clock regardless of the day of the week. Care was taken not to employ women who had children so that they had no need for time away except for a weekly or fortnightly afternoon off.

The governors organised themselves so that two governors visited the hospital each day. Governors put themselves forward for this so there were some 'inactive' governors who did not take part. Those who did volunteer would only have to visit infrequently. It is impossible to imagine that Thomas did anything other than visit as often as he could. The visiting governors would talk to the staff, particularly the steward and the matron, learn about problems, discuss issues and put forward new ideas. The governors would record their visits and report on what they had found and issues arising would be discussed in daily meetings and then, if necessary, raised in the General Committee meetings with the other governors. In this manner a strong link was created between those who were doing the work and those who were responsible for governing the organisation, a very beneficial way of working in these early days when so much was uncertain and experimental. This meant that problems could be spotted, reported and resolved with speed.

The governors were also working on recruiting women living in the countryside around London to take in babies so that they did not have to be kept in the hospital in their early years. A little over a fortnight after being brought into the hospital, most of the babies were given to these country nurses who travelled to London to collect them.

> The Governors and Guardians of the Hospital for exposed and deserted young Children. Desirous to receive and accommodate at their House in Hatton-garden, have within a few Weeks pass'd carefully sought out and agreed with good Nurses in the most healthy Counties, at proper Distances from London, who are to be under the charitable Inspection of some good Ladies, and other reputable Persons who live in the Neighbourhood: The said Governors and Guardians sent for those Nurses to London, who last Week received and carried with them to their several houses most of the children that were in the House.[4]

Sending the children to nurses in the country meant that the beds and staff in Hatton Garden were freed up so that more babies could be taken in. On Friday, 17 April, less than a month after the first reception, the doors of the hospital were opened once again to new babies. Again, like the first reception evening, more babies were brought to the hospital than could be accommodated inside, even though the project was still so new and word was still spreading. In May, there was another reception evening and then another on 5 June, bringing the total number of children received into the hospital to 113. But here is where the monthly reception evenings ended and no more children were taken in by the hospital that year. During the following year, 1742, just 47 children were received into the hospital, and 23 in 1743.

With so many of the children being sent out to country nurses, this must have left the hospital a strange and quiet place to be. With those exciting first months of admissions gone, many of the staff would have had very little to do and very few children to look after.

For the approximately 100 country nurses, however, they had crying, often weak, babies to look after. While the hospital got progressively quieter, the army of women looking after babies grew in size.

Country Nurses

A key part of Thomas's plan for the foundlings was that they would not spend their entire childhoods in the hospital building.

This was not a new practice and was not uncommon amongst wealthier people to choose to have their baby raised by a paid nurse in the countryside.[5] It was perhaps thought that what was considered a luxury by those most privileged in society should be used, in a very similar fashion, for those who were the least privileged.

When they were given to the hospital the foundlings were aged from a few days to two months old. As soon as a place could be found for them, they were sent, on a less temporary basis, to nurses who were living in the countryside. The country nurses were paid a weekly allowance to take a foundling into their home and treat them similarly to how they cared for a child of their own. The journey into the country would generally have been in a horse-pulled cart and may have taken some time. The countryside was thought to be the healthier option for the babies – fresher air than that in the towns and cities and space outside for play and chores to strengthen their growing bodies.

When foundlings were sent out to country nurses, it freed up capacity in the Foundling Hospital building for more foundlings to be brought in. In this way, there was a continuous movement of foundlings in and out of the hospital building.

Initially, based on the advice the governors had received that bottle feeding was healthier for the baby than breastfeeding, the nurses were chosen largely for their proximity to the hospital, whether they lived in the countryside and whether they had room for another child. Later, nurses who could breastfeed were preferred and the acceptable geographical distance from the hospital increased hugely as more and more nurses were needed.

Nurses who could breastfeed, known as wet nurses, were generally women who had recently had a child of their own, sometimes a child who had died. Alternatively, the wet nurse may have been feeding her own baby and a foundling at the same time. Country nurses used by the Foundling Hospital commonly had a working husband and perhaps other, older children of their own. The money they were paid was a welcome addition to the household finances.

The foundling, only a matter of weeks or months old at this point, would generally be brought up as one of the foster parents' own. As the foundlings themselves were so young, they would have had little idea that this was not his or her birth family or that this was not his or her own community of family, friends and neighbours. As such, the child was likely to build bonds with the countryside family far stronger than they were able to build in the short time they were with their birth family. The foundling often found itself with brothers and sisters, younger babies arriving, grandparents, aunts, and uncles that would have seemed like their own relatives.

In this fashion, what Thomas Coram's hospital created was a foray into formal foster care. And it was achieved on an enormous scale. Hundreds of children were found homes and nurses in the countryside. While it was nothing like the cautious and comprehensive assessment, recruitment and monitoring of modern-day fostering, an attempt was made to supervise the fostering arrangements. Volunteers were recruited to look after the fostered children in a location. While women could not become governors of the hospital, some well-to-do women chose to become inspectors. Their role was essentially to ensure that the foster nurse was paid, make sure that the records were all kept up to date, ensure the child had the clothing issued to it, and to make arrangements should the child die. They were also able to advise should the child be unwell. The governors preferred to appoint people they had links with to be the inspectors. In this way, some of the wives of the hospital governors were able to take a role in the institution alongside their husbands.

When the child was 3 or 4 years old, he or she would be returned to the Foundling Hospital, often accompanied on the journey by the local inspector. Once back in the hospital building, the child was slotted into the structure and routine of the institution with a regular daily timetable including mealtimes, lessons, church services, chores, work and training for apprenticeships.

At this age, the foundling would have formed bonds with their foster family and it may have been a confusing wrench to be taken from them so abruptly. 4 years old is too young to understand the concept of fostering but old enough for them to be aware that they were leaving their only family. This was no doubt a more painful separation for the child, than that from their birth parent when they were taken into the hospital as they were then too young to have any awareness of what was happening.

Leaving behind the sights and smells of the countryside and going into the large austere hospital building will have presented a huge change in the young child's world.

Of course, once in the hospital building they were no longer living with a family, but with tens or hundreds of other children and adult staff. Some children will immediately have found friendship and allies. Others may have taken longer to adjust to institutional life and have experienced extreme homesickness for their short-lived countryside homes.

But not all foster families will have been remembered fondly. Some children may have been relieved to escape the cruelty or neglect of their foster family. It has to be considered that not all foster families were happy places to be.

But it would not only be the foundlings who were having to readjust to their new situation. Many foster families themselves formed strong bonds with their fostered foundling. It is inevitable after some years of seeing a baby growing up within their own family, that some foster parents would feel bereft when their child was taken away.

There are many documented cases of foster families asking to keep their foster child. Sadly, regardless of the bond formed between the foundling and the foster family, staying permanently with the foster family was not allowed by the governors and the child had to be returned to the hospital.

However, it seems there were some exceptions made and there are recorded cases where the inspector and the family found a way to enable the governors to agree to the child staying with the family. This was dependent on the foster father having a business or trade which he could teach to the child. The arrangement could then be regarded as a live-in apprenticeship. In this way, the hospital fulfilled its role as providing a trade for the child's future and the family got to keep the child as their own. The child remained under the auspices of the hospital inspectorate until they were 24.

Similarly, when a country nurse died, the foundling was returned to the hospital even if the surviving husband, or other relative, appealed to have the child remain with them.

The complexities of the apprenticeship arrangement with a family is in sharp contrast with the common Victorian approach to adoption in which families wanting a child were invited into an orphanage where they could simply pick a child to take home with them. Both approaches have flaws of course, but the Foundling Hospital approach, which was cautious, considered and looked at whether a situation was appropriate for the child, is more akin to the modern view of adoption as an arrangement which cannot be entered into lightly and warranting careful assessment of how the child would fare in the family, not just how the parents feel.

In the vast majority of orphanages and barrack children's homes in this country since the Foundling Hospital, this sort of fostering arrangement has not been part of the childcare. In the Victorian era of orphanages, children spent their entire time in the orphanage building, individual children only being 'boarded out' as fostering was termed, as a prelude to permanent adoption. Thomas's fostering programme was extremely complex and hard to manage. Additionally, it was expensive as each family was paid a weekly sum for the care of the child for a period of three or four years. However, the fostering scheme was responsible for ensuring the hospital could survive during times of high intake and it inevitably saved the lives of many children as it was a healthier option than staying in the hospital.

Fostering, even in this early form, was by no means a new idea. Thomas had taken it from a very long tradition of country nurses established over centuries by the foundling hospital movement in Europe and the rest of the world.

Foundling Hospitals in the Rest of the World

The Foundling Hospital as it evolved in London in the eighteenth century was not a new idea. It is thought that there were around thirty foundling hospitals already established in or near significant European towns and cities by the time the London version came into existence.[6] And many more followed. Some researchers have suggested that foundling hospitals proliferated to a point where they were common. For example, it has been estimated that in Spain alone, there were 128 foundling hospitals by the nineteenth century.[7]

Some of the foundling hospitals of Europe had a very long track record; a foundling hospital was established in Barcelona, for example, in 1401. But the history of rescuing foundlings had an even longer heritage.

In the culture of the Roman Empire, child abandonment was seen as a necessary part of the management of societies. If a family did not have the means to look after a child, or the child's disabilities meant that it would not have the ability to look after his or herself when older, it was considered appropriate to abandon the child. Some children were abandoned in the market in the hope that someone else would take them in and perhaps bring them up or possibly be used to work for their adoptive family. Others, however, were left to die.

In Italy, centuries later, the first foundling hospitals were established to ensure a greater number of abandoned children were taken in. The first of these, in Rome itself, was founded in 1204. Foundling hospitals then spread through southern Europe, including Spain, Portugal and southern France and into Belgium, Germany, Austria and northern France. Through the eighteenth century, not only did Ireland and England gain foundling hospitals but also northern Europe, eastern Europe and the movement went into Russia with Moscow and St Petersburg establishing foundling hospitals in 1770.

For generations, thousands of children were being taken in by foundling hospitals in Europe. The concept of the foundling, which had gained legal respectability in the Roman Empire, was once more a significant part of the management of families and society in the eighteenth and nineteenth centuries. Abandoning children was part of family planning whereby both those babies which were unwanted because they were outside the respectability of marriage and those who were simply a mouth too many to feed within the family, could be effectively removed. Foundling hospitals themselves were no longer founded only by Catholic Churches and societies but, like those in England and Ireland, were outside the Catholic Church and functioned to teach Protestantism to the infants.

The hospitals were given the name of foundling hospitals but the babies they took in were not actually foundlings. They were not found on the streets but instead were delivered to the hospitals. They were placed in baskets by the hospital gates or put into specially designed revolving contraptions, whereby once a baby was placed into a basinet on a wheel, the contraption would be turned so that the basinet went into the hospital and a new, empty basinet appeared on the outside ready for the next baby. What these measures had in common was that the baby was delivered anonymously and so there was no knowing whether it was born legitimate or its family circumstances. Thomas's

Hospital was unusual in having a ballot system where the individual handing over the baby was present, but still no questions were asked of that individual.

The idea on which the foundling hospitals were based is that, if the individuals had not been able to hand over their baby to the hospital, they would have created foundlings of the babies by abandoning them on the streets. Would the same person who took care to take the baby a distance to a hospital have left that baby on the streets to die? Would those same women who took their babies on the specified time and date to Thomas's foundling hospital to take part in the ballot have been capable of murdering their babies as Thomas conjectured?

The eighteenth-century proliferation of foundling hospitals raised concerns about the number of foundlings in Europe. There developed an idea that the existence of foundling hospitals was not simply in response to the need to care for existing foundlings but was also actually encouraging more foundlings. Thomas Malthus, the economist who wrote *An Essay on the Principle of Population* in 1798 to argue that population growth impacted negatively on the wealth of society and standards of living, was not pleased to see the large numbers of children being brought up by foundling hospitals. He believed that the presence of a place to put unwanted and illegitimate children encouraged a growth in the number of unwanted and illegitimate children.

Most of the foundling hospitals were excellent record-keepers so we know how many children were taken in and want happened to them. However, what we don't know about are the children not in the hospital. How many children were born illegitimately, or were abandoned on the streets or were murdered by their parents? Did these numbers change after a foundling hospital was founded? Were children still left to die on London streets? Did the number of illegitimate births rise or fall?

The foundling hospitals of the eighteenth and nineteenth centuries mostly followed the same basic way of working as had been outlined in Queen Caroline's report on the Paris Foundling Hospital. Sending infants out to be cared for in family homes away from the hospital building itself was a fundamental part of enabling the foundling hospitals to take in large numbers of foundlings at a time while keeping the costs of raising them as low as possible.

Thomas Coram's Foundling Hospital was following this way of working established over centuries by Europe's early foundling hospitals. Children were brought in with no questions asked; they were sent out to foster families; they came back into the hospital to receive some form of education (generally only in religious matters) and were put to work. They were then sent out to apprenticeships when they were old enough. This was the life given to thousands of children a year in the foundling hospitals of Europe for hundreds of years.

Part V

Great Losses

'That the present Method of Nursing is wrong, one would think needed no other Proof than the frequent Miscarriages attending it, the Death of Many, and ill Health of Those that survive.'

Dr Cadogan, 1748

Losing Control

In the December of 1741, nine months after the hospital opened, the governors met to discuss an issue that had arisen with the behaviour of the appointed matron. The governors agreed that the problems were so significant that she had to be replaced with immediate effect. They had already chosen another matron who they felt would do a far better job. This was no doubt an issue of great concern to Thomas as the matron was such a key position in the hospital. She managed all the nursing staff and all the resources – bedding, clothes, food – that the nurses needed to care for the children.

Thomas was also very much involved in the planning for the new building and the negotiations for the new building. This was a relatively quiet time in terms of new admittances of babies to the hospital but a very busy time in terms of what was going on in terms of governance and management.

In February 1742, the General Committee passed a resolution to build the new hospital on land purchased at Lamb's Conduit Fields. The purchase had involved a long drawn-out negotiation with the owner of the land, Lord Salisbury, who very much wanted to sell the hospital far more land than they needed. The Committee had agreed that they needed, and could afford, just two fields. After much discussion, during which it was explained that the hospital did not have enough money to buy the entire 56 acres, the situation was resolved by the Earl of Salisbury making the hospital a large donation which enabled them to purchase his parcel of land in its entirety. He donated £500 and the full cost was £7,000. Thomas was one of the key negotiators in this process. The successful outcome of this negotiation was later to have a very marked impact on the longevity of the hospital.

The Charter and the General Plan outlined very clearly how the governors were to run the Foundling Hospital and the democratic process by which they

Great Losses 97

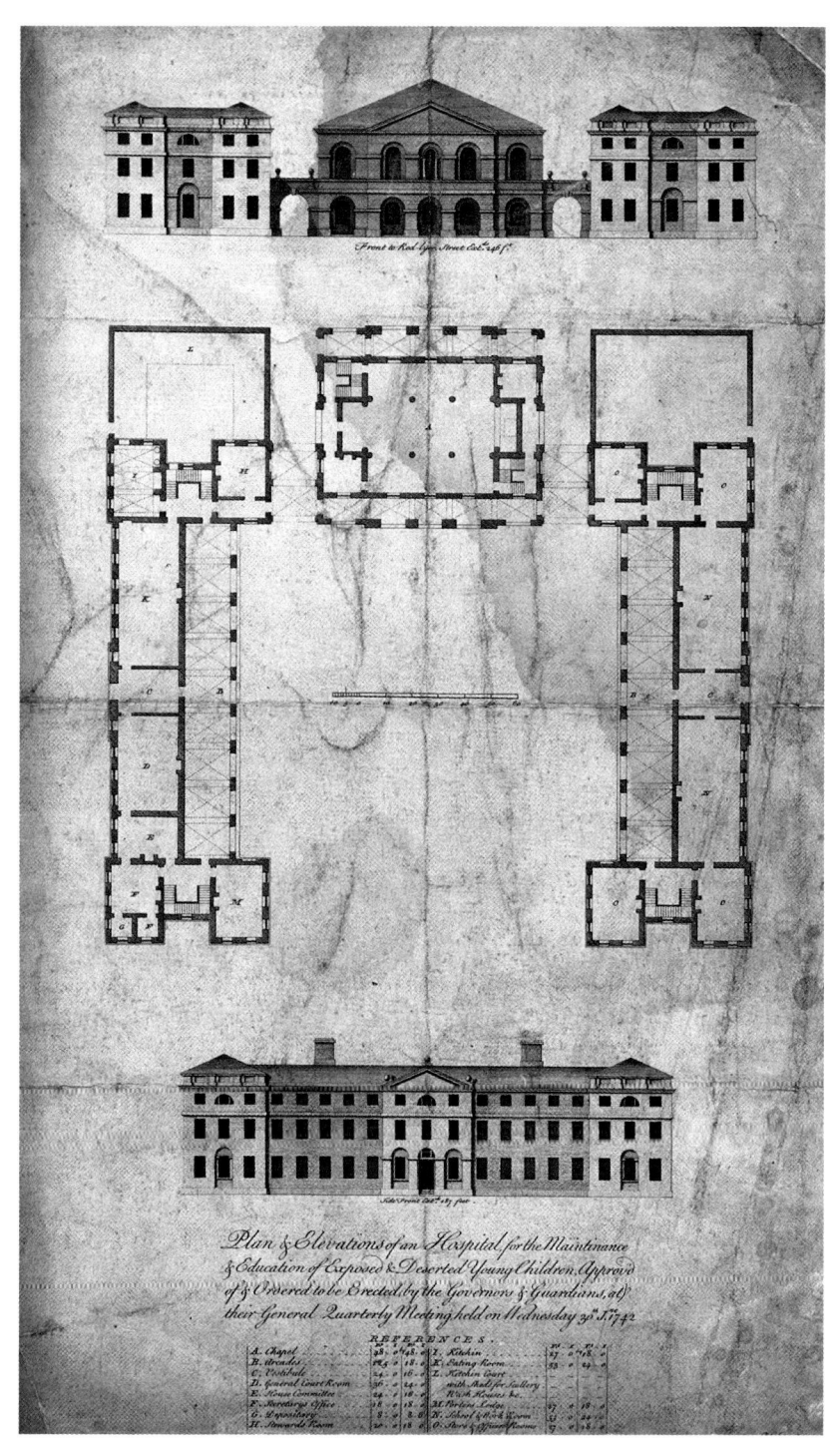

Foundling Hospital plan and elevations, with a scale and a key. Engraving by P. Fourdrinier [after T. Jacobsen, 1742]. (*Wellcome Collection*)

stood down after their term and stood for election. Thomas had been very much involved in designing and agreeing this whole process. They had settled on a plan which involved the hundreds of governors, but which enabled the more enthusiastic and active members to be more proactively involved through the General Committee.

Each year, the governors elected which of their number were to sit on the General Committee. From the outset, in 1739, Thomas had been one of the most active governors and stood on the General Committee as soon as it was first formed. In May 1742, he stood for election again as did others of the 'active' element of the governors. On this occasion, however, Thomas did not receive enough votes from his fellow governors to sit on the General Committee, so he was effectively cast out as a person of influence on his own Darling Project.

That Thomas, who had spear-headed the project for more than two decades and had been at the forefront of all the planning and decision taking since the Charter became a reality, was now not at the heart of the hospital was unthinkable. What could have happened to cause such disloyalty amongst his fellow governors?

Thomas's early biographers have different perspectives on Thomas's departure from the General Committee. Compston describes the failure to receive sufficient votes as an act of revenge carried out by a number of the governors who were angry about complaints of 'irregularities' Thomas had made about fellow governors.

Brownlow, however, writing in 1865 speculated that Thomas was upset that babies were taken in without trying to find out which babies had the greatest need.

> …He [Thomas Coram] … found that the managers were acting upon a principle which furnished no guarantee for the effectual operation of the charity, namely, -- receiving children without establishing any test by which the merits of each case could be ascertained. But after repeated admonition, finding his advice disregarded by the majority of the committee, he left the management of the institution in their hands.

However, Brownlow also acknowledges that there is no record of the disagreement. Brownlow, himself, worked for the hospital at a time when gathering evidence to make a case as to why a baby should be admitted was part of the everyday functioning of the hospital, so perhaps it was Brownlow who had an issue with the way the hospital was operating rather than Thomas.

Facing disagreement and even antagonism from those around him was by no means a new experience for Thomas and perhaps brought back memories of

Taunton, when he fell out with his community so badly that litigation brought between them all but ruined him and caused him and his wife to leave their home and resettle 3000 miles away in London.

In 1732, he achieved a dream of being made a trustee on the Georgia project but arguments between him and others on the committee caused him to leave. And now it had happened again. We know that he was a stubbornly determined man; it was, after all, sheer stubbornness that made him persist with the hospital project despite repeated rejection for seventeen years. Did this stubborn determination make it impossible for him to work effectively with others? Was he being punished as a man with ideas above his station? He was, after all, an uneducated man from humble beginnings in a world of titled aristocrats and wealth. Or was he simply a man of principle who occasionally failed to suffer the fools who surrounded him?

As Compston said: 'Coram was not the sort of man to be content to bask in the favour or the condescension of distinguished people'.[1]

Only thirteen months after the first children were admitted into Hatton Garden and his dreams were realised, he had lost his say in how the hospital would be run. He remained a governor in name but was no longer active in that role.

The project, Thomas's Darling Project, had been a very personal endeavour. It was he who had seen the babies dying on the dunghills of London and it was he who had decided what should be done about it. And it was he who had walked from house to house, literally, to talk people into pledging money and signing the petition that he himself had worded. It had reached this stage because it was personal – that was what had motivated Thomas during those seventeen years of his epic quest for the Charter. There is no doubt that without his own stubborn determination to keep going, the hospital would not have happened. Losing control of it at this key stage of its development must have been painful for him. There is no indication it had ever been his intention to hand control of his hospital over to others and walk away at this very early stage.

For a man who always liked to have a project on the go, his response was probably not surprising. He began a petition to set up another foundling hospital in London. Based on his knowledge that, in the first year of the hospital at Hatton Garden, only around half of the foundlings brought to the gate were admitted, it made sense to him to set up a second hospital to cater for the unmet need. He achieved 120 signatories. The determination of a man prepared to start the whole project again from scratch can only be admired. The project never got off the ground, instead the governors of the Foundling Hospital were attempting to accommodate more children themselves by building a brand new purpose-built hospital. And that was going to go ahead with or without the further input of their founder.

Thomas's last act on the General Committee had been to provide the only vote opposing the purchase of bricks needed to begin the build. There was no reason not to support the purchase of the bricks, so was this simply a vote in anger at his treatment by the rest of the committee? The purchase of the bricks was agreed without his co-operation.

Later that same year, the foundation stone of the new hospital building was laid and work on the western wing of the hospital began in earnest soon afterwards.

How much his influence shaped what the hospital was to become in the following years, we will never know. There are stories that, in later years, Thomas was seen at the gates of the hospital, offering the children treats such as raisins, wearing the same red coat he wore in Hogarth's portrait of him. These are perhaps just stories. Certainly, Compston's version of the story was very romanticised: 'There he would sit, often with tears in his eyes. Those little children, munching gingerbread, owed all their well-being to that shabbily dressed, broken-down old man'.[2]

Sadly, the Foundling Hospital was not the only dream that was lost to Thomas that year. He also finally sold the house he built for him and Eunice in Dighton, Massachusetts. Perhaps he had put it up for sale because the hospital was finally happening, or because he no longer had Eunice, or simply because he was now, aged 74, an elderly man who would likely find it difficult to move and resettle. The sale of the house was the physical manifestation of the end of the dream that he and Eunice had to return to Massachusetts one day.

Keeping the Babies Alive

Whether Thomas was aware of it before he was voted out, when he left the General Committee, he left them with a very serious emerging problem.

Through their daily visits to the hospital and reports received from the steward and the matron, it was becoming apparent to the governors that the hospital was not necessarily saving the lives of all those babies who were brought to the hospital.

Tragically, most of the thirty babies brought in on that first evening the hospital opened were dead. Two had died before they could even be christened.

Three years later, by the end of 1744, 183 babies had been brought into the hospital to be taken care of. All had passed the initial visual inspection for signs of disease, most had been sent out to nurses in the country, but 101 of the babies had died. Although the governors did not yet know it, more of them were to

The Foundling Hospital, Holborn, London: a perspective view looking north-west at the main building, happy children dancing round a statue of Flora [?]. Engraving by C. Grignion and P. C. Canot after S. Wale, 1749. (*Wellcome Collection*)

die during their time in the hospital. 137 (amounting to 75%) of the babies from those first years died while in the care of the hospital.

On a humanitarian level these losses were a terrible tragedy. It must have been awful for all those in contact with the babies to see them die, one after another, despite the care given to them. There was genuine doubt that the hospital was not going to save any more lives than would have been saved with no intervention at all.

There was another level to this, however. The hospital was reliant on public goodwill and the generosity of individual donors to keep going. There was by no means universal support for the hospital as many thought that they were already contributing enough to support poor people through the Poor Rates and should not have to fund a hospital as well. The news that the hospital was failing to keep children alive would have been very bad for the hospital's wider reputation as well internal morale.

While detailed statistics weren't kept about the death rates of infants in London at the time, many researchers have attempted to estimate the levels, and all agree that infant mortality was horrifyingly high in London at the time. There were many reasons for this high death including lack of medical knowledge, poverty, poor hygiene, overcrowding and malnutrition. The 75% death rate suffered by the hospital in those early years was probably similar to that being experienced in many areas of London and, for babies physically abandoned on the dunghills, the mortality rate was no doubt much closer to 100%.

No questions were asked of the people who brought their babies and gave them into the care of the hospital but it has been assumed by commentators of the time, and researchers since, that it was not only the poor and destitute who brought their babies into the hospital's care. Those who were wealthy, even aristocratic and perhaps royal, gave up those babies whose illegitimate births would otherwise have brought scandal and shame to the families. Although the babies came from privileged backgrounds and would have experienced a rather higher survival rate should they have been brought up by their families, they were also dying in the hospital. For these babies who would have been fed well and kept warm in the family home, there is every reason to suppose that they were far more likely to die in the hospital than they were if they had not been taken there.

For a hospital which had had the input, both in terms of time and money, of hundreds of people, losing so many of the babies in their care was a matter of great concern. The causes of death were varied; there was not one epidemic that affected all the children, nor a single set of circumstances that contributed to their deaths.

74% of those who died in those early years, died before they 2 years old. Tuberculosis (known as consumption) and measles were two of the biggest killers of such young children in the eighteenth century. Both were extremely infectious and there were no treatments available for either.

There were two immediate responses. Firstly, the governors greatly reduced the number of babies being admitted to the hospital. While 113 were admitted in 1741, 1742 saw just 47 babies admitted, which went down to 23 in 1743. The governors decided to admit no babies at all in 1744.

Secondly, the governors asked advice of doctors about what they could do. Most famously, the governors asked the eminent physician, Dr William Cadogan for his advice. He wrote a letter in reply to the governors and later published the letter as *An Essay upon Nursing and the Management of Children from their Birth to three Years of age*. Subsequently he was appointed as a governor and then as the physician to the Foundling Hospital. As his knowledge and experience of the Foundling Hospital grew, he published more and more editions of his Essay with revisions and additions to the text each time. It was to become a key document in terms of childcare at the time.

Dr Cadogan did not himself have children until 1747, but he nevertheless had very strong views on childcare. He felt that the large number of babies dying in the hospital was principally due to poor nursing. Women caring for children, he felt, relied too much on myths and superstitions passed down through their families and did not have the expertise to take care of foundling children. Their primary mistakes, he felt, were to keep the babies too warm and to overfeed them. He believed not only that babies could withstand illness and disease much better than adults ('for the same Reason that a Twig is less hurt by a Storm than an Oak') but that poor people were not as affected by illness as rich people:

> The Mother who has only a few Rags to cover her Child loosely, and little more than her own Breast to feed it, sees it healthy and strong and very soon able to shift for itself, while the puny Insect, the Heir and Hope of a rich Family lies languishing under a Load of Finery that overpowers his Limbs, abhorring and rejecting the Dainties he is crammed with, till he dies Victim to the mistaken Care and Tenderness of his fond Mother.

It was with these beliefs that he analysed the needs of the children in the Foundling Hospital. He perceived that the children in the hospital building were wrapped in too much bedding so that when they went to their country foster homes, which he felt were bound to be damp and draughty places, they would not be able to tolerate the cold and would inevitably die:

> Nature has made Children able to bear even great Hardships before they are made weak and sickly by their mistaken Nurses.

For the children of the Foundling Hospital, he prescribed a flannel waistcoat without sleeves with a petticoat attached, a light flimsy flannel gown over the top and a cap for the child's head. The swathes in which babies were initially wrapped were not needed he said. At night, a flannel shirt should be warm enough. He also stubbornly argued that young children should never wear shoes and socks. He said that bed linen should be cleaned as often as possible, dismissing the common view that clean bedding and clothes dried out the body and robbed it of its 'nourishing Juices'.

He felt that the newly admitted babies did not need to be fed immediately, as fasting was a natural part of a newborn's early days but that, when it was fed, it should be breastfed and not given other foods. He determined that they should not be fed whenever they cried but should only be fed at set times when it was known that the child was hungry.

Of the 113 children admitted to the Foundling Hospital between March 1741 when it first opened and 5 June that same year, 59 babies were sent out to nurses in the country and 54 remained in the hospital. By that September, 76 of the children had died – 44 died in the hospital while 32 died in the country with their country nurses.[3]

It was clear to Dr Cadogan that sending children out to country nurses was the healthiest option for them. He felt that the ideal nurses would be middle-aged as they have more milk than younger women, and that they should have a good diet of daily meat and vegetables. They should only drink milk, water or a small beer while they were breastfeeding, and not wine or strong liquors. The foster family, he felt, should keep the baby entertained and alert and not let it sleep too much.

As babies grew older, he recommended adding fruit and vegetables to their diet. He acknowledged that many women were scared to feed their babies fruit and vegetables as they carried the eggs of insects and mothers feared that this would be harmful to their child. However, Dr Cadogan was sure that the digestion of young children could cope with such things.

For older children, he recommended a diet which included meat and vegetables, and bread and butter. It was primarily plain food but perhaps as healthy as it could be in the circumstances. He advised that portions were restricted as greed and over-indulgence should not be tolerated.

Dr Cadogan's regime included actions that we might now consider unhealthy – such as not giving very young children in a poorly heated house enough clothes, while others, breastfeeding babies being a prime example, probably saved many lives.

Foundling Infants, *The Strand Magazine*, September 1891.[4]

Dr Cadogan's influence created a strict regime to promote hardiness in the foundlings which, looking at it from our modern perspective seems unduly harsh and cold but he also had a very positive effect by encouraging more children to be sent to country nurses, championing the need for inspectors, and insisting on a move away from dry nursing (feeding with cow's milk) to breastfeeding. He also promoted a diet for the older foundlings which, in terms of balance and protein still seems reasonable in today's terms. His learnings from his time in the Foundling Hospital also filtered through to other doctors and the wider population.

One issue that the Foundling Hospital had difficulties with was influencing how the country nurses looked after their charges. With limited visits from inspectors and only occasional letters to communicate with families between those visits, it was not easy for the hospital to share ideas about how the children should be cared for and to ensure that these ideas were taken up. In the early days of the Foundling Hospital, the country nurses were essentially left to bring the children up as each felt fit. As Dr Cadogan developed his ideas about how best to look after children and wanted the country nurses to follow these ideas, this lack of effective communication became more problematic and his influence on the care that children received from the foster families was limited.

There was an improvement in the number of children surviving their first years of the hospital throughout the 1740s and early 1750s. While 55% of those admitted in 1741 to 1743 died before they were 2 years old, in 1754, this had reduced to 44% and 35% of the babies admitted in 1755 died before they were 2 years old.[5] For the time, this was an excellent outcome.

The New Building

It was not unusual for social care projects of the time to be small. For example, Westminster Hospital was established with just eighteen beds in 1720. However, it was not in Thomas's vision to have a small home. His aim had always been a large hospital. The obvious advantage of a large building is that it can house a large number of children and therefore he could take in as many children as possible off the streets. But that was not the only advantage. Thomas was interested in achieving maximum impact and then capitalising on that in fundraising terms. The bigger the splash, the more people would take notice and join in. And larger numbers of children could achieve impact – particularly in terms of protecting the country and populating the New World, both of which were in his sights.

He never gave any impression that he would be happy with a small project and it is also easy to imagine that his supporters, including the twenty-one women of distinction, had each been told that they were contributing to a project of significance, not a small house in Hatton Garden with only a handful of children. Even as the signatures were still wet on the lease for Hatton Garden, Thomas was active in the sub-committee of governors who were focused on the new building – the big vision. Before the first children arrived at Hatton Garden, land for the new hospital building was purchased and plans for the build were already in an advanced state.

The land purchased was in what was then the countryside north of the city. They had purchased four fields, surrounded by more fields. This was perfect as the benefits of fresh air were well known (even if not fully understood) and on Lamb's Conduit Fields, the children would have fresh air in abundance and plenty of space away from the noise, stench, and smoke of the city.

The site was just north of where Great Ormond Street Hospital is now. The northern extent is now marked by Regents Square.

There was a small ceremony in September 1742 when the foundation stone was laid:

> *On Thursday the Foundation Stone was laid of the Hospital for Exposed and Deserted Young Children, to be erected in Lamb's Conduit Field. Wherein was placed, between two Plates of mill'd Lead by John Milner, Esq; Vice President, in the presence of several of the said Hospital, a Copper-plate, whereon is the following Inscription: The Foundation of the Hospital, for the Relief of Exposed and Deserted Young Children, was laid 16 Sept 16 George II 1742.*[6]

Almost exactly three years later, the empty fields had been transformed into a large hospital building capable of accommodating up to around 200 children. The first children moved in on 1 October 1745 when the west wing was completed. These twenty-seven children were transferred from Hatton Garden. All the others, around fifty-five children, were living with their country nurses and were yet to experience hospital life.

The idea of the building was that it was a self-contained community of children and staff. Medical attention was within the hospital, as was schooling, as was the work the children carried out. Their exercise, gardening and husbandry experience was all within the hospital grounds. In 1753, a chapel was opened with the grounds, followed by a cemetery. The children had no reason to ever go through the large gates at the front of the hospital site, even in death.

Unfinished hospital building in 1753. Engraving, *c.*1750. (*Wellcome Collection*)

The idea of cutting children in care off from the community around them persevered as the preferred way of working in England into the twentieth century. Families were thought to be bad influences on their children and so needed to be kept away. Further, it was thought harder to mould and control children who were meeting other children at school for example, or in church. In an isolated community, the influences on the children could be controlled and monitored. It also served as a way by which diseases and infections could be limited. Although of course, once infectious diseases came into the building (via a staff member, or governor, for example) there was no escape.

The 1745 move into the new building coincided with the age at which the first intake into the Hatton Garden site were being removed from their country nurses and brought into the hospital building. Even with the twenty-seven already in the hospital building, this would not have amounted to many more than fifty children at most. With 56 acres of land and a building designed to accommodate 200 children, those little children must have felt very small indeed. For those children who had been in family homes with their country nurses for all their lives so far, it may have felt very strange – a large amount of space but also a large number of rules and restrictions.

The governors, however, felt that there wasn't enough space at all. A few months after the children moved into the west wing, newspapers announced that another wing, doubling the number of children who could be accommodated, was going to be built. The governors had plans for far more children to be brought in off the streets.

A Lottery

No children were admitted to the hospital in 1744, when it was still based in Hatton Garden. In 1745, admittance began once more. 45 babies were brought into the brand-new hospital building in that year. 52 more babies arrived in the following year and 101 in 1746. This was still not as high as the 113 admitted in 1741 but numbers were certainly rising.[7]

However, there were still far more babies being brought to the hospital than the governors felt that they could accommodate. They were concerned from the very first reception day that mothers who were turned away with their babies might cause some sort of trouble and these concerns remained.

> As the Hospital became more generally known, it will readily be supposed that the applications for admission greatly increased so that there were frequently one hundred women at the door when twenty children only could be received. This gave rise to the disgraceful scene of women scrambling and fighting to get to the door so that they might be of the fortunate few to reap the benefit of the Asylum.[8]

People gathered outside the hospital with their babies on the evening of the reception, but some arrived early. Queuing was difficult and not always fair. Women were often ill, usually upset and always desperate. With all the pushing and shoving, there was not always any guarantee that those who arrived first got to the door first to deliver their babies. The porter could do his very best to track which woman was where but, with increasingly large numbers of women, it was a near impossible task on many occasions.

With queuing so difficult to police and a fear that uncontrolled, disappointed people would rebel and riot, the governors hit upon a solution which they felt was both fair and gave them control over the situation. They put as many white wooden balls into a bag as they had places to give to babies on that evening. They then added five red balls for every twenty places they had available for babies and then put in a number of black balls that meant, when added to the white and red balls, there were approximately the same number of balls as there were babies waiting to be admitted.

The adult bringing each baby, in turn, selected a ball from the bag. If the ball was black, they were sent away, although, if the child was young enough, it could be presented again at the next reception evening. If the adult picked a white ball, they could take their baby to the governors where, with a doctor, the baby would be inspected. If it was not found to have any obvious signs of disease and looked to be under the age of two months, it was taken into the hospital.

The women who picked a red ball were told to wait until it was known how many of the white ball babies had been rejected because of age or illness. There would then be another process of selecting balls. If, say, three babies had been rejected, their three white balls would be placed back in the bag with a number of black and red balls. Those who picked a white ball second time around would be sent to have their baby inspected. This process would continue until all the white balls had been selected by those whose babies passed the inspection.

In the new building, there was a court room with long benches on which the women sat with their babies. Those selecting red balls may have found themselves sat there for as long as it took to inspect thirty babies, and then redo the ballot of the wooden balls as many times as was necessary. It must have been a long, distressing wait for many of the women. How must it have felt to leave such a life-changing event to chance, to the random selection of the right wooden ball? It may have been a fair way of allocating hospital babies in that everyone who selected a ball had the same chance of selecting a white ball, but it was a method entirely devoid of humanity.

For some, putting their hand in the bag and picking a ball was literally a matter of life or death. Most often the life in question was that of their baby, but for others it may have been the life of the mother as well. If mother and child selected a black ball and were turned away with nowhere to go, how would they survive the night?

Brownlow was not even convinced that it was always fair. 'This plan, it is true, prevented the disgraceful scenes described; but a charity so unguardedly dispensed as to the selection of its objects, could not but open its door to fraud and abuse of the worst description. We know that no human institution, however cautiously managed, can be wholly free from abuse.'[9]

The introduction of this form of ballot was another distinction between the London Foundling Hospital and those in the rest of Europe. Babies brought to the Paris, Rome or Madrid Foundling Hospitals, for example, were simply left outside and the people bringing the babies never met anyone from inside the hospital. What the London Foundling Hospital had devised was a complex process which, it could be argued, dragged out the process of delivering babies, putting distressed mothers under great emotional pressure. Was the practice designed to deter mothers from getting into the position whereby they had to bring babies to the hospital? Or was it a punishment for the mothers who did so?

Fame and Fortune

It would appear that Thomas Coram knew the value of showmanship. From the very first reception for babies in March 1741, there was an audience watching as people brought their babies to the door of the Hatton Garden house that was the first home of the Foundling Hospital. People arrived in carriages and watched the misery of women queueing with their tiny crying babies. They saw the pain of handing over a baby and they saw those that were turned away either because the child was evidently poorly or because they were simply not far enough ahead in the queue to receive one of the limited places.

The audience could then see the end of this story of reception by attending the baptisms of the selected children just a few days later. The babies were each given names, some taking on the names of famous people of the time. Many of the governors attending the baptisms had babies named after themselves. Older foundlings were present at the services and often took around the collection plates passing from person to person to smile and receive a donation.

The new building meant that there was far more room for spectators and much more comfortable facilities for them. However, such was the demand for seats at the Sunday evening service in the chapel when the christenings took place that tickets had to be issued for spectators to ensure they were not oversubscribed. Never before had there been so much interest in illegitimate babies.

In part, the large number of governors, up to a thousand at times, meant that a large crowd was almost inevitable. Not only did many of the governors want

The hospital chapel filled with visitors by Thomas Rowlandson and Auguste Charles Pugin; aquatint by John Bluck.

to see the reception themselves as they had contributed financially or in some other way to the project, but they encouraged their friends, family and colleagues to attend to see what good deeds they were responsible for. The newspapers, local to London and further afield, took a regular interest in the proceedings and reported on the goings on in the hospital. Unusual news was reported, say an accident with the builders of the new hospital, the death of an officer, or a fundraising event, but also more mundane news such as the numbers of children received or baptised, the date of a General Committee meeting or the election of governors. Newspapers also took an interest in rumours, perhaps a baby with noble connections being left at the hospital, or gave ghoulish attention to fights breaking out amongst the women waiting to give their babies into the hospital. There was no shying away from these tragic or desperate details in respect for those involved.

Making a spectacle of this no doubt brought in further interest in the work of the hospital and donations followed. The Foundling Hospital became more fashionable as a cause as the size of the crowds watching the spectacles of reception and baptism increased.

It is remarkable that a hospital caring for children who were generally thought of as being evil because of their illegitimate births had become so fashionable in wealthy London society. Thomas had struggled for the best part of two decades to encourage people to take the smallest interest in his project, and now the upper echelons of London society were vying for space to witness these babies being rescued. This was a feat achieved by Thomas and the Foundling Hospital alone; no other organisation in London had even attempted such a thing. Had Thomas even envisaged that he would create such a sea change in the popular view of illegitimacy?

However, the spectacle of the babies was not the only reason for the exceptional popularity of the Foundling Hospital as a cause. During Thomas's times in London (and by the time the Charter was written, he had been in the city for thirty-five years) he had amassed a wide range of friends and acquaintances in high places. Many of these he persuaded to be signatories on the 1739 Charter and became governors of the hospital. In this fashion, the hospital had literally hundreds of exceptionally well-connected governors. Casting the net so widely meant that awareness of the hospital travelled throughout society.

Two of these supporters were particularly notable for the contribution they made to the fashionableness of the hospital as a cause. These men were William Hogarth and George Handel.

In 1739, when William Hogarth became a governor of the hospital, he was in his early forties. His childhood in London had been with two working parents, although Hogarth was aware of the problems of poverty in the city as his father had spent some time in a debtor's prison when William was a young man. William Hogarth had undertaken an apprenticeship in engraving and worked as an engraver for other people for a time. However, his primary and enduring interest was in his own art, particularly satirical works which focused on such issues as the bursting of the South Sea Bubble. He developed into a very keen observer of human nature, particularly at the less palatable elements of society – both amongst the wealthy and the poor. By the time of his association with Thomas and the Foundling Hospital, he had already completed *A Harlot's Progress* about a girl who turns to prostitution and *A Rake's Progress* which took as its subject a wealthy individual who spent his life on prostitution and gambling.

Self-portrait of W. Hogarth in a Montero cap, with his dog Trump. Stipple engraving by B. Smith after W. Hogarth. (*Wellcome Collection*)

It is perhaps not surprising that an issue such as illegitimacy was a subject he had already considered and did not shy away from and when he was introduced to Thomas by his association with the Ladies of Charity and the Hospital Charter was granted, he decided to become involved. And he became involved in every way possible.

Famously he painted a portrait of Thomas which he then gifted to the hospital. The painting has since become one of those considered to be amongst the greatest works of art he produced. He also made a donation to the new hospital of some 120 pounds (worth approximately £18,000 in today's terms). He designed various aspects of the hospital's 'branding' including the hospital's coat of arms, the letterhead and even the uniforms of the children.

William Hogarth had married his wife, Jane, some ten years before the hospital opened and, like Thomas and Eunice, the couple had no children. Being some thirty years younger than Thomas and Eunice, William and Jane fostered children from the hospital. It is also thought that Jane may have acted as an inspector to other country nurses in her neighbourhood. Willam and Jane were ideally located as they had a large house in what is now Chiswick, before London had enveloped it. When they lived there it was in the countryside, away from the unhealthy air of the city and so a great location for the children to grow up away from the unhealthy atmosphere of London.

But Hogarth did something that had much wider implications for the positioning of the hospital as a popular cause in London society.

In May 1750 a lottery called 'Mr Hogarth's Subscription' was held. 1842 of 2000 tickets were sold in aid of the hospital funds with the unsold tickets being donated to the hospital. The winning ticket was selected at 2 o'clock on 4 May, before 'a great number of persons of distinction' and the ticket numbered 1941 was the winner. It was one of those that had been given to the hospital. Thus, the hospital itself won one of Hogarth's pictures – *March to Finchley*. The Duke of Ancaster is said to have offered the governors 200 pounds for it, but they refused, preferring instead to keep the art.[10] This decision, to keep the painting rather than sell it, turned out to be a very significant one for the future of the hospital and for art in London.

After this first 'accidental' donation of *March to Finchley* from William Hogarth, he made further donations of his work. As he was an artist of some renown in London, his donations encouraged other artists of the time to also donate their work to the hospital. Thomas Gainsborough gave his work (his depiction of the Charter House, was hung in the court room), as did Sir Joshua Reynolds (including his portrait of the Earl of Dartmouth, one of the vice-presidents of the hospital). Again and again the governors agreed not to sell the art but to display it in the hospital. Some of the works presented to the hospital had subjects related to the hospital, or depicted scenes designed to give the children comfort. Others had no relevance. The paintings were hung around the hospital. Of course, portraits of the men behind the hospital also adorned the walls – Hogarth's portrait of Thomas was joined by Shackleton's portrait of George II, and portraits of numerous governors shared the wall space.

As Bernard (1797) wrote: 'The whole of the building … was intended to be plain and devoid of decoration; but the talents and public spirit of several artists benevolently varied the institution'.[11]

At first, artists were simply supporting the hospital with their art and following Hogarth's lead. But as more artists contributed their work, visitors were drawn to the hospital specifically to view the works on display. Artists began to give their work so that it would be seen by the visitors, rather than to support the hospital. Remarkably, at the time, London did not have a public gallery where artists could display their work for the appreciation of whoever wanted to visit. The hospital took on this role and became, not simply a place for the care of

The walls of the hospital's court room were adorned with art. The Foundling Hospital: the interior of the court room, with people in eighteenth-century dress. Wood engraving. (*Wellcome Collection*)

children, but a place in which art was exhibited for art's sake. London society now had even more reason to visit the hospital.

The governors elected those artists who had donated their work to the hospital as governors. These artistic governors were so numerous that they decided to hold an annual Artists' Feast in the hospital each year on 5 November to celebrate their art and discuss their future plans. It was reported that during the Artists' Feast of 1757, as many as 154 artists were present.[12] In 1761 the artists agreed to appear at their annual feast each wearing outfits made entirely by foundlings. The children in the Ackworth branch foundling hospital were given the task of making all the clothes.

The art hanging in the hospital was now such a draw for the public that a visit to the Foundling Hospital became 'the most fashionable morning lounge in the reign of George II'.[13]

The annual feasts continued and other meetings were also held to plan these events and other exhibitions. From these came the founding of the Royal Academy of Arts.

Inspired by Hogarth and the other artists who were not only supporting the Foundling Hospital but also making it a place for art, the musician George

Frideric Handel, already famous in London, approached the governors with an offer they could not refuse. He offered to put on a concert of his own works with the money raised to go to the Foundling Hospital. The concert was held on 27 May 1749 and was attended by a thousand people including the Prince (eldest son of George II who had granted the hospital its charter) and the Princess of Wales. Handel composed an anthem for the hospital especially for the occasion. The event was a tremendous success.

Handel was offered the position of governor of the Foundling Hospital and, to mark his acceptance, he gifted the hospital an organ which was placed in the hospital chapel.

It is not known why Handel chose the Foundling Hospital as the cause to which he would give so much time. Handel was already an established musician and so while popular public performances were no doubt beneficial to him, this is unlikely to have been his motivation. He may have been introduced to the idea by the Ladies of Charity as he certainly had noble connections in London. Handel had no children of his own (he never married) but perhaps his own father dying when Handel was only 12 may have given him some empathy for the foundlings.

It is also possible that he was influenced by the ideas and work of Professor Francke who worked at the University of Halle when Handel studied there in 1702. Professor Francke established schools and an orphan house in Halle from 1695 for the children he saw living in poverty on the streets of Halle. The scale of his philanthropic work was such (at the time of his death in 1727, 2300 children were in his schools) that he helped shape both education and orphan care in Germany. Even if the two men had not met, it is hard to imagine that Handel was not aware of Francke's work.

The concert was so successful that it became an annual event at the hospital. For the 1750 event, Hogarth's coat of arms was used on the grand ticket.

Under Hogarth's design were the words 'The gentlemen are desired to come without swords, and the ladies without hoops'. These space-saving measures had to be taken so that the maximum number of people could attend the concert. At this, the second of Handel's Foundling Hospital concerts held in May 1750, 1200 'persons of distinction' were there to hear him perform.[14] It is astounding to think that so many people would go to, and thereby support, an institution for illegitimate babies when illegitimacy had been such an unpopular cause.

In April 1751, another concert was held with the Messiah performed and Handel playing on the chapel organ he himself had donated. It was reported that there was the 'greatest appearance of persons of distinction, with 600 pounds raised from the sale of tickets'. Another concert was held in 1752 for

Foundling Hospital, Holborn, London: interior of the chapel. Etching by John Sanders, 1774, after himself. (*Wellcome Collection*)

which 1200 tickets were sold at half a guinea each. For the event, the chapel was newly fitted with three finely gilt chandeliers, a gift from Francis Bedwell esq.[15]

Sadly, after an accident, Handel went blind in 1752 but he still performed at concerts in the Foundling Hospital chapel in 1753 and 1754. He died in 1759, only ten years after beginning his association with the hospital.

The presence of music and art in the hospital building fuelled further support from artists and those in the wealthiest echelons of London society. The newspapers covered Foundling Hospital events regularly, broadening its sphere of influence. Within a few years of opening its doors to the first children, the hospital was arguably so famous that it had become London's most important charity.[16]

By the late 1740s, it must have felt as if the hospital could do no wrong. In May 1747, newspapers reported that at one of the regular Sunday christenings of the newly received babies, there was the greatest number of gentry that had ever been seen there. Foundlings were a topic of conversation in the new coffee houses of London.

Thomas was witness to much of the initial growth in the fame of the hospital. He certainly knew of the donations of art from his friend, William Hogarth, and the success of Handel's first concert in the hospital chapel. But while the fortunes of the Foundling Hospital he founded were in the ascendency, his own fortunes were very much in decline.

Thomas's Death

Thomas did not live far from the hospital that was his Darling Project. He was said to have been seen near the building, perhaps with treats for the children living there. It is said that he bent down with raisins for the foundlings while he was still wearing the red coat of the Hogarth portrait. But is this just romantic conjecture? Even as the foundation stone for the new building was laid, he was no longer a part of the management of the Foundling Hospital, and he had new projects of his own.

We know from the length of time he remained angry with his neighbours in Taunton quite how long he could maintain bad blood. He and the rest of the Committee never repaired their rift sufficiently for him to return to the meetings at his own Foundling Hospital.

His home in Leicester Fields was only a short walk from the hospital and he would no doubt have seen the building work taking place. We certainly know that he liked walking as this was his practice throughout his time in London. He may have witnessed, from the outside, the first twenty-seven children being taken from Hatton Garden and walked into the completed west wing in October 1745 and the work continuing on finishing the rest of the hospital.

He was no longer a part of the Georgia project, having fallen out with his fellow trustees, and his house in Dighton was sold. However, this did not stop his thoughts returning to the New World. As these late projects did not come to fruition, there are scant records of them so there are no doubt more schemes that we do not know about. It was reported in his obituary, that he had spent these last years in forming 'new Schemes full of Goodness, and which had a tendency to spread the Influence of Britain, and to expand the Nation's Glory'.

A few examples of what he was plotting remain. In 1748, he was reported as preparing a petition for a large tract of land in North America which was to be cultivated with the proceeds from the sale of the produce being used to fund the Foundling Hospital. He lobbied actively for a college to be established in Cambridge, Massachusetts, which would be for the education of native Americans. It is thought he also had an idea for educating native American girls. In 1749, one of the projects for which he had been petitioning came to fruition after some years of delay: the colony of Nova Scotia was founded. He was not involved in the project by this time, but he surely took a great interest in such a success.

It is clear that he had gradually increased his contact with the Foundling Hospital once more. He attended some events such as the christenings of newly received babies, even giving his name to some of the boys. There are also letters

A bird's-eye view of the Foundling Hospital courtyard. Coloured engraving. (*Wellcome Collection*)

he wrote to the governors enquiring after some of the children, but it seems he was being careful not to interfere.

However, it became clear to himself and to his close friends that, despite being busy, he was destitute. Seven years earlier he had finally sold the house he built in Dighton but, by 1749, it seems that the proceeds from the sale had gone. Perhaps the last of his funds were spent on his efforts to raise support for a second Foundling Hospital? Or perhaps there were other projects in which he invested his money, the details of which have since disappeared. It is said that he did not ask for help himself as 'Men of true Publick Spirit are, of all others, most ashamed to ask private Favours'.[17]

He himself is quoted (by many, including his twentieth-century biographer, Compston) as being very open about the predicament he found himself in:

> I have not wasted the little wealth of which I was formerly possessed in self-indulgence and vain expenses, and am not ashamed to confess, that, in this my old age, I am poor.[18]

However, he still had friends, some of whom were in very high places. When these friends asked him if he would mind some help, he accepted their offer. These friends rescued him from his poverty by contributing towards a small pension for him.

Dr Brocklesby, who is said, together with Sampson Gideon (a governor of the hospital) to have arranged the pension, had this to say about it:

> He [Thomas] was so attentive to the publick Affairs as to be a little too careless of his own ... but his Friend, Mr Gideon, who loved him for loving the Publick, interposed and obtained a Subscription for his comfortable Support upon which he subsisted for some Time which gave him an Opportunity to form new Schemes of the same Kind with those he had executed already; Schemes full of Goodness…

Most of the subscribers to Thomas's pensions were not his fellow governors, but merchants with whom he was probably associated through his work in colonial trade and his campaigning about New World settlements.

Even the Prince of Wales made a contribution. This was Frederick, the eldest son of King George II who was himself a great supporter of the Foundling Hospital. The Prince had become a governor of the hospital and attended Handel's first concert there with his wife. This loyalty to the hospital, was also loyalty to its founder. The Prince was said to have given 20 guineas to Thomas each year punctually, a not inconsiderable sum.

Thomas's work, either in the colonies or the Navy or in the Foundling Hospital, was never rewarded with a knighthood or other title but to have the Prince of Wales himself think so much of him that he was willing to give a regular sum of money must have felt like some acknowledgement to Thomas of his many achievements.

In October 1749, at the age of 81, the Mayor of Lyme honoured Thomas with the Freedom of the Borough in a silver box. It had been seventy years since he lived there, but Lyme was significant to Thomas for many reasons. Not only was it where he was born but it was the place of his own family tragedies and also the place where he had first seen the impact and excitement of the New World and was where his career on ships began. The reasoning behind the honour was to thank him for what he had done for Britain, specifically his part in the Tar Act and what that had achieved for British trade with the New World; for his part in settling Nova Scotia (which took place earlier that year) and also for his part in the founding of the Foundling Hospital.

To be honoured must have been a comfort but, for a man who was so industrious, so dogged and who had so many ambitions, to be without an income, without a title, without a role in any of his projects, and entirely dependent on the kindness of others, must have been an immense disappointment to him. The majority of his ideas had come to nothing. A few had come into being, none had taken him with them.

On 29 March 1751, aged 83, Thomas died. There is no record of how he died, but old age would seem to be the most likely cause. He had been fit enough in the years leading up to his death to be able to keep himself busy. 83 was a remarkably good age for a man born in humble circumstances in the seventeenth century.

Two days after Thomas died, Frederick, the Prince of Wales, who had been such a loyal supporter of the hospital and Thomas himself, also died. Frederick was a relatively young man, only 44, and he died without being able to realise his birth right, the British throne. It is said that he died having been hit in the chest with a cricket ball. George II's subjects were understandably in shock and grief to hear of such a sudden end to the life of the king's heir.

With the nation so unexpectedly thrown into mourning, the governors of the Foundling Hospital had a choice to make. They could, legitimately, have given Thomas a very quiet, subdued send off as people were focused on the sudden loss of their future king. After all, Thomas had been estranged from the General Committee for nine years by this time. However, this is not the route they chose to take. Instead, they decided to celebrate his life and, most importantly, to laud him for his role in the founding of the hospital.

The funeral that they arranged for him very publicly showed off their gratitude to Thomas, despite the rift that had effectively removed him from the Foundling Hospital for almost a decade. The governors were also generous, giving a man who had no money of his own a grand send-off at their expense.

Thomas had requested that his body be interred in the chapel of the Foundling Hospital. This was done on 3 April, just a few days after his death.

Thomas's body was brought in a hearse from where he was lodging near Leicester Square. It was reported that there was a coach following the hearse carrying his mourners. With no close relatives alive at this time, the personal mourners were largely friends and acquaintances of Thomas's.

The hearse and coach were met at the gates of the Foundling Hospital by a number of governors and a small procession into the hospital grounds was formed. At the head of the procession, the secretary of the governors carried the 1739 Charter document on a crimson velvet cushion, a clear indication of the debt of gratitude owed directly to Thomas by the Foundling Hospital for petitioning successfully for the Charter.

Next in the procession were foundling children (both boys and girls) from the hospital. The coffin was carried by Sir Joseph Hanley, Peter Burrell, Joseph Fawthorpe, John Milner, Paul Joddrell and Sampson Gideon who were all governors of the hospital. Following the coffin was 'a great number of Gentlemen' including Taylor White, then the treasurer of the Foundling Hospital and chief mourner for this occasion.

When the procession arrived in the hospital chapel, there were many gentlemen and ladies in the galleries all there to pay their respects to him. Members of the St Paul's choir sang the Burial Service, giving their services voluntarily, accompanied by Dr Boyce, the organist of St Paul's Cathedral who was an eminent musician of the time.

Thomas was buried in the vault beneath the chapel with the following text to mark the place.

CAPTAIN THOMAS CORAM
Whose name will never want a monument
So long as this hospital shall subsist
Was born in the year 1668
A man eminent in that most eminent virtue, the love of mankind.
Little attentive to his Private Fortune,
And refusing many Opportunities of increasing it,
His time and thought were continually employed
In Endeavours to promote the Public Happiness,
Both in this Kingdom and elsewhere,
Particularly in the Colonies of North America.
And his Endeavours were many times crowned
With the desired Success.
His unwearied Solicitation, for above Seventeen Years together
Which would have baffled the Patience and Industry
Of any man less zealous in doing Good.
And his Application to Persons of Distinction, of both sexes,
Obtained at length the Charter of Incorporation
Bearing the date 17th October 1739,
FOR THE MAINTENANCE AND EDUCATION
OF EXPOSED AND DESERTED YOUNG CHILDREN,
By which many Thousands of Lives
May be preserved to the Public and employed in a frugal
And honest Course of Industry.
He died the 29th of March 1751, in the 84th Year of his Age,
Poor in worldly estate, rich in Good Works,
And was buried at his own Desire in the Vault underneath this Chapel
(the first there deposited) at the East End thereof, many of the Governors
And other Gentlemen attending the Funeral
To do Honour to his Memory.
READER

Thy Actions will show whether thou art sincere in the praises thou may'st bestow on him,
And if thou hast Virtue enough to commend his Virtues,
Forget not to add also the Imitation of them.[19]

Thomas Coram was a master of showmanship in terms of the Foundling Hospital and, through this, he created the first truly fashionable charity. We can suspect that he knew that being buried in the grounds would be a great story to carry the hospital through into the future and the governors knew this too. Thomas Coram, although 'divorced' from the charity legally, was a great back story for it in his death. The funeral was covered widely in the local and national press with repeated mentions of his role in the creation of the Foundling Hospital.

Shortly after Thomas's death, a document was published entitled *Private virtue and publick spirit display'd in a succinct essay on the character of Capt. Thomas Coram who deceased on the 29th of March and was interr'd in the Chapel of the Foundling Hospital (a charity established by his solicitation) April 3rd 1751*. The text, written anonymously, served as Thomas's obituary and, as it was written so soon after Thomas's life, remains the key document in our understanding of who Thomas was and how he was understood by those around him. Although anonymous, it has since been attributed to Dr Brocklesby who was a personal friend of Thomas and was instrumental in arranging the pension for him only a few years earlier. From the details of the Foundling Hospital contained in the document it is highly probable that he consulted with past or current governors of the hospital when writing it.

The hospital was not named after Thomas and, aside from the Freedom of Lyme, Thomas received no formal permanent accolade for his founding of it. There was no statue outside the building, marking the project as his, nor did Thomas write any sort of autobiography. However, the obituary clearly makes the connection between Thomas and his hospital and, by doing so, that connection has maintained for centuries since. This was helped by John Brownlow, when he was writing about the hospital in the mid-nineteenth century, as he reproduced the obituary in its entirety. John Brownlow was brought into the hospital as a foundling in 1800 and remained living and working there as an adult, becoming the treasurer in the mid-1800s.

Brocklesby's obituary tackles some of the issues which we may not have expected to be tackled at such a delicate time; it would have been understandable to shy away from them.

For example, there is perhaps a recognition that he had not received the praise during his lifetime that was due to him for what he had achieved: 'There may indeed be some kind of Restraint, some Check upon our Zeal, during the life of the Party; from an apprehension that Praise might be mistaken for Flattery'. As his friend, perhaps Dr Brocklesby knew that Thomas would have been uncomfortable to have received in his lifetime the sort of gratitude and recognition that was shown to him during his funeral. However, Dr Brocklesby also suggested that the public would appreciate some form of lasting memorial for him: 'The late Capt. Thomas …was a person whose Merit and Virtues were so extraordinary, exerted with such Vigour, and with so great constancy, for the Benefit of Society, that an Attempt to raise some little Monument to his Memory, cannot fail of being well Received by the Public'.

The obituary was also disarmingly honest about Thomas's own character and personality and included some thinly veiled criticism. Thomas was described as having an honesty that was 'a little rough' and as having 'stubborn obstinacy'. His lack of education is also referenced more than once, and the eulogy also noted that he never 'raised to any conspicuous Station in Life'.

Conversely, the obituary was also very complimentary, particularly in relation to the Foundling Hospital, describing him as 'Our Advocate for the Helpless and the Unborn, [who] left no stone unturn'd, let no Opportunity slip, but continued to solicit where he had no Interest, with as much Ardour and Anxiety

A statue of Thomas was erected outside the gates of the hospital. He was depicted holding his Charter document. The Foundling Hospital, seen from Lamb's Conduit Street. Wood engraving after P. Justyne. (*Wellcome Collection*)

as if every deserted Child had been his own; and the Cause of the unfounded Hospital, that of his Family'.

In terms of his other achievements, his plan to settle Nova Scotia, so recently come into being, was mentioned; his role in achieving a British interest in the naval stores imported from the Colonies; and his role in protecting the business interests of the hat makers who rewarded him with a lifetime supply of hats.

Throughout the obituary, Dr Brocklesby refers to him mostly as Captain Coram but a reference to Mr Coram also makes it into the text. That Thomas Coram was a sea man there is no doubt, and he probably captained ships during his long career at sea. However, there is no record that he ever reached the rank of Captain in the Navy and there is no record that he ever publicly called himself Captain Coram.

In his death, however, the title of Captain was commonly given to him by courtesy. Perhaps this started with Hogarth who titled his portrait 'Captain Thomas Coram'. Perhaps it was a mark of the respect with which he was viewed in the absence of another title. Since this time, numerous biographers writing about the Foundling Hospital and its founder have also referred to Thomas as Captain Coram (notably Brownlow and Compston) and he is now very commonly referred to as Captain Coram. We can only assume that he would have been delighted with this posthumous promotion in the service he loved.

Thomas was interred on 3 April. Ten days later, on 13 April, the Prince of Wales was buried in Westminster Abbey and the nation's attention turned to him. Thomas's pension was given to a popular baroque singer and composer, Richard Leveridge.

For the hospital, after Thomas's funeral, life very quickly went back to normal. Building on the east wing continued unhindered by Thomas's death and was finished the following year. A year later, the chapel building was completed.

Part VI

Life in the Hospital

'From three years old to six, they are taught to read, and to learn the catechism; and at proper intervals employed in such a manner as may contribute to their health, and induce a habit of activity, hardiness and labour.'

Dodsley, 1761

Thomas's Ideas for the Hospital

In 1749, two years before Thomas died, the governors decided that they had sufficient funds to start work on the east wing of the hospital. This was important for continuing Thomas's plans for the hospital as it meant that the girls and boys could be kept separate.

The following description was written of the hospital buildings in 1761:[1]

These wings are directly opposite to each other, and are built in a plain but regular, substantial, and convenient manner, of brick, with handsome piazzas. It is well suited to the purpose, and as fine as hospitals should be. On the farthest end is placed the chapel, which is joined to the wings by an arch on each side and is very elegant within. Before the hospital is a large piece of ground, on each side whereof is a colonnade of great length, which also extends towards the gates, that are double, with a massy pier between, so that coaches may pass and repass at the same time; and on each side is a door to admit those on foot. The large area between this outer gate and the hospital is adorned with grass plats, gravel walks, and lamps erected upon handsome posts: besides which there are two handsome gardens.

The children slept in dormitories which were, by their very nature, simple rooms. The children did not have possessions of their own (aside from perhaps a small token which was kept with their papers, not on their person) and other items such as combs, clothes, shoes were only given to the children as and when necessary. There was thus no clutter, no need for shelves and cupboards beyond shared storage of the basics. Decorations were generally reserved for public areas only.

The buildings have been described as plain, particularly in comparison with the grandeur of some of the foundling hospital's European counterparts. But, while perhaps not over-ornate, they were certainly grand with a large entrance with three arches on either side of two entrances, each with a large gate. A walkway of some significance took visitors to the main building. A central building had a west wing and an east wing on either side. In total, 400 children could be accommodated making it approximately the same size as Christ's Hospital was at the time, following its rebuild after the Great Fire of London. With babies being accommodated in the country until they were 3 or 4 years old, the scale of the whole project was exceptional.

The total cost of the build of the hospital was £48,500 which has a value of around £13.5 million in today's terms. The huge sum raised for this is thanks largely to the work of Thomas as a fundraiser and the connections made through his Ladies of Charity. The king himself made a donation of two thousand pounds.

The second wing of the hospital gave the governors much more scope to run the hospital as they wanted to, with the girls and boys kept separately and all the staff attending to them similarly separated. As soon as the west wing was completed, the girls were immediately moved from the west wing, which they had been sharing with the boys, and into the newly finished east wing. This was a separation that had been desired by the governors for some time.

As Thomas envisaged, the girls were trained in domestic housework and in sewing. Both of these were very time-consuming tasks, and both were of great benefit to the hospital so the girls tended to have far more fully occupied time than the male foundlings.

> The boys and girls are kept entirely separate; the girls under their mistresses; by whom, as soon as their little hands are capable, they are taught to knit and afterwards needlework and reading; the elder girls are instructed in household world, being employed to assist as servants in and about the eastern wing of the Hospital.[2]

The girls and boys did not meet. They would have seen each other across the chapel, or through the windows but did not get close enough to talk with each other. The girls always had female staff with them and so were not left alone at all. The boys, encouraged to be more independent and to spend more time outside, were afforded slightly more freedoms.

> The girls are to be kept in wards, entirely separate from the boys to be dressed plain and neat with numbers visible in some part of their cloathing to rise at the same hours with the boys, to clean the house, make the beds,

and do the household business until the hour of breakfast after that to be employed in making linen or cloaths or such other labour as is suitable to their age and strength, or in some useful manufactory. They are always to be kept apart from the boys, and to be attended by the Mistresses of their wards.[3]

Allin[4] has looked at the number of children in the new building in its first ten years and the closest to full it reached was in December 1754 when 238 children were in residence. In 1755, there were fewer than 200 children in residence. It must have felt a very large, under-used building for the staff and children inside.

Thomas's role in the Foundling Hospital may have been diminished through being ousted from the General Committee but his influence remained strong. In the early days, he had been very much involved in the formulation of the General Plan and he was a fundamental part of the choosing of the land on which the new buildings of the hospital were sited. He was also part of the sub-committee that designed the new building. His stamp was all over the hospital and, as the hospital continued to function very much unchanged for decades, that imprint remained on the childhoods of thousands of children.

Thomas's ideas as set out in his early petitions were very straightforward. He wanted to establish a hospital for infants where they would be maintained and receive a proper education until they were old enough for service. The ultimate goal was to produce good and faithful servants and to supply the Government with useful hands.

The early years of the children's lives, when they were not of an age to be taught the necessary skills, was taken care of. Country nurses would see to the children's care. The foster nurses had been asked to ensure the children in their care received some religious instruction but little more than that.

The older years were also taken care of. The Charter made all the foundling children wards of the Foundling Hospital until the boys were 24 and the girls were 21 (unless they married sooner) but the plan was that they would either be employed in the hospital itself – primarily this involved the girls who were employed as domestic servants – or they would be sent out to apprenticeships. This meant that, by the time they were no longer the responsibility of the hospital, they had learnt a trade and could be useful to the nation.

The hospital building was to be home to the children for around only eight of their twenty-one or twenty-four years with the hospital. By the time they came to the building, the foundlings were already walking, talking children who could be taught and respond to instructions. When they left to go to apprenticeships, they were barely reaching puberty.

The hospital building was of course, not just the place where they lived, it was also where they were taught lessons, where they began learning skills for work and undertook work, where they took religious instruction and attended religious services, where they received medical care, where they ate and where they played. For many, tragically, it was also the place where they died.

When the children arrived in the hospital building, they lost all their freedoms. They had no choice in how they lived their lives from that point. They could not choose when they got up or went to bed, what they did with their days, what they wore or what they ate. They had very few choices about what they could do with any spare time they might have or who they spent that time with. They could have no contact with their foster families or their birth families. If a child's parent or parents did happen to come to Foundling Hospital to claim their child, it was the decision of the governors whether the child could leave with them, not the decision of the child.

The idea of essentially imprisoning people who had done nothing wrong other than experience poverty was by no means a new one. The workhouse movement was in its infancy at the time, with the main growth in workhouse provision coming in the nineteenth century, but workhouses were certainly in existence in London at this time. Their ethos was to remove the freedoms of the individuals there so that they had no choice other than to do the work presented to them. Only those who were fortunate enough to have an alternative to keep themselves alive were able to leave.

While Thomas certainly never aimed to provide accommodation as harsh and feared as that of the workhouses, there were many lessons to be learnt from a successfully run workhouse for the governors. The governors were forced to be frugal because of the level of donations they received and yet had to provide everything for the children and keep order.

As each child was a clean slate with nothing known of their backgrounds, cultures, family status, or religion, each child was treated the same regardless of what their expectations may have been.

A Structured Life

The key element the Foundling Hospital took from the workhouse to aid the accommodation of so many people at one time, was structure. The hospital was run on a very rigid structure, with virtually no times of deviation from that arrangement. The daily and weekly routine was rigid and had to be followed by both children and staff. Both were discouraged from taking a more relaxed approach to the routine by threats and acts of punishment. The governors in the General Plan of 1740 introduced structure from the very start, despite initial intake numbers being small. A well-defined routine was also an excellent preparation for the children in their working life after their time in the Foundling Hospital.

These rigid principles meant that the care of the large number of children taken into the hospital could be carried out as efficiently and cheaply as possible. Treating every child the same and making all decisions for them was the only way in which the hospital could function.

The timetable for each day followed this pattern:

Summer
5.00 am – children woken up
5.15 am – work for the boys; cleaning for the girls
8.00 am – breakfast
9.00 am – back to work
12 noon – dinner
2.00 pm – work
6.00 pm – diversion
8.00 pm – supper
9.00 pm – bedtime

Winter
7.00 am – children woken up
7.15 am – work for the boys; cleaning for the girls
9.00 am – breakfast
10.00 am – back to work
12 noon – dinner
2.00 pm – work
dusk – diversion
8.00 pm – supper
9.00 pm – bedtime

The children would be woken by the nurses each morning at daybreak. They would then be given just fifteen minutes to perform their ablutions. The first task of the day was to empty the chamber pots by each bed. Older children would empty the pots of the smaller children who were not yet strong enough to carry them. Each pot would be emptied into a large pail in the dormitory which was then to be carried outside. Inevitably, although chamber pots were provided, some children would have wet the bed. This was perhaps particularly so for those who had only recently left their country nurses and were still getting used to life in the hospital.

The children would then wash themselves using jugs of water. The water was not heated and so, in the winter, a layer of ice would have to be removed first. Blocks of soap made from animal fat and wood ash were shared between the children as were hair combs made of wood or bone. With this rudimentary washing done, the children dressed, slipping their day clothes over their linens.

The girls stayed in the dormitories to help the nurses in cleaning. Wet beds would need to be stripped. The girls made the beds, if the children hadn't done so themselves, and swept the dormitories, sweeping carefully underneath each bed. A nurse would check that each child was doing what they needed to do. The activities, however, were so much a part of the routine that the children would invariably get on with their duties largely in silence.

The boys went with the Master who allocated their tasks for the morning.

Prayers were a very important part of the daily routine in the Foundling Hospital and prayers were said before breakfast with the children taking it in turns to say prayers out loud to the other children or the children all saying them together.

Breakfast was generally some variation on water, milk and oats. A thin gruel of water and oats on some days, a thicker variation with milk and oats as a pottage on others. In winter, the pottage could be warm. Sundays would sometimes see bread given to the children as a treat.

In the dining room. *The Strand Magazine*, September 1891.[5]

Dinner generally lasted an hour and was followed by an hour in which the children could play or rest, depending on their age. After an afternoon's walk, children were again afforded some play time at the end of the afternoon – games, talking, singing or a nap for the younger ones. Supper was served at six. This was primarily bread with water to drink. There may also be some cheese. After supper, children could play again until it was time for evening prayers followed by bed at 8 o'clock. Play could be outside in the summer when it was still light.

On Saturdays, the afternoon's work would be replaced by outside exercise. Children were, however, not allowed to do anything that might encourage gambling: 'On Saturdays in the Afternoon, they may be allowed to divert themselves with such exercises as will increase their strength, activity and hardiness; but are never to play at Games of Chance, which they are to be taught to consider as base and effeminate; and some punishment is to be affixed to this offence.'[6]

Sundays were very different in nature with children attending church services and scripture lessons instead of work and schooling. Church services were held in the Foundling Hospital. Some of the foundlings were given the task of taking the collection plate around after the services in the hope that this would encourage the generosity of the churchgoers. Others would join in the singing, or simply watch the goings-on.

Church services were held within the grounds and, after 1753, when the hospital chapel was finished, they were held in the chapel. Sunday's evening service was no doubt an exciting weekly event for those children who were able to attend. They would have witnessed the baptism of the new intake of infants but also have seen the grandeur and elegance of the visitors of nobility.

This daily structure varied very little. Events such as Christmas brought little change to the routine. The birthdays of the children were not known so were not celebrated. Major national events, such as the death of the Prince of Wales in 1752, were marked by church services. When Thomas Coram died, many of the children were there for the funeral.

Events such as haircuts, smallpox inoculations, the annual allocation of new clothes or visits to the sick bay were otherwise the only changes to the daily and weekly routines.

Significantly, the routine did not include the children leaving the hospital site at any time. Once the children had returned from their stay with their country nurses, they had no reason to go through the gates of the site into the land beyond.

Despite being kept within the same walls of the hospital site, as much of the children's time as was possible (particularly for the boys) was spent outside. Older boys were encouraged to eat their breakfast outside and were encouraged to be outside for the 'down time' say, after dinner and before supper. Much of the work the boys were given to do was outside such as tending the garden, hanging out washing, hedging, growing crops, or looking after animals. They would be given exercises to do and they could walk and play. Fresh air was considered healthy for the children, and only extremely bad weather would prevent their time outside. City air was highly polluted with smoke from the London chimneys and stank because of the open cesspits and sewage and rubbish left to fester on the streets. There was little understanding at the time of the health problems of pollution and sewage, but common sense had told Thomas and the governors that country air was better than city air. The hospital was, for the first decades it was in Lamb's Conduit Fields, in the open countryside, north of the city.

Despite not leaving the hospital, the children did have opportunities to see people from outside the hospital. Because it was a popular venue for London Society, the hospital was visited by many people. The children would have been able to see governors and visitors in their finery at the church services in the chapel, particularly when baptisms of the new admissions were taking place. People would also visit at other times to see the art displayed and the governors had a walkway installed so that people could perambulate around the building and take in the healthy country air while viewing the hospital. The children must have looked with wonder at these visitors dressed in their finery, perhaps smiling and waving at the children while they worked or played. It was a meeting of the poorest of the city with some of the wealthiest.

Food

The hospital was established for the *Maintenance and Education of Exposed and Deserted Young Children*. One of the most important aspects of the maintenance of the children was feeding them. It was also the most expensive aspect of life in the hospital warranting several staff and provisions. The right diet, while there was a need to be economical, was essential for the health of the children but also their ability to study and work. However, knowledge about diet was in its infancy in the eighteenth century.

Mealtimes were also a very important part of the day's schedule for the foundlings. They acted as a break from the day's routine of work or schooling and were a time when the children could be with each other and relax but also, of course, take in calories essential both as growing young people and for the work, exercise and play ahead of them. Meals were also a time when prayers were offered.

Life in the Hospital 133

Because of the need to be frugal, the diet of the children was based primarily on what could be grown within the hospital grounds by the children themselves. The Hospital Regulations of 1757 state:

> The Diet of the Children in the Hospital is to be plain and good of the Sort, and to consist some Days of Meat, and others of Roots or Herbs [such as cabbage], raised by the Children's Labour; their Drink Water, their Bread good, but coarse, and made of a different Sort of Corn as Wheat, Rye, Barley, Pease, Oats &c. occasionally so that they may be inured to these accidental Changes. Strong Drink, Coffee, and Tobacco are never to be permitted to be used by any Child in the Hospital nor any Butter allowed them.

In the kitchen the cook was responsible for managing her team of paid servants and female foundlings to get the meals ready. She was given provisions which were decided upon by the governors through the steward and the matron. The children were also involved in both preparing the food and serving it, as well as cleaning up afterwards.

The food was generally plain although much of the perishable produce was preserved with salt. The only cooking was on an open fire but, as there was little way of keeping food warm for so many people, it was often served cold. There was no formal understanding at the time of the importance of vitamins, minerals, roughage, and protein, all of which would be needed to provide a healthy menu now. Instead, the priorities were vegetables that were in season, food that would keep or be easily preserved with salting or drying, food that could be bought cheaply in large quantities and food that would fill up the bellies of hungry children. Supplementing what the children grew in the hospital grounds, food could be bought in from the surrounding farms.

Children were taught to eat what they were given; menu options were not provided. And it was not the practice to give extra food in addition to the meals provided. The concept of 'seconds' was not encouraged. This was not just because of the need to save money, or to discourage the sin of greed. Dr William Cadogan, who was influential in the food given to the children in the hospital, felt that eating too much was harmful: 'The Feeding of Children properly is of much greater Importance to them than their Cloathing … nothing be given them than what is wholesome and good for them, and in such Quantity, as the Body calls for towards its Support and Growth; not a Grain more.' He felt it was as important not to give the children too much food as it was not to give them too little.

Breakfast would not have differed hugely from the working poor living elsewhere in London. Gruel or pottage was a common option for those who could not afford meat and bread, and not just for breakfast but as a basic throughout the day. As it was thin, it could just be drunk out of a bowl or cup without need of cutlery and other crockery. Those children who had been living in the country would no doubt have been very used to gruel.

The morning's work finished at noon when they would all stop for dinner. Grace would be said before the food was eaten. Dinner was generally boiled meat – mutton, beef or pork – or root vegetables with some greens and bread or potatoes. Perhaps dumplings would be added. The morning's pottage could make a reappearance with peas or other vegetables added to make a thin stew. Sundays were often noted for having roast beef on the table.

Having meat most days would be unheard of in the families of those living in the poorest parts of the city. As London's population grew and the built-up area spread outwards, it was increasingly difficult for the residents to keep any sort of livestock – there simply was not enough room for both people and animals. Thus meat, particularly beef, was dropping out of the poor Londoners' diet as they could not afford the costs of buying in meat from the rural outskirts and refrigeration was not an option.

The diet of the foundlings may have been bland and basic by today's standards, but having three meals every day was a luxury that most of their contemporaries in the city would not have had. And the health of the children must have been improved by the milk, vegetables and meat that they were regularly served. The availability of particular foods depended very much on the season and the weather as there was no way of keeping food fresh. The children would certainly have been used to a much broader sense of what was fresh enough to eat than we have. Milk going sour, meat on the turn, vegetables that have seen better days tend to end up in the bin now but would have been eaten without question in those days before refrigeration was possible.

At each mealtime, the children sat to eat. Each child carried a pewter porringer which was filled with their helping which they scooped up and ate with a spoon. The Lamb's Conduit Fields on which the hospital was built were named after the water pipe, the conduit, which took fresh spring water to London. The hospital was able to use the spring to give the foundlings what was probably the freshest water in London. At each meal, the foundlings were given cups of water to drink.

Apart from seasonal changes in the vegetables and meat, the children were given the same diet every day. One exception of great significance was 17 October each year when the hospital celebrated Charter Day. The children would be given a special meal to celebrate this key date in the Foundling Hospital's calendar.

Clothes

Following the lead of Christ's Hospital and the other charity schools, the children of the Foundling Hospital were each given a uniform to wear. For those in the local charity schools, a uniform was important as, when they were in the community, it was easy to spot the charity school child and thus notice if they were lost or absconded. For the Foundling Hospital children, who rarely left the hospital grounds, it was arguably less useful. However, as it was down to the hospital to provide all the children with their clothes throughout their childhood, it made sense for them all to wear the same clothes. A tag was added to the uniform which carried the child's admission number.

While a uniform made sense, what is perhaps less expected is that the uniforms were designed by the very famous artist, who happened to be a friend to Thomas Coram, William Hogarth. Hogarth, in the very early days of the planning of the hospital, had used his artistic talents to design the hospital's coat of arms, a letterhead and had spearheaded the hospital as London's premier art exhibition location. He also then put his mind to designing the children's clothes.

Ultimately, guided primarily by the needs of economy and practicality, Hogarth's uniform design did not differ enormously from the clothes that were

Girls wearing the Foundling Hospital clothes. *The Strand Magazine*, September 1891.[7]

given to charity school children. The outfits were long-lasting, smart, flexible and modest (covering the whole body) and yet suitable for play and work.

He chose brown as the main colour and gave the clothes a red trim. The girls had a brown dress initially made of drugget which was a coarse thick woven or thick felt fabric which had scarlet trimming. Stockings were grey. The boys had brown drugget breeches with a buttoned jacket with a red woollen waistcoat, white linen shirt and a cap.

The girls had a brown drugget dress and the addition of a white apron and bonnet gave the uniform the look of what they would likely be wearing in the future in their anticipated roles as domestic servants. To ensure their modesty, girls also wore a tippet which was a white scarf around their necks. In general, modesty was a very important element of the uniforms as the children's entire bodies, arms and legs were covered; even the younger children in the hospital wore full length tunics.

The clothes were undoubtedly heavy for play and work but warm for outdoor activity, especially in the winter. The summers of the early 1750s were notable for being exceptionally wet. The heavy fabric of the children's clothes must have made them uncomfortable in the rain and difficult to dry.

The drugget was replaced with leather, equally warm and hard-wearing but perhaps easier to source at the time, or simply more waterproof. Lighter serge was used in later years.

The older children were given stockings and heavy boots to wear.

The heavy drugget or leather clothes were not just warm, but they were also very hard-wearing so were expected to last. The foundlings were taught how to stitch tears and add patches. The girls were employed in making new clothes while young boys learned how to make the stockings. Each year, the children were issued with a new set of clothes if they needed it, should they have outgrown theirs or they had damage which was beyond repair.

The linen items – the boys' shirts and the girls' shifts, aprons and tippets – were washed once a week. It was common practice for people to use their shirts and shifts as nightwear as well as day wear. Every six weeks, the bed sheets were also changed and washed.

The younger children living with their country nurses were sent a new set of clothes from the hospital each year. This clothing allowance was carefully distributed and monitored by the network of local inspectors and recorded in registers set up for the purpose. The influence of Dr Cadogan meant that, for many years, children with their country nurses were not given shoes or stockings to wear as it was thought to be unhealthy. In his *Essay on Nursing* Dr Cadogan stated: 'Shoes and stockings are very needless incumbrances, beside that they keep the Legs wet and nasty, if they are not chang'd every hour, and often cramp and hurt the Feet; a Child would stand firmer and learn to walk much sooner without them. I think they cannot be necessary "till it runs out in the Dirt"'.[8]

The hospital uniform designed by Hogarth stayed remarkably unchanged throughout the eighteenth and nineteenth centuries. In those early days when the children were undertaking hard outside work and clothes were washed only infrequently, the uniforms undoubtedly got very dirty, as well as being hot and heavy in the summer months. However, they were certainly far more robust, warm and smarter than anything the street children of London were wearing. The ragged schools of the nineteenth century got their name precisely because of the state of the clothes worn by street children.

Education

Thomas considered education for children to be important. He had petitioned the Government about the education of native Americans, feeling it to be a route out of the poverty and their limited options. His early petitions for the Foundling Hospital Charter had included his view that the foundlings should be given a 'proper education'. This was not necessarily a view widely shared.

Education for children was not compulsory in the mid-1700s. It was not until 1880, more than a century later, that there was a legal obligation for children to have an education and, even then, it was only applicable to children up to the age of 10. Thomas Coram's Foundling Hospital kept children until they were aged 10 or 12, when they would be sent out to apprenticeships; this puts him approximately 150 years ahead of the state as compulsory education for 11-year-olds was not brought in until 1893. It was not until 1973 that education became compulsory up the age of 16.

Part of Thomas's understanding of the importance of education before it was enshrined in law, was that he was not educated himself beyond the very basics, and was honest about his shortcomings in writing, for example. While he was in the British colonies of the east coast of America where he had spent so much of his adult life, he had seen how education was given a much higher priority and was offered to all children, not just those who could afford it or who were expected to achieve status in society. And nor, significantly, was it offered only to boys; girls too were thought to be worthy of education.

This is what he wanted for the foundlings in his care. His view that education for the foundlings was so embedded in his plans that the very name of the establishment included it – the Hospital for the Maintenance and Education of Exposed and Deserted Children. At the time, this must have felt revolutionary.

Thomas did have a precedent for this approach, however. The Charity School movement was very much in the ascendency in London during the time of his quest when he was no doubt making his plans, although had declined before the hospital began work. Inevitably, however, only those families who could afford for their children not to be in work, could allow their children to attend and there was no compulsion for any to turn up to lessons.

What Thomas was planning was education for all the foundlings with no options to drop out, a move which was not to exist on a general basis in the UK until the end of the nineteenth century. Outside of the Charity Schools, children's education was very much only for the upper and middle classes. Those who could afford to give their child an education were at liberty to do so. It was common for wealthier families to have a governess living with the family to take on the education of the children of the household. However, many families chose not to educate their female offspring in anything beyond needlework and the harpsichord while the boys received a more rounded education in numeracy, literacy, history and other subjects.

Children from working class families were put to work. The family structure was such that any children born into the family would have to work in order to help with providing for the family. It was normal for children to begin working at an early age, perhaps 4 or 5. While in the mills and factories of the nineteenth century, this turned into large-scale exploitation of children labouring for wealthy industrialists, in the eighteenth century it was more a part of ordinary family life. In rural areas the work children did was varied – from picking vegetables to scaring off birds; there were many jobs which did not need the physical strength of an adult. In towns, many of the jobs were less healthy – sweeping chimneys being a famous example. They were also given the jobs that adults did not want to do, such as emptying cess pits. Some jobs used their small fingers like sewing or making matchboxes. Others scavenged, begged or stole.

The need to work for the family meant that there was no time for education but, more than that, it was not thought that there was any purpose to education for children other than the middle and upper classes. Why educate a child who was not going to do anything other than the same menial work of their parents? And why educate girls?

What happened in the Foundling Hospital is that no single approach to education was developed and adhered to. Part of this was an issue that had impacted on the Charity School movement, a belief that teaching the Catechism was as useful for poor children as teaching reading and writing. This arose from the idea that foundlings were not going to achieve anything whether they had lessons or not so they might as well know about religion so that they could at least be godly. Interestingly, however, a criticism at one time levelled at the Foundling Hospital was that there was not enough religious education. Samuel Johnson, the writer, visited the Foundling Hospital in around 1757 and

Girls taking lessons in the Foundling Hospital. *The Strand Magazine*, September 1891.[9]

was highly critical that the children appeared ignorant of religion and had not enough teaching about the Catechism.

Some of the education the children received was, of course, outside of lessons. Some of the people involved in the hospital were giving the children informal learning. Not least of these was Taylor White who became treasurer of the hospital in 1746 and who was a great fan and scholar of natural history When he moved into the treasurer's house in the east wing of the hospital with his family, he also brought all his collections. The hospital became home to a large collection of plants, shells, coins, skins, specimens and, it is said, many live birds. Any child who was able to visit this would have been astounded to see such things.

The General Plan was not very informative about education stating only that 'The Children, when taken from Nurse, are to be taught to read, and instructed in the Principles of the Christian Religion, and brought up to Labour, fit for their Age and Sex'. It is also pertinent to note there was no mention of who should do the teaching and no teachers listed in the staff to be employed in the hospital.

Through the life of the hospital, the occurrence of lessons was variable, as were the subjects taught. Sometimes all children had lessons, at other times, it was just the younger children and sometimes, just the boys.

A key problem in the education of the foundlings, however, was not related to discussion about who should receive education and what that education should entail; it was a far more basic consideration. The hospital needed funding and, as such, the children needed to work to earn money to pay the running costs of the hospital. The Charity Schools of London had found themselves with the same issues as the hospital. The pupils in the school also had to spend time working to pay for the schools to exist.

The regulations of the hospital in 1757 stated 'The Master is to call the Children from their Work to reading Class, as such times as shall be convenient, so that each may be instructed once, at least, every day'. This firmly put work as the priority task with education as an extra to be slotted in when the Master could.

If Thomas had remained involved in the hospital would education have retained the importance that it was given when naming the hospital, when it was second only to maintenance? Would he have allowed learning to take second place to paid work?

The *idea* of education in the Foundling Hospital, however, was of great significance. Britain was on a journey of realising the worth of children, particularly the worth of poor children and female poor children. That Thomas got so many people – signatories, governors, the general public – to think that education was appropriate for foundling boys and girls was a great step towards shifting popular opinion.

Work

In the eighteenth century there was a belief that working poor people were in poverty at least in part because of laziness. There was work there for them to do but they chose not to take it on and thus could not afford to keep themselves and their families. It was in this spirit that the first workhouses were established to force people into work. The primary role of the workhouse was not care, but forcibly eradicating laziness. Laziness was even thought to be immoral: 'Idleness and Sloth are Immoralities as well as publick Nusances: and, as the Apostle commands. They who are guilty of them ought not to eat, if they will not work.'[10]

For the Foundling Hospital, giving the children work to do served three purposes – it both trained them for their apprenticeships and for the work they would need to do after they left the institution. Thomas was always very firm that he wanted the foundlings to become useful to the nation. Secondly, giving the children work to do for the majority of the day meant that, while they were so occupied, they did not need other entertainment and would not get up to mischief. Thirdly, the work they did could be sold and bring in funds to help keep the hospital going or save the hospital money by doing tasks that they would otherwise have had to pay staff to do.

Looking at children from the age of 6 taking on work in a children's home, seems wrong from today's perspective. However, children working from a young age was common in working families in the eighteenth century and the move that the country was making into workhouse provision meant that people were used to the idea of poor people, regardless of how young or old they were, having to work for their keep.

The initial daily timetable gave the children eight hours of sleep, three hours for mealtimes, three hours of diversion (exercise and play), and, for the older children, more than eight hours of work each weekday, with a minimum of five hours work on Saturdays.

Masters had the option of taking older children out of their work duties for an hour each day for education. If they did not do this, older children would be left with nine hours' work. Younger children had some schooling in the mornings. The ages of children participating in this and the amount of schooling they were given varied throughout the time of the Foundling Hospital. Education was not always considered as important as it was at other times, and as perhaps Thomas had envisaged it.

For girls, the work was focused mainly on domestic duties. Girls were given the tasks of cleaning, sewing and mending the clothes the children wore, or working in the laundry or kitchen. These jobs were not without their learning qualities and the children would no doubt have picked up skills useful in their future employment and daily lives as most of the girls went into domestic service when they left the hospital. With the girls looking after the younger children, cleaning up after the boys and giving them their meals, the girls were taught important lessons in their place in society as women and in subservience which were going to be useful attributes in both their work as domestic servants and as the wives of working men.

The hospital would have had to employ countless cleaners, kitchen helpers and seamstresses without the girls there to share in the workload with the servants of the hospital.

When the girls were not employed in the work of the hospital itself, they were given work to do which brought in an income for the hospital. For example, in 1751 the girls completed the following list of garments:

Clouts 188 dozen (2256) [clouts were nappies]
121 dozen + 4 shirts and shifts (1456)
101 dozen caps (1212)
6 dozen and 8 day caps (82)

86 dozen and 10 pin cloths (1042)
3 dozen lap bags (36)
7 dozen and 2 tuckers (86) [a tucker was the collar or neckline of a dress]
183 pairs of cuffs
6 dozen handkerchiefs (72)
93 girls bib aprons
24 boys aprons
46 dozen and 5 neckcloths (557)
41 dozen biggins (492)
42 dozen long stays (504)
255 pairs of sleeves
65 pairs of sheets
35 pairs of sheets turned and mended
12 counterpanes
3 dozen pudding bags (36)
6 dozen table cloths (72)
4 aprons for kitchen and laundry girls
80 grey coats
77 bodice coats
75 petticoats
84 grey mantles
133 white bays blankets
34 grey coats for the country
12 brown coats for the house
Plus marking all the linens of the house

107l 9s 9d had been made from selling purses made by the girls and nets made by the boys.

The regulations stipulated outside, manual work for the boys and suggested that too much time spent making things would perhaps raise their expectations that their future work would be just as satisfying. It was felt that mundane, monotonous tasks would give them more realistic expectations of their future: 'Their Work is to be such bodily Labour as is suitable for their Age and Strength, and may be most likely to fit them for Agriculture, or the Sea Service, such as Digging, Houghing [cutting an animal's hamstrings to prevent it moving], Plowing with Ploughs manageable without Horses, Hedging, cleaving Wood, carrying Burdens and such like Employment. Manufactures in general seem improper for the Employment of the Boys, being likely to incline them to a way of Life not intended for them; if any are ever made use of, they must be only such as are simple and laborious, as spinning and twisting Thread and small Ropes, or the like.'[11]

It seems that making fishing nets for the boats of the Thames was a task that both brought in money and was sufficiently dull as to keep the boys' expectations at an appropriately low level as this was a common task of the boys for many years in the Foundling Hospital.

With children working so many hours each day, primarily on the most mundane of tasks, was there any real difference between the workhouse and the Foundling Hospital? The short answer is that for the children, the work was probably very similar on many levels. In the workhouse children would generally have had a parent with them, although they may not have spent time with them. The food was no doubt as basic but there were some fundamental benefits to the Foundling Hospital. The first was that the conditions in the workhouse were certainly less comfortable than those in the Foundling Hospital where the children were given time outside and time for play and exercise.

In the workhouse there was always the threat of being thrown out while punishments in the Foundling Hospital were less harsh. For example, in the workhouse, a daily quota was not uncommon whereby children would have to complete a certain amount of work and have to continue working until they had reached their quota. If a person refused to work in the workhouse, it could be treated as a criminal offence and the individual sent to magistrates to receive punishment. The Foundling Hospital had two very significant advantages over the workhouse for children. The first was that schooling was provided, albeit in varying levels of quality and quantity and the second was that the hospital always had an eye on the children's futures and trained them in a way that would make them appealing as apprentices or domestic servants so that they had a good chance of being able to earn themselves a living in the future.

Health in the Hospital

The institution, when set up, was named as a hospital. This did not carry the same meaning as we now understand – an institution giving medical treatment – but instead meant an institution providing hospitality or care. Likewise, the nurses employed to care for the children were there to act as care givers rather than providing medical nursing. However, despite medical treatment not being the institution's focus, medical and health issues were still of enormous significance for the hospital.

When babies were first brought to the Foundling Hospital, an apothecary or doctor, together with one or two of the governors, looked over the babies. In the few minutes that they were with the infant, they made a judgment on whether or not he or she was healthy. They could feel if the child was hot, and thus may have a temperature, or could hear whether the child had a cough. The men could see if the child had the rash of smallpox, for example, or whether they looked obviously too thin, or too limp. Those who appeared to be ill were given back to their mothers while the others were admitted. But the assessment was limited to this very cursory examination; the doctor had no way of testing to see if the child had any disease which had no obvious visible symptoms. Despite best intentions, the medical knowledge of the time meant that it was inevitable that some babies with disease, and some with contagious diseases, were admitted into the hospital. Conversely, they may also have turned some babies away who looked ill but were merely hungry or drugged and could have benefited greatly from being taken into the hospital.

Tuberculosis or TB (then known as consumption) and measles were two illnesses commonly experienced by children in the Foundling Hospital. There was no effective cure for either and deaths were common. The diseases were also highly infectious and so could spread through the hospital quickly with devastating consequences. Fevers could also be deadly. Many of the illnesses which affected the foundlings may not have had a name, or had a name we would not recognise today.

Diagnosing, understanding and treating illness was still in its infancy when the hospital was founded and, indeed, throughout its first century of operation. In those early years, treatment was often herbal or based on theories around an imbalance of humours or bad air. The causes of illness were poorly understood and knowledge about the links between nutrition and hygiene and health were in their infancy. Surgery was at best brutal – amputation without anaesthetic being one of the limited options – and at worst brought in more infections and problems than it solved. There had been developments in understanding bacteria, for example, but these, while of long-term significance, had little impact on the treatment of individuals in those early days of the Foundling Hospital. It was to be two hundred years until the use of penicillin was widespread in the UK, and the NHS was founded.

The governors of the Foundling Hospital did what they could. They engaged a physician for the foundlings who treated them to best of his abilities with the limited knowledge and medications that were available to him.

Nurses were, from the start, appointed to care for the children only if they had already had smallpox as it was known that having smallpox once effectively made a person immune to having it a second time. Ensuring those in contact with the children had already had smallpox was a great way of limiting the children's risk of coming into contact with it. Very early on, however, the hospital started to take great strides in getting smallpox under control. In April 1744, it was reported that 'a fortnight ago fourteen of the children in the Foundling Hospital were inoculated, at the same time, for smallpox, and all did very well'.[12]

In 1751 it was decided to build a sick ward alongside the new hospital building. This was designed with isolation wards so that children with diseases thought to be contagious could kept away from the other children and thus limit their spread as best they could.

Being in London, the hospital had many physicians around. These doctors were able to earn an excellent living from giving advice to the wealthy residents of the city and so many could be persuaded to give their advice to the hospital for free. In return, many doctors, such as Dr Cadogan, used their studies of the foundlings to write papers and increase their own knowledge and status as experts.

Some of the advice, in those early years when the governors were very much starting from scratch, was useful. Other advice has not stood the test of time. For example, when the governors were thinking about the first intake of babies at Hatton Garden, they went to the College of Physicians who, it is reported, advised that bottle feeding was healthier for newborn babies. For years, the young children were not given shoes and stockings to wear as Dr Cadogan had advised against them.

In truth, the Foundling Hospital was probably creating far more knowledge about caring for babies and children than already existed. The hospital began with virtually no real experience or knowledge of looking after large numbers of children and so all those involved were on a very steep learning curve. However, from the outset, the governors kept detailed records of the numbers of deaths but were also fully aware of the children needing medical attention and how diseases would travel through the hospital. When there was not a paid doctor in the hospital building in the early years (the majority of children being out with country nurses), several of the hundreds of governors were practising doctors and some took a very active interest in the learning to be had.

Motivated by the need to reduce the amount of illness and the number of deaths in the hospital building, the governors were looking at the numbers they collected, at the daily reports from the matron and sick bay, and worked towards resolving the issues, learning all the way.

Taking this active learning on the job a step further, it was not unusual in the foundling hospitals of Europe for medical experiments to be conducted on the children and the London Foundling Hospital was no exception. Smallpox was a big problem in the hospital as it was so contagious, caused such suffering to those who caught it and was so deadly. Smallpox was, for many years, one of the biggest killers of children in the Foundling Hospital, being cited as the cause of around a fifth of all deaths. It was also one of the few diseases for which inoculation was in use, Lady Mary Wortley Montagu having brought it to England in 1721.

The governors had been inoculating children routinely for many years with some success when Dr William Watson was appointed as the hospital physician. On his advice, in 1767, the governors decided to become involved in a trial relating to inoculation against smallpox. Such a trial would struggle to get past the ethics committee of any modern hospital, but it proved to be an exceptionally wise move and the effectiveness of the programme saved countless lives both within the hospital and in the wider population.

Dr Watson could see that the inoculation that had been developed was effective but that the means of preparing each person for the inoculation was impacting on just how effective it could be. He designed a series of experiments to test the effectiveness of what each child was given to prepare them for inoculation. In each experiment the children were divided into three groups. Two of the groups were given a preparation such as mercury, rose syrup or a laxative, while the third group was given nothing and so acted as the control group. Once the children had been inoculated, the number of pustules they developed was counted. Through these experiments, Dr Watson was able to determine with quantitative evidence, which preparation led to the most effective inoculations. This work was not just at the forefront of inoculation development but was amongst the very first experiments which can be compared with modern clinical trials upon which medical developments now depend.

But it was not just disease which was an ongoing issue for the hospital. Children (and no doubt staff members too) suffered greatly from what was known as 'The Itch' which generally was a form of rash. It is likely that in the close quarters of the hospital dormitories fleas and bed bugs were an unavoidable part of daily life for the children. We know that bedding was washed only eight or nine times a year, with linen-wear (shirts, shifts and aprons) being washed weekly. But without soaps and detergents, it was not possible to clean them to hygienic standards. Head lice, scabies and worms probably added to the itching, but treatments were a long way in the future. Boys had short hair while the older girls' hair was longer and tied back.

Some of the children inevitably arrived with or went on to develop (through diseases such as smallpox) long term or permanent disabilities. While none of the initial documents or plans mention this as an issue, the hospital developed means to assist such children: 'Of so large a number of children as had been admitted, it could not be hoped that all would be capable of being placed out, as apprentices in the world. Some unfortunate instances of imbecility of body or mind, were to be expected.'[13]

Brownlow put the presence of children with disabilities amongst the foundlings as a consequence, not of disease, but as the result of the young age of the foundlings brought into the hospital meaning that pre-existing disabilities could not be seen: 'At the Foundling Hospital they are received at so early an age as the prevent the possibility of their state, in either case, being ascertained; consequently as they grow up some of them are found, from time to time, incapable of being placed out in the world either being idiotic, blind, deformed, or constitutionally incapable of earning their living.'[14]

During their time in the hospital, children with disabilities were given activities and work which the governors attempted to match to their abilities. However, it was at the time when the children were due to leave the hospital to take up apprenticeships that extra thought was given to how this could suit children with disabilities. Bernard reports that some of the governors felt it was best that their future was not outside the hospital but that they should remain on the grounds doing whatever they were deemed capable of. 'They still remain in the Hospital, as comfortable and useful as their capacities will allow.'[15]

A benevolent fund was set up to pay for these foundlings to stay in the hospital. The governors could not fund their expenses out of the general income of the hospital as that was intended for children, not adults.

Keeping adult foundlings in the hospital was perhaps not the most imaginative or satisfying future for the children but, as with so many matters, it was probably far better than what would have happened to people with disabilities outside the hospital. For poor families, a child with disabilities was another mouth to feed with little hope of them being able to earn money to help the family. With no support on offer to help families of children with disabilities and a very narrow range of potential work opportunities, many people with disabilities had to resort to begging. Life on the streets as a beggar was harsh and cruel.

There are documented instances, however, where foundlings were trained in the hospital to enable them to get work which was not only outside the Foundling Hospital but was potentially rewarding and lucrative.

In 1758, the governors decided to fund music lessons for Tom Grenville, a foundling who was blind. He was to be taught by the assistant chapel organist at a cost of two guineas a quarter for four lessons a week. But the governors' attention did not end there. When they found that the teaching of the assistant organist was not up to standard, they appointed another teacher, Mr Cook, to take his place. Mr Cook was then an assistant organist in Ross, Herefordshire and in 1767, nine years after starting his lessons, the parishioners of Ross employed Tom as the organist with a pay of 25 pounds a year. Work for blind people was not easy to find in the 1700s, and the Foundling Hospital was unlikely to have been successful in achieving an apprenticeship for Tom, but investing in music lessons for him meant that he could live independently with a respectable job as a church organist.

The music teacher appointed to Tom then took on John Printer and in 1771, Blanch Thetford. Both of these children were also blind and had their music lessons paid for by the Foundling Hospital. The lessons were funded from the collections during services at the chapel. [16]

Part VII

Leaving the Hospital

'You have my heart, though we must part'
Words left on a token with a foundling.[1]

Escape

There were essentially four ways a child could leave the hospital's care: escaping; returning to their parents; apprenticeship; or, tragically and most commonly, death.

We know from accounts of more recent residential care institutions that absconding is a significant issue and many children have attempted escape with some achieving some success, at least until they were caught and sent back.

In the Foundling Hospital, there is little evidence that children escaping was a significant issue in terms of numbers and, as an institution which has become famous for its record-keeping, it would have been difficult to hide the existence of large numbers of absconders.

While other institutions (such as the foundling hospital in Dublin, for example) could only account for what happened to a proportion of the children in its care, the Foundling Hospital in London rarely lost track of a child in its administration. The meticulous hospital registers show that between 1741, when the hospital opened, and 1800, only 0.3% of the 18,619 children admitted to the hospital were unaccounted for and were thus potential escapees.[2] That amounts to 59 children who did not die, were not apprenticed and discharged, and were not reclaimed. This amounts to an average of one child per year unaccounted for in the 59 years since the hospital opened. Of course, they may not all have escaped – some may have been taken, others may simply represent some form of administrative error. No children went missing during the time the hospital was at Hatton Garden as they were far too young to consider or achieve escape.

One possible reason for the low number of escapees overall is that the children knew nothing different. For older children taken into care from their families, they may miss friends, family and the outside life and be desperate to return to their former life. Those brought to the hospital were very young babies with no memories of the life they had and so they had nothing to miss or with which to compare their life in the hospital. Those living with a country nurse were arguably too young to execute an escape. It is also significant that, once they had returned to the hospital, the children did not leave the confines of the institution and the high walls and gates surrounding them made any escape incredibly difficult.

Hospital records do detail some escapees from apprenticeships where opportunities for absconding must have been all around. Significantly, the children who fled their apprenticeships tended to return not to the Foundling Hospital but to the homes of their country nurses, despite having left there some years before. It is perhaps no surprise that the homes of the country nurses felt to the children like home as they had spent all their earliest years in memory there.

Apprenticeships

The stated aim of the hospital in the 1739 Charter that brought it into existence was that the boys would go to sea with the Navy to help protect the country from the wars which were going on in Europe but also to protect British trade with the Colonies.

At the time, there was much going on at sea relating to British interests and the Royal Navy was rapidly becoming the largest maritime force in the world. Wars within Europe were needing men to fight. The New World needed ships to bring people and resources and take raw materials back to England. The slave trade was growing and British interest in it was growing enormously. All slaves were transported by ship from Africa to the Caribbean and around the world. Ships needed protection from pirates and others at sea and also from mutinies on board. Thomas Coram knew, from the very first moment he conceived the idea of the Foundling Hospital, that what Britain needed was men to go to sea to do this essential work for the country. His time in London must also have shown him the value of good domestic servants in the houses of those in power in the city. As Britain's power and wealth grew overseas, the importance of those running it, and benefitting from it in London grew. And those households needed to run smoothly.

Thus, Thomas designed a Foundling Hospital which could produce well-trained men to go to sea and women to go into domestic service. It was an excellent scheme to help the nation right at the beginnings of the British Empire and, as such, it was a scheme close to Thomas's heart. Aside from his patriotic concerns, Thomas himself had been in an apprenticeship from the age of 11 when it had quite literally opened up his world.

The 1740 General Plan document specified that the boys would be in apprenticeship until they were 24, the girls until they were 21 or, until they got married, when they would become the legal and financial responsibility of their husbands.

Until every such Male Child shall attain his age of Twenty four years, and ever such Female Child shall attain her age of twenty-one years, or shall be married or to bond any such child or Children Apprentices to any Person or Persons who shall be willing to take the same or to place them out as servants, or as mariners.

As the Charter gave the Foundling Hospital the responsibility for the children from the time they were admitted until they were in their twenties, finding an apprenticeship for each became an imperative not simply so that they could become useful citizens but also for reasons of finance. The Foundling Hospital needed them to be out earning money rather than in the building, costing money to feed, clothe and train, and taking up beds needed for other foundlings.

But there was another need to move the children out of the Foundling Hospital, far more significant than saving the costs of feeding them. Poor relief was the way in which a destitute person could apply to their parish church for help. One of the conditions of having the Foundling Hospital in London was an agreement that the local parish, St Andrew's, would not bear responsibility for the inhabitants of the hospital in terms of giving them parish relief if they fell on hard times. This was a wise move which made the idea of the hospital more appealing to Londoners and reduced the risk of St Andrew's Parish collapsing under the financial burden of taking on so many potentially poor residents. As soon as a child moved in with their apprentice master, the child had the right to apply, should they ever need to, for parish relief from that parish. If they stayed in the hospital, they had no such rights at all.

The training given to the children by the Foundling Hospital was all very much geared towards making each child 'attractive' in terms of apprenticeships. They were trained to be obedient, reliable and able to take instruction readily and carry out the types of tasks which might be needed of them in an apprenticeship. For an apprentice master looking for a hard-working, obedient apprentice, literacy and numeracy skills were of secondary importance.

The governors worked hard to find tradesmen to take on apprentices from the hospital. The 1757 Regulations, in line with Thomas's vision, very much focused on the boys spending their apprenticeships at sea hoping that 'an order may be obtained from the Lords of the Admiralty, to the Captains or other Officers of his Majesty's Ships, to take a certain number of Boys, from time to time, according to the Rate of the Ships and their Proportion of Men; and if the Captain of every Merchant-ship, of a hundred tons or upwards, was oblig'd (if required) to take one or more, it would greatly increase the Number of Seamen; and, the Hospital keeping an Account of them, the Government on any Emergency would be directed where to find them'. This level of mass apprenticeship of foundlings at sea did not happen on the scale Thomas hoped it would and the governors instead placed many boys out in manufacturing and trade.

In terms of the girls, the hospital regulations stated: 'The girls are to be placed out, as Household Servants, or put out for a Term of Years to be employed in the Linen or other Manufactory, as soon as possible, but not without due Enquiry after the Character of the Persons who take them'. The governors attempted to avoid placing the girls with unmarried men. The preferred apprentice master for the governors was a protestant.

When the foundlings were sent to their apprenticeship, they were given a Bible and printed instructions. The governors endeavoured to keep in touch with all their apprentices throughout the length of their apprenticeships to ensure that all was working well. As apprenticeships were long, lasting up to fourteen years, and often at sea, this was not always possible.

At the end of the apprenticeship. The Foundling Hospital gave each young person a sum of money to help them set themselves up in independent life.

Death

Tragically, the numbers of children going into apprenticeships was dwarfed by the numbers who died. Looking at the overall figures prepared by Allin from 1741 to 1800,[3] 5941 children were sent out to apprenticeships. More than double this number, 12,355 children, however, died while in the care of the hospital; the vast majority dying before they were two years old. Death was by far the most common way the foundlings had of leaving the hospital's care.

There were a number of factors which lead to this tragic outcome. The main factor is that researchers are confident that the death rate in London was very high generally. As population statistics and birth and death data were not kept in those days, we have to rely on the estimates generated by researchers of the time. For example, John Lander's calculation of childhood mortality in London in that time period found that only a quarter of children reached the age of 10 – approximately two or three in every ten children born. It is reasonable that mortality would have been higher for those children living on the streets as is assumed would have been the case for the hospital's foundlings; certainly a death rate in excess of 75% is likely.

There were many causes of death in the hospital, whether at nurse or in the hospital building itself. Smallpox, tuberculosis, measles, infected wounds, diarrhoea, dysentery and smallpox could all kill a child. Babies recently admitted might also die of malnutrition or injuries inflicted before they came to the hospital. Modern medicine would mean that most of these deaths could be avoided. Sadly, there were few effective treatments available to the hospital.

Despite the high mortality rates, every time there was an admission evening, people queued up and fought for a place in the hospital for their baby. We can only guess now whether they left their baby thinking that it had a good chance of surviving there or whether there was some outside knowledge that each baby was more likely to die than to live to adulthood.

However, improvements in the hospital were seemingly having an effect on the deaths of children. Looking at the hospital in three distinct time periods, a definite pattern is in evidence. In the years from the hospital opening and the beginning of the period known as General Reception, ninety-one children were admitted each year on average, and the death rate was 64%. More than six children in every ten admitted died.

In the period of General Reception, 3734 children were admitted each year on average and the death rate increased to 70%; only three children in every ten admitted survived.

In the forty years following the end of General Reception, just 57 children were admitted each year and the death rate was 46%.

From the data available, it also seems likely that the London Foundling Hospital fared better than other foundling hospitals. For example, at the Paris Foundling Hospital, of the 3631 children admitted in 1751, 2487 died before they were even a year old – leaving only four in every ten children to reach their first birthday after which there were further deaths. Death rates in the Dublin Foundling Hospital were even higher.

Part of the reason for the high death rates in foundling hospitals, particularly those who were very young, may be the circumstances of the foundlings themselves. Being born into poverty, perhaps to a mother unable to feed herself properly and unable to breastfeed her baby in his or her first days, is likely to have had an effect on how robust and healthy the baby was. Equally, the care given to the foundlings by the hospital, or the country nurses may also have played a part.

No one looking at mortality in the Foundling Hospital, and indeed in other foundling hospitals could say that the results were not tragic. But it is possible to say that more children were likely to have died had the Foundling Hospital not existed.

Reclamation

When the General Plan was written in 1740, the governors had agreed on how the children would leave the hospital. The boys would leave when they were 24 after an apprenticeship, the girls could leave when they were 21 or if they got married. But they also considered another route to departure: being collected and taken back to their birth family home.

This was not simply seen as a remote possibility, but as a likelihood the governors needed to prepare for. The General Plan was very clear that children would be a completely blank slate when they arrived. No details would be recorded of them or their birth family and the children were christened as soon as possible after being taken into the hospital, usually the following Sunday, whether or not there was any information that they had been previously christened. Each foundling was, at this point, given a new name – both a first name and surname.

While preserving this principle that each child arrived at the hospital anonymously with no baggage or reminders of their previous life, the General Plan detailed how a paper trail would be created for each child so that, when a parent asked for their child back, the hospital could identify which child was theirs without using their birth name.

While no details of the child's name, or the birth parent's name were recorded, the child was given a number which was linked to their new name given at their baptism and carried with them on a tag attached to their bodies and clothing.

> Immediately upon Reception of each Child, the Steward shall enter on a Sheet of paper, its sex, supposed Age, the Year, Day and Hour when brought, Description of the Child, the marks (if any) on its Body, and the Child's Dress; and particular mention to be made of any Writing or any other Thing brought with the Child.

This was not an easy task. Meticulous records had to be kept in large handwritten registers which were then cross-referenced with other registers such as the register of children with country nurses, apprenticeship registers and of course, registers of those who had died. The infants would need to be tagged constantly as, once they were without their identifying tags they could each be confused with the others and thus their identities lost.

The entire reason for this paper trail to the original nameless infant brought into the hospital was so that the baby could be reclaimed by the parent that gave them up to the hospital's care.

Giving us an idea of the importance the governors gave to the idea of parents reclaiming their child, more words were devoted in the General Plan to how a parent would go about reclaiming a child as were given to the issue of children being sent out to country nurses.

> When any person shall reclaim a child, they shall attend the Daily Committee, and shall be examined by them what Right they have to the Child, what are their circumstances, whether they are able and willing to provide for the child, and to pay for its maintenance in the Hospital a Sum to be limited by the Daily Committee ... the proper Registers shall be searched.

Parents reclaiming children who had been given to the hospital as an infant certainly did happen.

For example, in December 1742 (only two years after the Foundling Hospital first took children in) a man and his wife who had given up their child when he was only weeks old, went to the hospital to ask to have him back. They had been forced to give him up because of poverty but had since come into enough money that they felt they could afford to look after him themselves. The couple applied to the governors of the hospital and were able to give the exact date and time at which the child had been left with the hospital and also details of what the child had with him. Through the series of registers kept by the hospital, the child was tracked down and found to be with a nurse in the countryside. When the birth parents agreed to pay for the expenses incurred by the hospital for caring for their child up to this point, the governors agreed that he could be brought to the hospital and handed over into the care of his birth family.

Despite the plans for this type of reclamation in the General Plan, this happy story of parent and child reuniting turned out to be a very unusual event. In the 59 years of the hospital up to 1800, only 218 children are recorded as having been reclaimed by their parents. This amounts to 1.2% of all the children who were admitted to the hospital.

Given that giving up a child cannot be an easy decision for any parent and many mothers who have given birth to, breastfed and held a baby will have developed a bond which leaves them missing their child for many years, the number of children taken back seems far lower than might be expected. For the governors, having devoted so much of their planning to ensuring it would be possible that each parent could be matched with the right baby, they were no doubt also surprised at the very low take-up.

A key reason for the few reclamations is that many of the children in the hospital died during their time there. Any parent applying to the governors to check on their child, or request taking him or her home, was likely to hear the terrible news that their offspring had died. Thus, many parents who were willing and able to take their child home may have been turned away for this most dreadful of reasons. If we look at the number of children who didn't die while they were in the care of the hospital (6264), the 218 who were reclaimed represent 3.5% of the total. This remains a very small proportion who were reclaimed.

Most people gave up their children because they could not afford to keep them. This level of extreme poverty is very difficult to get out of. For many parents who had had to give up their child due to poverty, the sheer difficulty of pulling themselves out of the situation which caused them to have to give up their baby in the first place, was insurmountable. For this reason, many families simply never managed to get themselves to a position where they could afford to look after their own child and so could never apply to have their own children. For others, a new husband may not have wanted his wife to bring home a baby that was not his, or the shame of explaining away why they suddenly had a 3-year-old child may have been too much.

The General Plan stated that a person wanting to reclaim their child would have been questioned by the governors about whether they could provide a suitable home and could afford to keep the child. At times in the hospital's history this assessment was carried out with more gusto than others. Some mothers were simply deemed unsuitable because they were unmarried.

After 1800, the governors developed a much stricter policy of interviewing the parent or parents to discover if they were financially and otherwise suitable to bring up their child. This may be one of the reasons that, in the century after 1800, only 126 children were successfully reclaimed by their parents.

However, even if parents were assessed as being in a suitable circumstance to reclaim their child, there was another particularly challenging hurdle they had to surmount. This was the insistence that the birth family could not reclaim their child unless they reimbursed the hospital for the expense it had incurred in looking after the child up to that point. This would have been a significant lump sum that a parent had to find. If the child had been in the hospital for a number of years, this is likely to have been a sum of money out of the reach of the majority of people, particularly when it is considered that most foundlings were in the hospital because of their family's poverty.

And worse still, before 1764 parents were asked to pay for the costs incurred for their baby's care in the hospital even if their child had since died there. This may have put off many people from even enquiring about taking their child home.

A parent taking a child home with them would have saved the hospital the expense of the child's board and care for the remainder of his or her childhood. The General Plan made it very clear that frugality was important, but it seems that seeking reimbursement for the child's stay up until that time was a false economy as it prevented an unknown number of parents taking their child at all. Was there a fear that, if the hospital made it too easy for a parent to reclaim their child, the hospital would become a short-stay institution to look after infants only until the parents sorted themselves out? This might suit the parents, but it would mean the hospital could not fulfil its ambitions of providing poor children with an education and ultimately, producing useful citizens for the nation. Was this more important than mending families fractured by poverty?

Because of these barriers to reclaiming children, the vast majority of foundlings who survived their childhoods did so without ever meeting their birth families. And once the foundlings had left the hospital, they would have no clues as to their original identity and so no means of finding their birth family (or of recognising them in a chance meeting) even if that was something they wanted to do. The Victorian orphanages were based on a belief that children in poverty were best kept away from their families or they would be in danger of being tainted with their parents' problems and poor characters. In fact, the idea of the best place for a child being with their family, if at all possible, did not really come back into play for children in care until late in the twentieth century.

A token gesture
Despite the very small proportion of children who were ever reclaimed, one aspect of the reclamation administration in the Foundling Hospital has become extremely well-known and is now so famous that it is synonymous with the concept of foundlings.

The General Plan made provision for a complex process of taking away the child's identity but replacing it with an identification number that could potentially link back to the child's old identity throughout his or her time in the Foundling Hospital. But they also added a little extra security.

This extra security took the form of a token 'or other Thing brought with the Child' that was handed in with an infant when he or she was given to the hospital. Thus, a parent wishing to ask after or reclaim a child could describe the token even if they did not have other details such as the date and time that the child was given into the hospital.

Poems were sometimes given in with a child as a token:

> Go gentle babe, thy future life be spent
> In virtuous purity, and calm content;
> Life's sunshine bless thee, and no anxious care
> Sit on thy brow, and draw the falling tear
> Thy country's grateful servant may'st thou prove
> And all thy life be happiness and love.[4]

The General Plan mentioned that this could be a piece of writing, or any other thing brought with the child. As literacy levels were very low amongst the poor communities of London, most of the tokens left with the children were items rather than letters.

These tokens often took the form of a scrap of patterned fabric, a walnut or a bottle top. These items would have cost the parent nothing but the details of them could have been easily remembered. In 1757, a lottery ticket was given with the infant, perhaps in the hope that the child would benefit from the winnings.

Other objects included keys, coins, jewellery, lockets, lace, ribbons, hairpins and other such items. Some were personalised, perhaps embroidered or engraved with the child's name or a message of love. A coin cut in half was a precious token as the parent could carry with them one half, perhaps in hope that the two halves would be together again one day. Medals or jewellery were made for a child with heart motifs used frequently. They are a lasting reminder of how much parents may have loved the children they were forced to give up and how much hope so many of them may have had that they would see their baby again.

Some tokens hinted at a scandalous story. A gemstone, or a text in Latin perhaps, suggest the wealth or education of the person giving up the child. The Foundling Hospital had no barriers relating to the circumstances of the child and, as the only institution at the time which would take in illegitimate children with no questions asked, families from aristocratic, noble or even royal backgrounds are known to have given their illegitimate babies to the hospital rather than face the shame of a fatherless child and a tarnished woman in the family.

In November 1752, newspapers carried the story that a baby had been left in the Foundling Hospital with a ruby ring causing much speculation as to which aristocratic family it may have belonged. In August of the following year, a baby was left with a large red ribbon of the style worn by the Knights of the Bath, one of the most senior of the British Orders of Chivalry. The process was a thorough one however, the child was stripped of any identity when he or she arrived in the hospital – the fact that the child arrived with a ruby ring and a father of nobility, was never known by the child concerned or anyone else in the hospital.

These tokens, so carefully chosen for each infant, and some carrying messages of love for the child, were kept in storage; the child never got to see them. It is somewhat painful to remember the child who had no contact with their family, no love from a family, no possessions and yet, somewhere in a box in an office was an item such as an embroidered heart made by their birth mother as a keepsake for the child they were about to give away, probably entirely unaware that their child would never see the item.

Thousands of these tokens were left with infants over the years and they varied hugely in style, nature and monetary value. But it is not the worth of these in financial terms that has captured the imagination of those who have seen them since, instead it is the poignancy of giving a child, when it was time to say goodbye, a token of love, of hope for the future. And sometimes it is the very flimsiness of the item, the very fact that they were of absolutely no value at all, that makes them all the more poignant.

The hospital developed a storage system whereby the token was pinned to a billet which was completed for each infant, and which was given a reference number which was recorded in the admissions register with the child's new name once it had been issued at the christening. When an infant could not be identified by its admission date, someone must have had the job of going through stacks of billets to see if they could recognise one of the tokens from the description given by a hopeful parent.

Details written on the billet:[5]

Marks and Clothing of the Child

Ribbons	Mantle
Cap	Sleeves
Bonnet	Blanket
Biggin	Neckcloth
Fore-head Cloth	Handkerchief
Head-Cloth	Cloak
Long-Stay	Roller
Bibb	Bed
Gown	Waiscoat
Frock	Short
Upper-Coat	Clout
Petticoat	Pilch
Bodice-Coat	Stockings
Robe	Shoes
Barrow	Marks on the body

The person filling in the billet was tasked with indicating which of these items the child had and then giving details of each. These details would be linked to the register which gave the date of admission and the token (if feasible) would be pinned to the billet or described on it.

Sadly, while the Foundling Hospital archives still include many tokens, at some point in their more recent history they were separated from their original paperwork. Many hours have been spent recently trying to link tokens back to the foundlings they were left for. Some of the tokens are now on display in the Foundling Museum.

Part VIII

A Terrible Experiment

'The vortex cause by parliamentary interference.'
Brownlow, 1847

General Reception

General Reception was a period of just five years, years which commentators have since described as a scandal or a great mistake. It is a period of the history of the Foundling Hospital which has come to define the Foundling Hospital in many respects, and which has had a long-lasting effect on what the hospital was able to achieve.

Ten years after the establishment of the Foundling Hospital a great deal had happened. The hospital had lost its founder Thomas, but it had also built and opened an enormous purpose-built hospital building and all the children and staff had been moved into it. A network of country nurses and volunteer inspectors had been set up and children were successfully being fostered by largely rural families and monitored by the inspectors. The hospital had hundreds of governors who had donated funds for the work and also carried out much of the planning, monitoring and running of the hospital. They were holding regular meetings and seemed to be running a smooth ship with few disasters.

The level of mortality amongst the babies admitted was slowly declining. It was only a slight downward trend, but it was going very much in the right direction. It was certainly possible to say that the hospital's practices were improving. Of each hundred children admitted, current estimates suggest that between sixteen and twenty-five lived to adulthood who would have died had they not been taken in by the Foundling Hospital.

The work of the hospital was getting positive reports in local and national newspapers and a steady flow of babies were being admitted. Others were returning from their foster care in the country and were being given lessons and training. The oldest children in the care of the hospital were 10 years old and had been in the hospital for around four years. Sending children out to apprenticeships had not yet begun.

The hospital was an ambitious project which was running well although these were still early days. The numbers being admitted were not insignificant, but the hospital was certainly not at maximum capacity. The Hatton Garden building could initially only physically accommodate thirty children so that was a serious limiting factor from the outset. The east wing of the hospital had recently been completed and so the building could accommodate 400 children, so beds were no longer the immediate problem.

In the Hatton Garden years between 1741 and 1745, there was an average of just 41 children admitted to the hospital each year. In the first six years of the new building, this increased to 109 children admitted each year, with a peak of 199 children admitted in 1751. These were small numbers when considered against the 400 children who could be accommodated in the Foundling Hospital at any one time (with many more living with their country nurses) and the estimated 2000 foundlings in London each year who potentially needed to be in the hospital.

However, more children were still being turned away at reception evenings than were being brought into the hospital. For example, in April 1754, 110 babies were brought to the hospital to be considered for admittance but only 10 boys and 10 girls were allowed into the hospital leaving 90 babies turned away.

Newspapers carried stories of how people were trying to get babies into the Foundling Hospital by other routes than the official reception events. In October 1753, a basket was left hanging from a rail outside the Foundling Hospital. A passer-by saw the basket and took it with him to the local pub where he had opened it up and a look at what was inside. He found a boy about a month old. The baby was given to parish officers to decide what should be done with him.[1] In June 1754, three women went into the hospital saying that they wanted to visit. When they had left, it was discovered that they had left a baby on one of the beds. It is thought that one of them had the three-month-old child hidden in her petticoats.[2] The following month, a person who had failed to get through the wooden ball ballot at the reception event, took their baby to a pub called the Coach and Horses near the Foundling Hospital and left it there.[3]

In fact, in 1754, the year that these babies were abandoned, only eighty babies were admitted into the hospital. This must have been just the tip of the iceberg in terms of the number of babies needing the protection of the hospital and the number of women forced to endure the shame of bringing up a baby who was illegitimate.

Space was not the issue as the new hospital was large and furnished. Was it finance that was the issue?

Thomas Coram had been an incredibly successful fundraiser. He raised enough money in the first years of the hospital to get it set up and running and then the hospital continued to be successful – this is largely through bequests and donations. He had given the hospital a fantastic start which had enabled them to achieve a great deal in the very short time since the Charter was granted.

Most of the Foundling Hospitals in Europe, on which the Foundling Hospital was modelled in many ways, had much stronger connections with the Church – the Roman Catholic Church in Rome, for example, and the Protestant Church in Dublin, with the Paris Hospital supported by Vincent de Paul and the Daughters of Charity. This brought in a greater financial security than the London Foundling Hospital had. In London, the hospital was reliant on a large number of relatively small donors. This made fundraising time-consuming and essentially unreliable as donation levels could potentially fall at any time. Albeit an incredibly successful example of this type of fundraising, it seems it did not give the governors the confidence they needed to upscale the venture and fill the hospital.

The governors embarked on lobbying the Government to step in and take the Foundling Hospital to a new level; a level not previously achieved by any other social care institution.

Negotiations began between the governors and the Government to take the pressure off independent fundraising and take in public funding instead. The governors and the Government were, of course, very strongly linked, with many politicians also acting as governors which made the process of negotiation much easier and perhaps quicker.

The Government was prepared to give the Foundling Hospital funding, and a very large amount of funding, but there was a very important caveat – the doors had to be open to all babies no matter how many turned up and no matter from where in the country they came. Up until this point, the governors had been able to select specific dates when children could be presented to them and could select how many of the babies were admitted from all those who were presented. This ability to control just how many children were in the care of the hospital at any one time was to be taken away.

To this effect, a petition was presented to parliament to obtain an Act to receive and maintain all such children as are presented to the governors. "Tis greatly hoped this will meet the approbation of every humane breast, since it must naturally prevent many horrid murders, that mothers too frequently commit on their own flesh and blood'.[4]

Such was the respect that the Government had for the hospital and how it was run that it pledged to support it financially but essentially left the running of the institution to the governors. Thus, the hospital became state-funded but still independently run. As such, the Foundling Hospital was to become the very first state provision for children – the children admitted to the hospital became the first children 'in care'.

Bernard's distaste for the achievement is barely disguised: 'The Charity obtained the splendid name of a national establishment. The King declared himself its patron. Large sums of money were annually granted to the Corporation; and the number of children of an infantine and helpless age supported by the hospital was, in 1760, increased to above 6,000; a number which, at the rate of £71 6s each, required an income of above £45,000 a year to maintain.'[5]

It is hard to imagine that Thomas Coram would not have been pleased with the principle of General Reception and the opening of the doors to all those babies who needed help. While, in practice, in the time he was part of the management of the Foundling Hospital, the numbers of children brought in were extremely restricted, the new hospital building that he had a hand in designing was far larger than the temporary premises in Hatton Garden. Hatton Garden, with a very limited number of beds, admitted only children aged under two months and they were primarily from within walking distance. The 1740 Charter Thomas put his name to, however, was open-ended when it came to talking of the children who could benefit from his project. The wording allowed for 'any child or children whatsoever' to be received by the hospital – with no age limit, or geographical limit set or even suggested. It is also significant to remember that the petitions he presented to attain the Charter never mentioned that the children were to come from London. His ambitions presumably transcended the city limits.

> That it shall and may be lawful for the said Corporation, or any Person or Persons authorized by them, to receive, maintain and educate all or as many Children as they shall think fit, into any Hospital or Hospitals, House or Houses which shall be erected, purchased, or hired for such Purposes; and that it shall be lawful for all and every Person whatsoever to bring any Child or Children whatsoever to any such Hospital or House, as aforesaid, to the end that such Child or Children may be received, maintained, and educated by the said Corporation therein.

Was it Thomas's plan all along to have an open-door policy? The answer is probably yes – and maybe he had even come up with a scheme for funding it.

We know that one of Thomas's last great plans was to begin a settlement in North America which would raise enough money to fund the Foundling Hospital. In 1751 a proposal to put a tax on theatre tickets was put forward which would be used to fund the hospital. Was this another of Thomas's big ideas? It seems clear that he knew that subscriptions from individuals were not going to fund the hospital to the level he needed. The idea was not far-fetched. The Foundling Hospital in Cork and, in part, the hospital in Dublin as well, were founded by a tax on the import of coal. Unfortunately, during Thomas's lifetime, a scheme of this scale to fund the hospital did not happen. However, five years after his death, government funding was agreed.

Ceremoniously, on 2 June 1756, a basket was placed outside the Foundling Hospital gates. This was the beginning of General Reception, state-funded residential childcare for the whole country based in the London Foundling Hospital.

Into this basket, foundlings could be placed at any time and the child would be brought into the hospital to be cared for. No longer would someone have to bring the baby in person, no longer would they be subjected to a lottery of picking balls from a bag, no longer would each baby's admission be dependent on a medical check-up, no longer would there be any uncertainty about whether a baby would be accepted, no longer would there be queues, fights and distress at the gates of the hospital.

It is interesting to return to the drawing Hogarth produced for that first fundraising letter in 1739, before a building for the hospital had even been found. In the background of his hospital scene, a woman can be seen, in a private moment, placing a baby by a gate. It has long been assumed that this was a depiction of a woman abandoning a baby as it did not fit with the reception process which had been designed for Hatton Garden, but perhaps Hogarth was including an idea that Thomas had for his hospital all along wherein babies could be left at the gates at any time.

It would not have been surprising had Thomas had an open-door plan all along as the foundling hospitals in mainland Europe each allowed people to deliver babies by leaving them outside the gates of the hospital or into rotating basinets which delivered the babies inside the gates.

The potential benefits of General Reception were evident. So many babies, so many families in dire poverty or living under the shame of illegitimacy, would now be able to flourish with the babies safely cared for in the Foundling Hospital. This was the ideal that Thomas would have been proud of and news of this great change in the fortunes of the Foundling Hospital was lauded in the newspapers. It was surely a triumph for Britain, and certainly for London which now had a Foundling Hospital which could genuinely stand alongside those of the other great European cities. For the governors of the hospital, it must have been a great relief not to have to turn any foundlings away as, for many of the babies and their mothers, that would have had such terrible or tragic consequences. Seeing women distraught when their baby was handed back to them deemed too poorly to be admitted or the hospital too full, must have touched even the coldest of hearts.

How Many Babies?

On that very first day of General Reception in June 1756, 117 babies were left outside the gates to be taken into the Foundling Hospital. 117 babies in a single day exceeded the per annum total for most of the preceding years. What a feeling it must have been to say yes to all the babies in need.

It was a large number of babies to receive in a single day, but probably not a cause for any panic. The beauty of Thomas's foundling hospital was that it was expandable, as long as funding was in place. So, when more babies were brought in, more country nurses could be taken on; when more 4-year-olds were brought back from the country into the hospital, beds could be freed up by more apprenticeship places being found for older children. For this reason, 117 foundlings on the first day was likely to have been surprising – certainly a big change from the 30 or 40 the governors had been used to receiving at any one time, but perhaps not alarming as there was confidence that the hospital had the flexibility to cope.

That first day's reception was never equalled on subsequent days. However, the numbers did remain far higher than they had ever been before. In the rest of the month of June, a further 324 children were admitted. In the next six months of 1756, another 1342 babies were admitted.[6]

The flexible structure of the Foundling Hospital began to feel the strain.

If a project such as this were to be proposed today, there would be a very significant resource in place that simply did not exist in 1750s. That resource is data. Putting a plan together now, we would have the benefit of statistics – the numbers of foundlings, the potential peak periods, the projected availability of country nurses. These numbers would all help to create a plan for the likely level of service use. Computer modelling would enable the project planners to see what resource gaps might exist. The project could then be designed to an appropriate scale and a realistic budget allocated to it. When the Government agreed to fund the hospital, there was no real idea of how much money this might entail. When the governors placed that basket outside the hospital gates, there was no idea of how many babies would be placed inside.

Notably, Queen Caroline's report of the foundling hospital in Paris, on which so much of the running of London's hospital appears to have been based, did not mention numbers of foundlings, or potential problems of overcrowding. No data was provided at all. Likewise, in the Charter document of 1739, there were no numbers given for babies, for staff, for country nurses, or for inspectors.

The governors, when discussing the General Reception plan with the Government, would not have seen the lack of data as an omission particularly. The first census which counted the number of people resident in London did not take place until 1801. Basing plans on detailed data was not how things were done. The fact that the new hospital was built to accommodate 400 babies was probably as much about making it the same size as Christ's Hospital as it was about meeting the existing level of need. Or perhaps it simply was based on the size of the building that they could afford. Or the design of the dormitories.

Hospital nurses
The initial issue that the large influx of children brought to the governors of the hospital was the need to employ more nurses in the hospital itself. When each baby was left at the gates, after its details were recorded in the register, it needed immediate care.

The first day of more than a hundred new babies put the hospital under immediate strain in terms of providing this immediate nursing. Through that first year, an average of five babies were left each day to be nursed in the hospital until they could be sent to country nurses. In the following years of General Reception, this doubled to ten babies a day. And the unpredictable peaks and troughs in terms of the numbers of babies admitted each day brought additional complications in terms of staffing.

The governors knew from experience and the expertise of doctors such as Dr Cadogan, that the babies had more chance of surviving if they were breastfed. However, there was not an endless supply of wet nurses and dry nurses had to be recruited to make up the numbers. The wet nurses could literally be suckled dry on busy days.

During this time, there developed a fear that women were leaving their newborn babies at the hospital gates and then presenting themselves as wet nurses for the hospital, leaving the hospital potentially paying women to breastfeed their own babies. This was a situation that the governors almost predicated themselves as their adopted corporate seal, designed by William Hogarth for them, depicted the story of Moses who was found and adopted by the Pharoah's daughter who unwittingly paid his own birth mother to nurse him. Given the nature of the records held by the hospital which left the parents of each baby anonymous, it is not possible to determine whether Moses's story as a foundling being nursed by his mother was ever actually played out in the hospital or whether it was an early urban myth.

Even as a myth, this was not good publicity for the hospital, and it was in the best interests of the governors to reduce the demand for in-hospital nurses by sending the babies out to country nurses as quickly as possible.

The next big problem the governors had to face was recruiting sufficient country nurses. In the first year and a half of General Reception, in addition to those foundlings who were already settled with country nurses, the governors had to find an average of 290 placements with country nurses for babies.

The governors found it very difficult to locate this many nurses despite offering them what was considered to be reasonable payment. Initially, some of the existing country nurses simply took on more babies but this was not sufficient to take in all the babies and it left some babies malnourished as their foster mothers did not have enough milk to feed all their charges. While the initial country nurses had largely been within a day's horse and cart ride from the hospital, the governors were having to search much further afield for new country nurses while also resorting to recruiting more dry nurses who could not breastfeed the babies when the number of wet nurses was exhausted.

Increasing the number and spread of country nurses also created a greater demand for good voluntary inspectors covering the areas of the country to match that of the nurses. Initially, many of the inspectors had come through some sort of link with governors of the hospital, including their wives. Further away from London, the links with governors were not always there and the hospital had to take on some inspectors unknown to them and some were negligent in their work or simply failed to cope with the number of babies they were charged with looking after.

Transport

As the children were now coming into the hospital from all over the country, and the country nurses were based in a much larger geographical area, issues of transporting children became more significant. Taking very young, sometimes weak or sickly babies on long horse and wagon journeys was always going to come with challenges and not all babies survived the cold and the difficult conditions. It could take days to transport children from northern England for example.

Parents, without transport of their own, resorted to paying carriers to take their babies to the hospital. The hospital paid carriers to transport the babies to country nurses. Suddenly moving babies around the country was an opportunity for those who wanted to earn money. Unfortunately, the large volume of babies who needed moving between places allowed for unscrupulous people to take advantage of the situation. Drivers taking insufficient care of the children causing them to die on the journey became a problem and there were instances of drivers taking payment for transporting babies and then dumping them and leaving them to die instead of taking them to their destinations.

Dickens wrote powerfully of the issues: 'It is almost incredible but nonetheless true, that a new branch of the Carriers' trade was commenced. Baby carriers undertook to convey infants to the all-embracing basket from distant parts of the country at so much per head. One man who had charge of five infants in baskets, got drunk; and falling asleep on a bleak common, found when he awoke that three of the five were dead. Of eight infants consigned to a country waggoner, seven died before he got to London; the surviving child owing its life solely to its mother who followed the wagon on foot to save it from starvation'.[7]

To make matters worse, women found themselves under suspicion of killing their babies when their baby had been dumped by a heartless driver paid to take the baby to the hospital. It was thought more believable that a mother would kill her own (illegitimate) baby than a paid driver would do so, such was the vilification of unmarried women who became pregnant.

These difficulties were not simply a logistical nightmare for the governors. The impacts were far more serious. In the five years before General Reception started, 39% of the 663 babies admitted died within two years of being taken in by the hospital. Of the 1783 babies admitted in 1756, the first year of General Reception, 1132 died in the first two years, which is 63%.[8] While the numbers are tragic, the percentage increase would have been of great concern if the governors had had the benefit of such data. As the babies were with country nurses, in the main, for their first years, most of the deaths took place in these foster families. For rural families a child's death was not unusual; most of the foster families would have experienced a child's death before. The inspectors had to record the details of each baby that died and report this this to the governors.

To what extent the governors would have been aware that what was happening was an increase in the proportion of babies dying is unknown. They were dealing with a far more immediate crisis which was how to place the living arrivals, and the reports that they produced tended to focus on the numbers of children under the auspices of the hospital at any one time, rather than an analysis of mortality.

Branch Hospitals
The governors continued to fight back in the face of this seemingly unremitting influx of children in need. They did not close the gates but instead focused on trying to improve the situation for all the babies, no matter how many turned up. They introduced a system of receipts so that whenever a baby was handed to a driver to be transported to or from the hospital, a receipt was given to evidence that the baby had actually been given to that particular driver. This meant mothers could no longer be accused of killing their baby when it was dumped by the driver, and it also encouraged the drivers to take better care of their charges as there was now proof that they once had them.

The governors also took the decision to leave children with country nurses until they were older so that they would be in the Foundling Hospital building for less time. With only 400 beds and babies arriving in their hundreds each month, this was a sensible way to manage the future. Leaving the babies for longer with their nurses seems to have had the effect of strengthening the bonds between children and their foster families and increasing the number of families wishing to adopt their fostered foundlings. Additionally, the governors took the decision that they would send, where possible, children to apprenticeships at an earlier age. By these measures, children would arrive at the hospital building later and left earlier so reducing the demand for beds.

The next measure taken by the governors was quite remarkable. They embarked on a programme of opening more hospitals. They set up, in a very short time scale, six branch hospitals – satellite versions of the Foundling Hospital in London.

It was hoped that the new hospitals would not simply provide more beds for the endless incoming stream of foundlings but also, being spread around the country, mean better access to potential country nurses in other locations, and new local networks of governors and inspectors who were better placed to monitor foundlings locally. Importantly, no longer having London as the only place where foundlings could be brought, reduced the need for long journeys down the length of the country. Additionally, the branch hospitals meant that there would be far more beds available for when the foundlings left their country nurses. Looking to the future, the presence of branch hospitals opened up many new possibilities of places for apprenticeships when the children were older.

There was no set policy for where or how the branch hospitals were to be set up. The Foundling Hospital in Barnet, just north of the London Foundling Hospital, for example, was established there because one of the existing voluntary inspectors lived in the locality and thought it would be a good idea. Other locations were in southern, central and northern England. Some were established in rented houses, others were purpose-built. The first of the branch hospitals was up and running in 1758, just two years after General Reception started. It was located in Ackworth, West Yorkshire, east of Wakefield and some 200 miles from London which, in a horse and wagon was a journey that could have taken anything up to 50 hours. Having a branch hospital there significantly reduced the journey times of new foundlings.

In 1758 and 1759, the second two branch hospitals opened – in Aylesbury, Buckinghamshire and Shrewsbury in Shropshire. All three of these first branch hospitals involved the purchase of property or land, or both. In Shrewsbury, land was purchased and while the new hospital was being purpose built, children were temporarily placed in a rented building.

The branch hospitals did solve some of the problems that having so many children brought into the London Foundling Hospital was presenting the governors. They now had many extra beds and a way of recruiting and managing country nurses over a much larger geographical area. This was coming at a very significant expense, however. The governors were having to spend very significant funds in order to come up with a way of handling the huge number of babies coming in.

Despite the three branch hospitals, the Foundling Hospital continued to be beset with problems resulting from the high numbers of babies being admitted. The hospital had now been taking in an average of ten babies every day for three and a half years.

News spread of unscrupulous voluntary inspectors taking advantage of the situation by such means as creaming money off the pay of country nurses or claiming maintenance money for children who had died or failing to pay for sick children to be returned to the hospital building.

The transport problems continued. Some of the hospitals attempted to transport children en masse in large horse-drawn wagons but this was not always practical. The branch hospitals also struggled to employ sufficient good calibre country nurses and trustworthy inspectors.

There was also growing anger that that the parishes and workhouses around the country were simply passing the children in their care to the hospital rather than paying for their upkeep themselves. Worse, there were stories that women were being forced to give their children to parish officers who sent them without the parents' consent to the Foundling Hospital.[9] In this way, providing care for destitute children was being paid for twice – once through Parish Poor Relief and again through government funding of the Foundling Hospital.

These stories reflected badly on the parish officers but also severely dented the reputation of the Foundling Hospital itself. There was a growing public

A Parish Board of Guardians discusses what to do with a foundling. Engraving. (*Wellcome Collection*)

perception that the Foundling Hospital, far from a popular recipient of people's donations, was seen as becoming a waste of government money to do a job that parishes were already being paid to do and doing it badly.

Bernard, writing in 1796, was confident that these parish officers had been discovered and punished, and the babies returned to their parents: 'There was another species of abuse – Parish officers, in some instances by fraud, and in others by force, had sent in the children of poor parishioners, some from a great distance, in order to secure the parish against the risk of future charges. – The children were immediately returned to their parents; and the criminals, for they deserved no better name, prosecuted to convictions and punishment, at the expense of the Charity.'

Thomas's Darling Hospital Project which had received such positive press coverage, and unprecedented support from the London's high society, was suddenly experiencing criticism and complaints. Public support waivered, donations plummeted. And the costs went through the roof.

There was no sign of the flood of babies coming into the hospital abating, despite the money being spent on it and that the investment so far was not enough to fund this number of babies coming in each year into the future.

The End of General Reception

> The inconveniences, which attended the unmanageable magnitude of the establishment, drew the attention of Parliament in April 1759; when the House of Commons expressed itself strongly against the practice of conveying children from the distant situations to the Foundling Hospital. In the next session, an enquiry was instituted and, on the 8th February 1760, the House of Commons resolved that the general admission of all children indiscriminately, under a certain age, into the Hospital, to be maintained there at the public expence, had been attended with many evil consequences, and that it be discontinued.[10]

The Government, feeling the experiment had proved to have 'evil consequences', did what they felt they had to do and withdrew their financial support after nearly a little under five years of General Reception. They were not so cruel as to stop all income immediately but agreed with the governors to taper down the money given to the hospital.

On 25 March 1760, the basket was removed from the gates of the Foundling Hospital and no more new admissions were to be made.

Between June 1756 and March 1760, nearly 15,000 babies had been taken in by the Foundling Hospital.

At this point, the hospital still continued with its plans for three more branch hospitals. They were still needed as the large number of foundlings living with country nurses at this time would soon need beds and to receive the education and training that was an important element of the Foundling Hospital.

In the first years following the end of General Reception, admittances were at a negligible level, so much so that the daily intake of ten babies each day during Geneal Reception became practically the annual total. After General Reception ended, 1760 saw just nine babies admitted; in 1761 eleven were admitted with six babies in 1762. During this time, the majority of the General Reception intake were brought back from their country nurses and settled in the hospital buildings.

The second three branch hospitals that opened did not involve purchasing land or buildings probably because, by the time they were being set up, it was known that the funding from the Government was being withdrawn.

The Chester Hospital began advertising for nurses in 1763:

Orphan Hospital, Chester
This is to give notice that the Governors of this Hospital intend placing under the Care of Nurses in the Country several children of the age of three years; and whoever is inclined to receive one or more, may apply to the Governors of the Orphan Hospital at Ten of the Clock on any Tuesday morning, who will treat with the said Nurses, if properly qualified, on reasonable terms, and pay them per Week or Month, according to the Contract.[11]

A branch hospital was opened in a rented house in Westerham, Kent in 1760. Then a house was rented near Barnet in Hertfordshire which started taking in children in 1760 and finally, the Blue Coat School in Chester rented out some of its building to use as a branch hospital which opened in 1763.

However, the branch hospitals were a great expense and within just four years of the last, in Chester, opening, the governors began the process of closing all six of them.

The first branch hospital to close was Aylesbury in 1767; the following year, Barnet closed, and then the branch hospitals in Chester and Westerham closed in 1769. Shrewsbury closed in 1772 and finally, the last branch hospital, in Ackworth, closed in 1773, thirteen years after the Government had withdrawn funding. All the children still living in the branch hospitals were sent to London. Keeping the branch hospitals open so long after the General Reception period was over was a tremendous drain on the Foundling Hospital's so seriously limited finances. As well as the ongoing running costs, there was also the matter of the money which had been spent on the properties. A completely new hospital had been built at Ackworth and extensions on existing buildings had been built at Ackworth and Aylesbury. While the governors made efforts to sell the properties, this did not happen quickly and did not fully reimburse the hospital. For example, the Ackworth Branch Hospital cost £13,000 and sold for just £7,000 some years later.

> Between the villages of High and Low Ackworth stands a handsome stone edifice, built 70 years ago, partly by voluntary subscription and partly by aid of parliament, as an appendage to the Foundling Hospital, in London. This building cost £13,000. [The] dreadful mortality, the difficulty of obtaining proper nurses, and of providing humane masters, with the frequent contests from the opposition of parishes, and the cruelty of masters where they were apprenticed, proved such insurmountable obstacles to the well conducting of the charity, that the house at Ackworth was abandoned as a Foundling Hospital…[12]

Too Great a Price

The cost of General Reception to the Government was around £500,000 (the equivalent, taking inflation into account, of £84 million today). This was not only the cost of the experiment in the four years it lasted but the cost of maintaining the children who survived and lived out the remainder of their childhoods with country nurses or in the hospital buildings. The initial pledge from the Government was just £10,000. That is a cost of £111 for each of the 4500 children who did not die during their time in the experiment. That is an equivalent of just £19,000 in today's money, and is a pittance in relation to the modern-day costs of providing full-time care and education for a child for ten to twelve years. However, in 1760 there was no precedent for such an expense and the vast total sum was shocking.

Bernard reflected that the hospital bore the blame for the waste of government money but could not help but spend the money unless it was going to throw out the children: 'The source of private donations has been considerably diminished from the time, and in consequence of parliamentary interference. We must not therefore wonder that, for a series of years, it should have been generally, though unfairly aspersed for that waste of capital, which, without driving from its walls a number of helpless objects, could not have been prevented.'[13]

However, the real cost of General Reception was not the money but the fate of the children. The governors were very aware of the lower standards of care that they had been able to provide for the foundlings when their numbers increased so hugely. They were aware that the country nurses and inspectors that they employed were not always doing the best for the children; they knew that some parish officers were offloading the babies they did not want to spend poor relief on; and they knew that babies were treated cruelly and even murdered by those who were meant to be transporting them.

What we know now, and what has become the most famous aspect of General Reception is that thousands of children died. According to Bernard (1796) the Government did not even mention the deaths of children when considering whether General Reception should continue or not. After all, many of the children who were to die, were still alive when the House of Commons was considering the future of the Foundling Hospital.

During the General Reception period, 14,934 children were admitted, dwarfing the total of 1384 children who had been admitted throughout the previous fifteen years since the hospital opened. The yearly totals throughout General Reception were:[14]

1756: 1783 (from 2 June)
1757: 3727
1758: 4143
1759: 3957
1760: 1234 (up to 25 March)

This sudden and large increase in numbers of children admitted, brought with it an increase in the number of children who died. In the five years before General Reception, of the 663 children admitted, 104 died while in the care of the hospital – a death rate of around 61%.

Of the 14,934 children admitted in General reception, 10,413 children died during their time under the hospital – a desperate tragedy and a death rate of 70%.[15]

But the real tragedy was amongst the youngest of the new admittances. Most of those who died did so before they were 2 years old.

Of those admitted during General Reception, 61% died within two years of being admitted. In the five years before General Reception, 39% of the foundlings admitted died within two years. General Reception had been most cruel to the youngest.

One of the theories behind this increase in the death rate of the youngest is that, without that initial examination by the governors which meant that those with visible signs of disease could be excluded, sickly babies were allowed in who were then more likely to die.

Bernard was convinced that this was a significant factor in the 'ill consequences' of General Reception, so much so that he believed babies were brought to the hospital so close to death that they died before they could be taken to the nurses:

A charity so boundless and undistinguishing, and so unnecessarily varied from its original institution could not but be attended with ill consequences. The scite of the Hospital was in many instances converted into a burying ground; and parental care, though perhaps it would not have deserted an healthy or hopeful child, carried the diseased and expiring infant, in some instances almost stripped of its cloathing, to take the chance of a change of air and situation, and of the efforts of medical skill and care; and failing those, to receive the certainty of a decent internment. So far extended was this practice…that I have been informed by a late respectable and active Governor, that there were many instances in which the child received at the gate, did not live to be carried to the wards of the Hospital.[16]

As the initial examination was only cursory and could only detect very few illnesses, its absence is perhaps unlikely to be the whole reason for the significantly higher death rate. More likely it was down to a combination of factors about which the governors were all too aware. The shortage of wet nurses meant that many children had to go to dry nurses, or to wet nurses who were already overstretched. And there were those children who died during transport from home to hospital, either because of the length of the journeys or the cruelty of the drivers.

Many commentators, then and now, have debated the consequences of the attempt to have General Reception. Edward Walford, a historian writing in 1878, described it as a 'massacre of the innocents'.[17] It is true that the number of deaths increased and looking at the stark numbers – with nearly 15,000 children having been admitted and more than 10,000 having died – it is very difficult to see the whole experiment with anything but horror. But it is also true to say that the death rate throughout General Reception, while undoubtedly high, was actually similar to that in other foundling hospitals in Europe. Maybe it is thanks to the efforts of opening new branch hospitals and bringing in new processes, that the children were saved from suffering an even higher death rate. But there was also another consequence of General Reception – it is inevitable that the wellbeing of many of the children suffered. The increased calls on volunteer inspector time, and the shortage of sufficient new inspectors left some children unchecked and others at the mercy of incompetent or downright unscrupulous inspectors. Others were sent out to poor quality apprenticeships without sufficient monitoring to protect them from cruel or negligent masters.

Dublin Foundling Hospital

The Dublin Foundling Hospital was founded in 1704 at the time when Thomas and Eunice first arrived in London. It was very closely linked with the Cork

Dublin Foundling Hospital, c.1798. (*Unknown artist*)

Foundling Hospital which was opened in 1747. The stated aim of both foundling hospitals was to take foundlings from whatever fate would otherwise be theirs but also to teach poor Catholic children Protestantism and thus reduce the hold that Catholicism had on the Irish population. This proved to be a difficult task as most of the country nurses the children were sent out to live with in their early years were actually Catholic.

Both the Cork and Dublin Foundling Hospitals were funded to a large extent through a tax put on coal that the cities imported. This large amount of dependable funding meant that the institutions could open their doors to large numbers of foundlings. The Dublin Hospital had a cradle fitted outside the gates. When a baby was deposited into the cradle, a bell was rung which summoned someone to collect the baby and bring it into the hospital.

General Reception brought the London Foundling Hospital and the Dublin Foundling Hospital closer together in terms of admission policy and the number of babies admitted. However, between 1500 and 2000 admissions a year was usual for Dublin, which is still less than half the number of admissions in London's General Reception period.

There are many reports of the harsh treatment that foundlings received while they were in the Dublin Foundling Hospital from identity numbers being tattooed on the new admittances leaving them marked for life as foundlings to babies being moved between Cork and Dublin to prevent parents from being able to reclaim them. It was said that the foundlings were regularly given laudanum (an opiate) to subdue and control them. It was also reported that girls were sent over to Australia joining the damaging trend of British children being sent overseas to start new lives without the consent of either the parents or the children themselves.

Foundlings going into the Dublin Foundling Hospital experienced very high levels of mortality; it is estimated that death rates were consistently higher than those experienced in its London counterpart. A report written about the Dublin Hospital in the late eighteenth century found that, between 1790 and 1796, 5216 children were admitted.[18] Horrifyingly, all but three of these babies died. How must parents have felt to discover that by giving their baby to the Foundling Hospital, they almost guaranteed its early death?

The Dublin Foundling Hospital closed in 1830 after the Catholic Emancipation Act and its Irish equivalent the Parliamentary Elections (Ireland) Act 1829.

The Dublin Foundling Hospital was not the only place that suffered a high death rate (although it arguably suffered the highest). Recent research[19] finds that, with geographical and time variations, most foundling hospitals had a death rate usually above 60%.

Taking the Strain of General Reception

Five years after the General Reception experiment started in 1756, those children who had survived started coming into the London Foundling Hospital building at the end of their time with their country nurses. This began a period of high occupancy in the hospital which continued until they could all be found apprenticeships.

While children were left with country nurses until they were at least 5 years old and sent out to apprenticeships when they were as young as 10 to reduce the number of children in the hospital building, the key method of limiting the over-crowding was, of course, not letting any further children in. This meant that for years after the experiment ended, the hospital all but stopped taking in new foundlings.

In each of the years following General Reception, up to 1773, fewer than a hundred children were admitted. By 1773, the first children admitted in General Reception would have been there for seventeen years and thus all would be either in apprenticeships, or otherwise discharged or have not survived. Those who were admitted in the last year of General Reception would have been there for thirteen years, also certainly of apprenticeship age. The numbers of children living in the hospital building could return to something like the numbers pre-General Reception.

From this point, the Foundling Hospital began returning to something like the reception levels that had been in place initially. Around 100 children were admitted each year, limited to those born in London and aged less than six months. If there were more children than the governors wanted to admit, a ballot system was used with those unsuccessful being turned away. After 1782, the number of children received dropped by around 50% to 50 or fewer each year.

With numbers in the hospital down, the children who were admitted during this time were much more likely to survive childhood than those who had come before. Between the end of General Reception and 1774, 545 children were admitted and 245 of them died[20] which is around five in every ten of the children, a significantly lower proportion than either before or during General Reception. These were also the years of Dr William Watson's experiments with smallpox inoculations.

What would the Foundling Hospital have achieved if it had not taken the route of General Reception in return for government funding? The hospital was hugely popular, if not fashionable, and had the support of hundreds of governors who were in enormously powerful positions in British government, industry, religion, academia, medicine, the arts and, of course, aristocracy. The hospital was, admittedly, starting slowly, but it was accumulating vast knowledge which was very much at the cutting edge of understanding at the time. Could this slow, evolutionary development have achieved much more than the five years of sudden General Reception did? Would sustaining the popularity it had developed while Thomas was alive have achieved more, in the longer term, than the large injection of government money?

Between 1774 and 1800, a total of 1756 children were received into the hospital. Between four and five of every ten children admitted died during their time in the hospital, a level which was the lowest reached and sustained by the Foundling Hospital in the eighteenth century and meaning the loss of 817 children over a period of twenty-six years.[21] In relation to other Foundling hospitals in Europe, this was an excellent achievement.

Looking at the life of the Foundling Hospital during the eighteenth century as a whole is illuminating. The hospital was open for fifty-nine years from 1741 to 1800. Nearly 19,000 children were received into the hospital and just over 12,355 died, amounting to nearly seven of every ten children admitted. 218 children were claimed by their parents and taken to be brought up in a family. A total of 6000 children were sent out as apprentices to begin their useful lives and ultimately go out into the world on their own.[22]

It is not hard to imagine that Thomas would have been upset but not fazed by these numbers. He was a man of immense patience with the progress of his projects. He was a ship builder by trade and used to ships being built plank by plank over months and years. He spent seventeen years filling two pages of his battered notebook with the names of Ladies of Charity. He was used to failure and setbacks. He carefully planned, through hours of thinking and talking, and then constructed, word by word, several petitions to hand to parliament detailing one great scheme or another. Most of these were dismissed out of hand but, he was not one to give up, and the next scheme was quickly under development.

He was a man who would have recognised these first decades of the London Foundling Hospital not as a disaster, not as the end, but rather as a step towards the ultimate success of the scheme. He would not have been put off but would have determined to carry on, to achieve what he wanted to achieve.

While the mortality rates were high and the care of the children was not as good as it could have been, it is also important to recognise that 4000 children were taken in by the hospital over those five years of General Reception, saving them from whatever fate had for those destitute, abandoned and unwanted children. That is 4000 children who were sent to apprenticeships by the hospital and thus had the chance of a future with work, and perhaps a home and family of their own. General Reception was not what it *could* have been, it was arguably not what it *should* have been, but it was *something* for children who otherwise would have had nothing.

Within two years of the end of General Reception, only around 5500 of the intake of nearly 15,000 were still alive as so many had died when aged less than 2 years old, and others had been reclaimed by their parents. Most of these young children were living with their country nurses all around the country.

When General Reception ended, the governors had between 1000 and 1,500 children coming into the hospital and its branches each year for the next five years as the stays with country nurses ended. Over these five years, a further 1000 children died. Unlike the majority of deaths in General Reception, these 1000 deaths took place largely in the hospital buildings. This high level of mortality was a terrible problem for the governors and their staff as the sick bay was stretched to its limits and each of these children had to be buried.

Life in the Hospital After General Reception

> 'an happier, a more healthy, or a more innocent collection of beings does not exist in the world than is to be found within the walls of the Foundling Hospital.'
> Bernard, 1799

Bernard, who had successful career in law, lived close to the Foundling Hospital in London and, as a close neighbour, took a great interest in it. His interest was such that, in 1787, he became a governor of the hospital and between 1796 and

1806 he was treasurer. During this time, he proved to have a great business mind and he masterminded the process of turning the land owned by the hospital into streets of buildings which the hospital rented out, bringing in significant funding for the hospital. This land had only been taken on reluctantly by the governors when they were first looking for where to site the new hospital but Bernard's use of it effectively gave the hospital its long future.

When Thomas and other governors first approached the Earl of Salisbury to purchase two fields of his land in Lamb's Conduit Fields, he had managed the negotiations so that they could afford to purchase all 56 acres as he no longer wanted the land. Most of this land was left unused by the hospital for many years, although some was sold as burial grounds for the local parish. With the unused land developed in the nineteenth century, the rental income gave the hospital a future.

This, like so many aspects of the hospital, was thanks to the connections of Thomas's Ladies of Charity. Not only did they create links to the king and the Prince of Wales through Queen Caroline, but they also introduced Hogarth and Handel to the Foundling Hospital with remarkable consequences. It was a connection to another Lady of Charity, Mary Tufton, that linked the hospital to the large parcel of land on which the hospital was situated. She was the aunt of James Cecil, the 6th Earl of Salisbury, who owned Lamb's Conduit Fields. James was 20 when his aunt signed Thomas's petition and had already inherited his earldom. In later life, he gained a reputation as 'The Wicked Earl' when he left his wife, mother of his heir, to live openly with his mistress with whom he had several children. He was outlived by his aunt.

While the land was open farmland when they purchased it, it increased in value considerably as time went on and the built-up area of London enveloped the Foundling Hospital, enabling the governors to rent or sell off parcels of land earning an immense profit. This contributed enormously to the longevity of the hospital.

By the late 1700s, the hospital had been functioning for more than half a century and the period of General Reception had long since passed.

However, numbers of children admitted each year were still low. In the last five years of the eighteenth century just 341 children were admitted – an average of sixty-eight babies each year. Bernard's time there was typified by this small, but stable admission level but also a shortage of funding (warranting Bernard's efforts to liquidise the land assets). The number of deaths was greatly reduced from those in the first five years of the hospital when 47% of those admitted died in the first two years. In the last five years of the century, 23% died before they were 2 years old, equating to 79 of the babies admitted.[23]

Women waiting outside the hospital gates. The Foundling Hospital, Holborn, London. Engraving by C. Grignion and P. C. Canot after S. Wale, 1749. (*Wellcome Collection*)

Bernard found the time to write at length about the workings and life of the Foundling Hospital with his *An account of the Foundling Hospital, in London, for the maintenance and education of exposed and deserted young children* being published in 1799.

He describes how much things had changed since the days before the General Reception experiment.

Each Wednesday morning at 10.00 am, the governors received not babies, but petitions from the mothers of babies requesting that they be admitted to the hospital. These petitions were then assessed to gauge whether the baby could be taken in by the hospital. The governors were looking for babies who were under a year old and whose mother could demonstrate previous good character and that she had been deserted by the baby's father. She also needed to persuade the governors that them taking the baby meant that she could embark on 'a course of virtue' and find herself an honest way of earning a living. By this, Bernard describes a very significant move away not only from the anonymous drop-offs outside the gates during General Reception but also the protection of the anonymity of both the parent and the child that the governors enshrined in the General Plan of 1740. The identity of the mother was now not only known but she was subject to investigation by the governors.

Once the governors had ascertained that the father had deserted the baby and the mother, he was of no further interest to the governors and was not subject to their investigation. By contrast, the mother had to provide evidence of her previous good character, that is, she had to show that her pregnancy was not her fault and that she would ensure that it was worth the governors' while to take her baby because she would not only behave herself but she would find respectable employment as a result. It is clear, by this, that Thomas Coram's influence on his hospital had, by this time, waned very significantly.

Once the governors had gone through the petitions received, had conducted their investigation and had found appropriate wet nurses, the 'successful' mothers were instructed to bring their babies to the hospital. These reception times were held monthly on Saturdays at noon. The babies were christened during the evening service at the hospital chapel the next day and then immediately taken away by the appointed wet nurses.

The nurses were paid three shillings a week but given a 'bonus' of ten shillings if the baby survived its first year. Bernard suggests that this is a reason for the death rate of the babies being relatively low.

When the children reached 4 years old, the local inspector brought them back to the hospital. The baby had, by this time, been living with their foster family for at least three years, generally longer, and the nurse and her family had seen him or her grow from a baby through to the toddler years and was now a small child. It must have been a wrench to hand them over and see them leave on that journey by cart to London. For the child too, this was an age when they would have been fully aware of their sudden loss and the extreme change in their lives. For the babies, the nurse was their mother, and her family was their family, for better or for worse. To lose them so completely will have affected many of the babies.

Life in the hospital was very ordered for the children returning from the countryside. They were immediately inoculated against smallpox when they arrived. The boys were then placed in dormitories in the west wing, while the girls went into the east wing.

Woken at 6.00 am (or at daylight in the winter), the older boys helped the younger ones get dressed and ready for the day while the older boys had the job of operating a forcing pump to ensure that the hospital had a sufficient supply of water for the day.

There was an hour for breakfast from 7:30 am and then the boys went to lessons. Lunchtime was an hour from 1.00 pm with lessons in the afternoon until 5.00 pm. The lessons were in reading, writing and accounts. Thomas Bernard describes that there was then an hour for play or work, with supper eaten at 6.00 pm and bed at 8.00 pm.

The work that the younger boys were doing was knitting the stockings that the foundlings wore with the older boys taking on tasks such as working in the

Boys in the Foundling Hospital. *The Strand Magazine*, September 1891.[24]

garden and cleaning. There was also work that was taken in by the hospital for the children to do for which the hospital was paid. Thomas Bernard describes that spinning yarn was one such type of work taken in for the boys but the hospital had to put a stop to it when they realised that the potential apprentice masters were more keen on the boys who had learnt to read, write and keep accounts and work in the garden. Many of the apprenticeships that the boys took on were in shops where basic maths was a far more important skill than spinning. Thomas, who imagined that the apprenticeships for the boys, at least, would be at sea or in some element of manufacturing that would make them useful to their country, would no doubt have been disappointed to learn that the children were becoming shopkeepers.

Thomas may also have been disappointed at how different the education for girls had become from that given by the hospital to the boys.

In the east wing, the lessons given to the girls included reading, but not the writing or accounts as was taught to the boys. The girls were given housework to do and worked alongside the servants in the kitchen and laundry.

Most of the girls' time was spent on needlework. They made the linen elements of the hospital uniforms for those foundlings in the hospital building and also for those with country nurses. Other sewing work was taken in for the hospital for the girls to do to raise income for the running of the building. Thomas Bernard, as the treasurer, calculated that each older girl earned, in this way twelve pounds a year for the hospital, with those girls under 11 earning a little less than three pounds a year. Twelve pounds would have paid the wages of a skilled worker for around eighty days, so the girls were contributing significantly to their own upkeep.

When boys were aged 12 and girls were aged 14, apprenticeships were found for them which was relatively easy at this time as the hospital was receiving more requests for apprentices than there were children. The only children who did not go to apprenticeships were those who had disabilities of some form and so were retained in the hospital and given work to do in the running of the institution.

In May 1798 there were 252 foundlings from the hospital who were in apprenticeships. 166 were reported as 'doing well' with another 27 who were

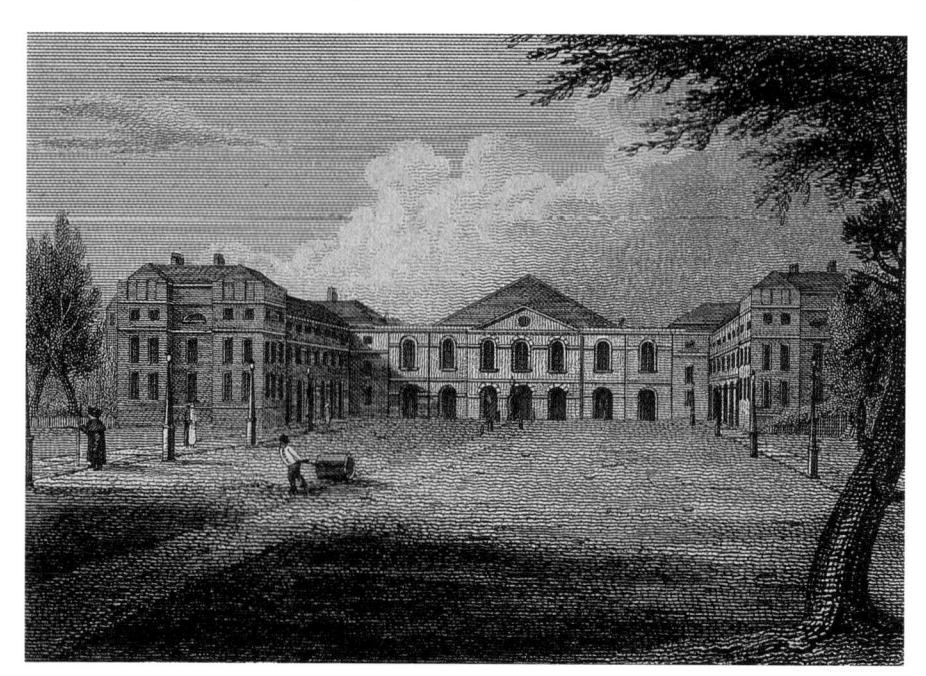

The Foundling Hospital: the main buildings seen from within. (Wellcome Collection)

placed too far away to visit but, as no complaints had been received about them, it was assumed that they too were doing well. Twenty-three were in apprenticeships with their own relatives and so had effectively been adopted back into the families although a full reclamation had not been sanctioned by the governors. Only two foundlings are recorded as having been claimed by their parents between 1785 and 1800.

Fifteen were found to have 'turned out ill'. Thomas Bernard pointed out in his report that was generally the fault of the apprentice master and not the child. Twenty-one of the apprentices were flagged as needing 'judicious management'.

For the hospital, this was an excellent result from the time the foundlings spent in the hospital. For Thomas Coram, who dreamed of saving the many babies he saw dying on the streets, were the numbers of children being cared for by the hospital enough? In 1797, there were 252 apprentices; approximately 287 children were with country nurses and 177 were in the hospital itself. However, we know that 40% of these children died during their time in the hospital. This means that, in the hospital in 1797, there were in the region of just 80 children.[25] For a hospital built to accommodate 400 children, this is a small number. Was this Thomas's dream?

The governors of the time had certainly found a way to structure the Foundling Hospital and to control the number of children coming in and the respectability of the women being helped. They had, to their credit, found a way to reduce the number of deaths. They had also found a good supply of apprenticeships for the older children. But, to reach this point, they had sacrificed the number of children who could be helped by the hospital and had arguably excluded those most in need – those mothers who were most desperate in society were probably unlikely to be able to evidence their past or projected respectability and thus their children would never benefit from the hospital's care. The governors were raising the children that they did take in to be shopkeepers rather than seamen or men of industry and were failing in the hospital's original mission to educate girls, putting them to work rather than teaching them to write.

The Hospital's Influence on Its Neighbours

Three organisations were established very shortly after the founding of Thomas's Foundling Hospital. It is hard not to believe that these were not in some way advantaged by the publicity and popularity of the Foundling Hospital. They were all related to 'unpopular' causes and had links with the hospital. At a time when there were few offerings for the destitute poor in London, these are unusual cases.

The first of these was set up in 1756, fifteen years after the Foundling Hospital first opened its doors. The aim of the Marine Society for Destitute Boys was very similar to that of the Foundling Hospital – to rescue destitute children from the streets and train them up to help the British war efforts, the focus, however, being boys who had already survived their childhoods and reached the age of 13. Like the Foundling Hospital, the architect of the Marine Society for Destitute Boys was a man, Jonas Hanway. He was not an aristocrat but a merchant who was well travelled.

He had achieved a degree of notoriety for being an outspoken critic of tea-drinking which he described as 'pernicious to health, obstructing industry, and impoverishing the nation'.[26] He went further, declaring tea to cause ugliness in its drinkers. He was also known as the first man in London to carry an umbrella, Previously, umbrellas had only been used by women, preferring them to hats to protect their hair from the rain. Like Thomas, it appears Jonas was not a man who feared speaking out and going against the flow.

Two years after founding the Marine Society, Jonas subscribed to the Foundling Hospital and became a governor. He took great interest in the failings of the General Reception era and was particularly critical of education in the hospital. Nonetheless, he stood by the hospital and what it was trying to achieve, becoming vice-president in 1772.

The Marine Society in many ways followed the lead of the Foundling Hospital. Jonas managed to gather around him a very influential group of men to govern the society including Lord Romney as the chair, and several other titled gentlemen in support along with members of the Society of Arts. The patron was George II, and the Prince and Princess of Wales were great supporters as they were of the Foundling Hospital. Hanway was successful in raising a significant sum of money from individuals and through legacies. A key difference, however, between Thomas Coram and Jonas Hanway is that Hanway was able to continue to be a significant part in the running of his organisation as it grew and developed, while Thomas could not.

In its first decade, more than 10,000 boys had been recruited by the Society. And, like the Foundling Hospital, the Marine Society still exists although its aims have developed and changed significantly in line with modern needs. Coincidentally, as the Foundling Hospital found itself at the heart of the development of Smallpox inoculation, the Marine Society, by giving their recruits free clean clothing and bedding and giving them facilities to wash before going to sea, did much to reduce the spread of typhus.

Just two years after the Marine Society started work, a large institution for girls was founded, becoming the third organisation set up by a lone male philanthropist. Again, there were strong links with the Foundling Hospital.

As with the Foundling Hospital, the aim of the Female Orphan Asylum was to take in destitute or deserted children and give them training to go primarily into domestic service. Girls were taken in from between the ages of 9 and 15. The girls were also taught to read and write. Without fathers, girls would be the responsibility of the parish. Those who were not in their home parish could find themselves with no support and it was feared that they would end up in prostitution on the streets of London. Instead, the orphanage took them in, to educate them and train them to be useful.

The asylum was founded by a magistrate, John Fielding, who was the brother of Henry Fielding, the famous novelist. Henry Fielding, also a magistrate, was a supporter of the Foundling Hospital and famously wrote *Tom Jones, a Foundling*, one of the first English novels. It is the comic story of the life of an illegitimate foundling published eight years after the Foundling Hospital opened its doors.

His brother's asylum attracted the support of prominent individuals including Queen Charlotte (wife of George III) and the Duke of Cambridge. The charity was governed by a committee of gentlemen, elected annually, who met at the asylum every Thursday at 11.00 am each morning. The work was funded through subscriptions.

Collections taken at the chapel each Sunday were a very important part of the asylum's early income as, like the Foundling Hospital, the asylum became

The female orphan asylum, Westminster Bridge Road, Lambeth. When the orphans were moved into a new building in 1824, the design was remarkably similar to that of the Foundling Hospital's 1745 building, with two wings flanking a central grand entrance. Engraving. (*Wellcome Collection*)

a fashionable place to visit by the wealthier members of London society. In particular, attending the Sunday church service attracted sizable crowds. Girls from the asylum were brought in to sing.

Also following the Foundling Hospital's lead, the asylum called in the services of gentlewomen who visited the asylum to check on how it was being managed and to observe that the girls were being instructed well. They were then asked to report to the governors.

The Magdalen Hospital was the third of these three organisations which were established following the Foundling Hospital's lead. Both John Fielding and Jonas Hanway played a part in the establishment of the Magdalen Hospital for Penitent Prostitutes in 1758 with Robert Dingley, a silk trader. This was a groundbreaking idea to take in women forced into prostitution as it was the only way they could feed themselves and their family, or pushed into prostitution by dint of their circumstances, such as having an illegitimate child. They were given shelter and, most importantly, work. The hospital taught the women skills such as sewing and took in crafts, sewing and other such work for the women to do. The women were given religious instruction, aiming for them to see the error of their ways and to encourage them to be penitent. As with the Asylum for Girls, the hospital's chapel became a fashionable place for the London gentry to visit.

This was a remarkable two years in which these three London organisations were set up – the Marine Society, the Female Orphan Asylum and the Magdalen Hospital. Each had connections with the Foundling Hospital, and it is clear to see that they were able to capitalise on what Thomas and the Foundling Hospital had achieved in terms of making causes such as destitution and illegitimacy and the plight of women more acceptable or, at least, superficially fashionable. Rather than simply being tolerated, each of these institutions themselves became fashionable in some way. The years 1741 to 1758 created real change. Did this upsurge in the acceptability of such causes last? Sadly, the upsurge did wane. The popularity of all the London institutions faded. Although each still managed to raise enough funds to keep their work going, they were no longer the fashionable haunt of London's nobility. And they were not followed by the establishment of other large philanthropic organisations for children.

While these four organisations made a difference, and to some individuals, what they achieved was lifesaving, the numbers in the country's growing towns and cities still suffering the impacts of destitution, abandonment and illegitimacy, were vast. What was needed was a large-scale response.

This was not to happen until Queen Victoria's reign.

Part IX

The Legacy of Thomas Coram

'The institution is continuing the good work begun so long ago by Thomas Coram. Some features of the system in force have always had their critics – the exclusion of children born in wedlock, the sudden and final separation of mother and child, the difficulty of securing a "home" atmosphere where hundreds are barracked together.'

Compston, 1918

The Nineteenth Century

The Foundling Hospital in the eighteenth century had been hit hard by the open-door experiment. It had cost nothing less than a small fortune to open to General Reception for just five years. The hospital had switched from being the most famous charity in London, the place to be for London society, to being the recipient of dwindling interest and negative publicity about the hardships and death experienced by its children. The money spent on General Reception was perceived to have been wasted. For years after General Reception, it was a hospital for children which simply could not take in children. It took twenty-four years – until the last male out as an apprentice was old enough to be discharged – for the hospital to be completely free of the impact of General Reception.

Incredibly, however, the hospital survived. The structure which had been developed for it – the hundreds of governors, the use of volunteer inspectors and the locating of children with ordinary families outside the hospital – had given it enormous structural resilience. The value of the land it was standing on gave it enormous financial reliance. Thomas would certainly have been proud.

During the nineteenth century, London and the area around the Foundling Hospital underwent huge changes. What had started out as fields in the middle of the countryside north of London had turned into a location near the centre of a large, dense urban sprawl. By the end of the nineteenth century to the north was Kings Cross Station (1852) and St Pancras Station (1868) and Euston Station was to the north-west (1837) with train lines to the east and west.

To the south-west was Great Ormond Street Hospital (1852) the Homeopathic Hospital (1895), and the Alexandra Hospital (1867); with the Royal Free

Sir Thomas Bernard. Stipple engraving by C. Picart, 1815, after J. or T. Wright after J. Opie. (*Wellcome Collection*)

Hospital (1828), the Royal Post Office (1889) and the Ophthalmic Hospital (1843) to the east.

The Foundling Hospital, once a giant of a building surrounded by greenery, was now one building surrounded by others, several of which were hospitals providing medical care.

The Foundling Hospital site itself was no longer fields but was a network of streets, some of which carried names familiar to those who knew the hospital including Coram Street, Bernard Street, Handel Street and Lambs Conduit Street (street names which still remain in Bloomsbury). The hospital was achieving a rental income of around £19,000 a year from this development.[1]

Such was the history, structure and wealth of the Foundling Hospital, it remained in existence, largely unchanged by the changing world around it. Despite the changes in the surrounding city, it stood firm for nearly two hundred years – a massive monolith commemorating the dreams of Thomas Coram.

Through the next hundred years, around 6000 children[2] were admitted to the hospital. That is around a third of the number of children who were taken in during the five years of General Reception. Thanks to huge advances in medicine and our understanding of all aspects of health, survival rates of children, both within and outside the hospital, were rising over this time so far more of these children lived through their time under the hospital and reached adulthood.

Since Thomas embarked on his quest to encourage wealthy and titled people to support social welfare, little had happened to further social care provision for the country's most impoverished and vulnerable people. The eighteenth century saw the Industrial Revolution surge forward and the impacts on the people were numerous. As well as bringing jobs and wealth for some, the Industrial Revolution brought misery for many. Jobs in rural areas were depleted as work became mechanised. People were pulled into urban areas in a mass move away from the countryside. It was a migration like no other. According to census data, the population of London rose from a little over a million in 1801 to 6.5 million in 1901.[3] Once in the towns and cities, the competition for work left millions homeless, jobless and helpless.

The Poor Law of the eighteenth century moved away from out-relief provided through the parish church which could no longer cope with the numbers in poverty and the need to provide for those who migrated away from their home parish. Instead, the focus switched to large, looming workhouses which dominated the area and terrified the workless into doing whatever they could to keep out of them.

The Poor Law Amendment Act of 1834 grouped parishes into Poor Law Unions which took over the care of the destitute and were instructed to do so largely through workhouses. In London, a number of Poor Law Unions were formed – the City of London Poor Law Union built the Bow Road workhouse; the East London Poor Law Union built the Homerton Workhouse; the West London Poor Law Union built the Upper Holloway Workhouse. This was the Union in which the Foundling Hospital found itself. The workhouse was on Cornwallis Road, near Archway, three miles north of the hospital.

The workhouses could take in large numbers of people at relatively low cost and give them work to do which helped pay for their upkeep. The work was generally monotonous, menial, unpleasant and hard. When Dickens sent his Oliver Twist to the workhouse he was charged, although only a child, with 'picking oakum'. This was the splitting of old, smelly, tarred rope into strands so that it could be reused. It was hard on the hands and even tougher on the body and mind as food was sparse, the workhouses were cold, and the hours were long.

Such was the scale of poverty in the nineteenth century that what has become known as the greatest era of philanthropy was born, with the Victorian era typified by the provision of social care by philanthropists and the Church.

This was also a time when there was a phenomenal growth in the number and type of players in the world of social care. Ragged schools, orphanages, cottage homes and other children's care providers were springing up all over the country, with many also in London. These formed alongside the new, much-feared, workhouses. While the Foundling Hospital had a century of experience, the rest of social care was in its infancy.

More than a hundred large orphanages throughout England were built by wealthy philanthropists during the early part of Queen Victoria's reign. Many others were established by churches or professional groups such as the Merchant Seamen's Orphanage in Snaresbrook, the Police Orphanage in Twickenham, the Military Orphan Asylum at Chelsea, the Clergy Orphan Home in Marylebone and the Actors' Orphanage in Croydon.[4] Smaller institutions proliferated such as ragged schools, children's homes, asylums and training homes, each established outside the Poor Law system.

In the late nineteenth century the large charities put down roots which saw them through into the twenty-first century. Three philanthropic entrepreneurs: Thomas Barnardo, Thomas Stephenson and Edward Rudolf each set up small homes from which seedlings sprang the large charities of Barnardo's, National Children's Homes (Action for Children) and the Children's Society. All three set up their first homes in London.

Most cities and large towns had at least one large orphanage, each of which could accommodate hundreds of children. Despite being called 'orphanages', these institutions rarely restricted their intake solely to children who were, strictly speaking, orphans. In fact, the admission policies of these orphanages of the nineteenth century reflect the many twists and turns of the admissions policy of the Foundling Hospital in the eighteenth and nineteenth centuries. Some of the children admitted had lost both parents, some one parent. Others went in because their parents were unable to care for them because of disability or illness, for example, and a large number of other children went in because of poverty. Some orphanages insisted parents were of a particular religion, others that they lived in a particular area. Some took in children straight off the street. Many orphanages insisted that the children were born within a marriage.

The orphanages founded in London in the nineteenth century were numerous, including the Alexandra Orphanage in Islington; the Home for Waifs and Strays in Marylebone; the Mount Hermon Orphanage in Hampstead; the St

Mary Orphanage in Hammersmith; the St Agnes Orphanage for Girls in Kensington; the St Barnabas Orphanage in Hanover Square; the Gordon Boys' Home in St George in the East; St Ann's Catholic Orphanage in Marylebone; St Mary's Boys' Orphanage in Streatham; the Hambro Orphanage for Girls in Putney and the Boys' Orphanage in Lewisham to name but a small proportion. Not all of the institutions established in the Victorian era were long-lasting, some lasted only a matter of months, but some remained functional into the twentieth century.

It was these orphanages set up by Victorian philanthropists which have strong parallels with Thomas's vision of the Foundling Hospital a hundred and fifty years earlier.

Portrait of Josiah Mason by Henry Penn, 1870.

Parallels With Sir Josiah Mason's Orphanage[5]

Like Thomas Coram, Sir Josiah Mason was a driven and dedicated man who saw a need and then worked on his own to provide a solution, albeit Josiah Mason's orphanage was two hundred years later than Thomas's hospital.

Both men saw poverty on the streets as they were going about their work which motivated them to build their institutions. While Thomas saw babies dying on the streets, it was beggars that made Josiah realise the need. He walked to his factory site and had beggars asking him for money as he passed by. While he gave them money, he felt that something more long-term should be done to help the poor people of Birmingham.

Like Thomas Coram, Josiah Mason received little education as a child. Josiah taught himself how to read and write when he was an adult. These were skills that Thomas felt deficient in all his life. For both men, this mean that they understood and appreciated the value of education and what it could do for poor children.

Both men were open about their own weaknesses in reading and writing. Because of their own poor education Thomas and Josiah felt that one of the key aims of their institutions was to teach the children. Both men aimed to give both boys and girls education; Josiah's aims including reading, sewing and arithmetic, as Thomas's had, but also many other subjects in line with the importance that education was being given nationally by the Government.

Both men, despite being in long marriages, found themselves childless.

While Thomas was an Anglican, Josiah was a methodist. Both men decided that, while religion would be an important part of life in their institutions, they would not go to the Church for funding. They wanted to build establishments that were independent of the Church.

Thomas had a respectable career in shipping but Josiah, also starting small (selling fruit and vegetables from his donkey's panniers) became one of the biggest pen nib manufacturers in the world and gained very significant wealth from it. Josiah's relative success made his journey into social care provision very much easier. While Thomas spent years soliciting the support of those with wealth, or with access to that wealth, Josiah simply used his own vast fortune.

Both men were in the later years of their life when their plans came together. Josiah was 63 when his first orphanage was opened; Thomas was 72 when Hatton Gardens opened.

Josiah started small, with a modest orphanage in Birmingham with room for just a few children and some almshouses for women in poverty. He then invested in a large purpose-built orphanage in the countryside on the outskirts of Erdington, which was then a small town north of Birmingham and is now very much part of Birmingham. The foundation stone was laid in 1865 and the orphanage opened in 1869, more than a hundred years after the Foundling Hospital in Lamb's Conduit Fields was opened.

Josiah's orphanage, distinguished by its Italianate style and two immense towers, cost £60,000 to build and could house 400 boys and girls in dormitory accommodation, matching Thomas's Foundling Hospital. In both, most of the staff lived on the premises. With the exception of the intake from the General Reception years, neither the Foundling Hospital nor Josiah's orphanage were ever full to capacity.

Both buildings had a chapel and a sick bay and all lessons were held in the building. On the orphanage site there was also a purpose-built school for younger children. In the twentieth century, older children went out to local schools from the orphanage. Both institutions had their own burial ground.

In both institutions efforts were made to produce much of the food eaten by the staff and children in-house, with crops grown in the grounds tended by the children themselves. The children were also given jobs to support the management of the buildings – cleaning, cooking, mending clothes – in both Josiah's orphanage and Thomas's hospital.

Despite all the similarities, there were two key differences in the two institutions. Firstly, the children taken in by Josiah's orphanage spent all their time in the orphanage building and were not sent out to country nurses. When it came time to leave, the children left at school-leaving age and were no longer the responsibility of the orphanage.

Secondly, unlike Thomas's no questions asked policy, admission to Josiah's orphanage was by application and most children had lost at least one parent, although the original deeds stated that 'every child shall be of or under the age of nine years, the legitimate child of poor parents, both then dead'. Like so many eighteenth- and nineteenth-century institutions, illegitimate children were not welcome at Josiah's orphanage.

Josiah went on to found what became the University of Birmingham and was knighted in 1872. Thomas died when he was 83, Josiah when he was 86. Both men were widowed and spent their last years living on their own but were said, in their old age, to have visited the children in their institutions for comfort. Both men were interred in their institutions, and both had to be moved when the buildings were demolished and replaced with residential development.

Despite being founded more than a century apart, Josiah's orphanage stopped taking in residential children in 1960, just five years after Thomas's hospital closed its doors. Both Josiah's orphanage and Thomas's hospital became schools, a fitting end for two men who truly appreciated the value of education.

A State Response

A series of Education Acts in the late nineteenth century made full-time schooling compulsory for children aged between 5 and 13 and all the orphanages and children's homes of the time, including the Foundling Hospital, had to make a switch towards providing formal education rather than ad hoc lessons they scheduled themselves. Many institutions began sending children to schools in the local community rather than continuing to try to educate them in-house. Josiah's orphanage turned their school building into a fully-fledged school which served both the children of the orphanage and those of the local community. What the Foundling Hospital did was to transition into a school.

In 1926, nearly 200 years after first opening to children, the hospital made a physical move. The site of the hospital was simply too embedded within the city to be useful as a residential children's institution with the noise, pollution and complex traffic completely surrounding them.

Initially the hospital moved to a temporary new home in Redhill, Surrey. Thomas's remains were moved to St Andrew's Church in Holborn, a short distance from where the Foundling Hospital was, and where they remain today.

The land owned by the Foundling Hospital was sold to a developer for £1.65 million,[6] a sum which, taking into account inflation, would have a value today of £126 million. The site was subsumed into the wealthy area of Bloomsbury. The Earl of Salisbury's fields that he was so desperate to be rid of, became prime real estate in one of the wealthiest cities in the world. Not all was lost to development however, a green space was preserved to be known as Coram Fields, forming a lasting memorial to the hospital and its founder. An infant welfare centre was also left to continue some of the Foundling Hospital's work for children.

The Foundling Hospital then moved in 1935 to Berkhamsted, a purpose-built school closely resembling the Foundling Hospital building and also, importantly, housing the organ that Handel had gifted the hospital in 1751.

It was still a large institution but now the focus was far wider than simply offering bed and board as the institution made the transformation into a school. In 1955 this metamorphosis was complete as the doors closed to all but day pupils. The Foundling Hospital no longer provided residential care. The residential children who were in the school at the time were transferred to foster families.

Towards the end of the nineteenth century there was a government move to develop a state response to the necessity of looking after children in need, alongside the philanthropic response which had begun decades earlier. To this end, Poor Law Unions began taking children out of workhouses where children were living both with and without parents. Some Poor Law Unions put children in barrack-style large children's homes with dormitory style accommodation. However, following a model developed in Europe, it became common in England and Wales to build what were known as cottage homes. Some of these, such as Aston Union Cottage Homes in Birmingham, were next door to the Poor Law Union's workhouse. Others were some distance away such as Greenwich Union's which was located in Sidcup, then a small town in rural Kent.

The idea of the cottage homes was, like the Foundling Hospital, that everything was on one site so that the children never had to leave. Children lived, not in barrack-style accommodation, but in large houses along a private street. Each house accommodated up to thirty children with a live-in matron.

A chapel, school rooms, infirmary, training workshops and staff accommodation were all within the gated grounds. It is estimated that around 750,000 children spent all or some of their childhoods in cottage homes in England and Wales.[7]

When the Poor Law Unions ended, and their role was taken over by local councils in 1930, Cottage homes became local authority children's homes. Some remained functional until the twentieth century.

The Second World War brought great disruption for children with thousands being evacuated out of towns and cities to the countryside. Many urban children's homes also despatched their charges to the country. Partly because this mass evacuation brought rural families into contact with urban children, with whom they had previously had no contact, there was a sea change in how children were viewed.

This resulted in the Children's Act of 1948 which really placed children at the heart of their families and was the start of children receiving rights as young people. For children's homes the effect of the Act was marked. No longer was it considered that large institutions were best placed to look after children in need. These were closed and replaced, during the 1950s and 1960s, with small children's homes which were designed to mimic a family unit.

No longer were children prepared for going into the services and domestic service, but the aim was to give them a more rounded upbringing with a full education so that they were more prepared to have their own families and careers of their choosing. The Foundling Hospital idea that Thomas had developed, of a large institution with dormitories of beds, uniforms, rigid regimes of chores and strict discipline, no longer has a place in childcare in this country.

For this reason, the Foundling Hospital ceased to provide residential care, as was the case with many of the orphanages set up in the philanthropic Victorian era. Instead, councils placed children in small houses on housing estates rather than in grand buildings in the countryside. The children were cared for by live-in staff who acted more as foster parents than as council employees.

As the small houses proliferated, the care paradigm transformed once more. With the advent of Social Services in the 1970s, residential care work developed as a profession, warranting formal training and supervision and shift work rather than 24/7 live-in arrangements. The live-in foster parents of the small children's homes were replaced by teams of care workers who were with the children in shifts.

It became clear that, in most cases, fostering and adoption were better options for children than life in a children's home, whatever the nature of the home. So began a huge move towards finding appropriate foster families and supporting them in their care for children. Looking after children in need developed in a huge circle and came back to the ideas of the foundling hospitals of Europe who learnt that children were best cared for within the families of nurses acting as foster parents.

Was It Just Too Soon?

Thomas Coram knew that children could not be left on the streets to die and that some support was needed for them. Motivated by national pride, he embarked on a grand project that mimicked both the very wealthy Christ's

Hospital, which was already successful in London, and the many foundling hospitals which existed in other countries.

In very basic terms, what Thomas achieved by soliciting support and donations, was a facility which was used for the care of children for 181 years.

He founded a hospital that took in, educated / trained and saw through to adulthood in the region of 10,000 children who may otherwise have perished on the streets. Importantly, the thousands of women who brought the babies into the hospital were also given a chance to make a go of their lives, without the shame of their illegitimate child, or the mouth to feed that they could not afford.

It is not possible to calculate what proportion of all those children who needed help went into the hospital. Nor is it possible to know to what extent the hospital achieved its aim of saving children from being murdered by their parents or abandoned on the dunghills; nor, indeed, do we know how many of those who were admitted were illegitimate.

It is not possible to know how many children would, had the hospital not been there, have been exposed and deserted. Nor do we know how many children continued to be abandoned on the streets and dunghills even though the hospital was an option. These sorts of statistics do not now exist. And nor did they exist in Thomas's time. People supported the hospital knowing that the children who went in might otherwise have died, but no more. The hospital was built, not on statistics but a faith that each child who went in stood a better chance than those who didn't and that the mothers who gave up their children had a better chance of being able to get on with their lives, free from the shame they would otherwise have faced.

The hospital was plagued by a high mortality rate in those first decades but managed to fare better than other foundling hospitals in Europe in this respect. The fear of re-visiting the high mortality and other problems of the General Reception period, however, held admission levels to a very low level for most of the hospital's functional life.

The question has to be asked, was the Foundling Hospital just founded too soon?

With medicine barely off the ground, was it simply too soon to have so many people living in such close proximity? The dormitories of the Foundling Hospital were, quite literally, a breeding ground for germs with illnesses being inevitably passed from person to person. The Foundling Hospital had provision for putting children they believed to be infectious in isolation from other children, but infectious diseases were not always recognised as such in time to prevent them spreading amongst the children and the staff. Medicine at the time had no real way of effectively treating the childhood diseases that, left to run their course, were so often fatal.

It was 187 years after the Foundling Hospital opened that Alexander Fleming discovered penicillin and two centuries before antibiotics started to be widely available. Think what the Foundling Hospital could have achieved if they had had access to antibiotics for the children.

Additionally, there was little understanding of the use of antiseptics to prevent wounds becoming infected until the late nineteenth century and the use of general anaesthetics was not widespread until the mid-twentieth century. Any surgery would have undoubtedly led to the death of an ailing infant.

It was arguably just too early to create a building of 400 children and to expect to be able to control the illness, infections and disease that occurred. And too early in the development of medical knowledge to be able to offer very much help to the foster mothers whose charges became ill.

Communication was also in its infancy when the Foundling Hospital was trying to look after a network of country nurses and inspectors around the country. The posting of a letter was an established way of communicating although, where distance was involved, a letter could only arrive as fast as the horses that carried it. And rural areas would have had only very limited access.

The Foundling Hospital employed a messenger who was primarily concerned with conveying messages between the hospital staff and governors. Getting urgent messages between foster mothers in the countryside, branch hospitals and the governors was a more challenging problem. It was not until the mid-twentieth century that home telephones became commonplace. The volunteer inspectors whose role it was to visit the foster children and answer the questions of the foster mothers had to rely on letters or visits, negotiating country lanes in horse-drawn carriages.

It was to be another century before children could travel in the comfort of trains and two centuries until they could travel by car. For the foundlings fostered to countrywide homes, they had to endure long, cold, uncomfortable journeys which many were simply too weak to survive. Others, being transported to the hospital in London, were poorly treated or 'lost' by unscrupulous paid carriers who were way outside the control of either the governors or the people who employed them.

While human beings have, of course, been having babies for generations, it was not as easy as perhaps the governors initially thought, to settle on the most effective way to bring up babies. Our knowledge was, like so many things, still in its infancy. This led to the initial decision that babies were most effectively cared for by so-called 'dry nurses'. Seeing a very high death rate, and presumably many babies in the Hatton Garden hospital showing signs of hunger and starvation, the governors switched to the idea of attempting to find a wet nurse for every baby to give them the nourishment of a mother's milk. It also gave rise to the decision that shoes were unhealthy and should not be given to the foundlings. Add to this difficulty in deciding how best to look after a baby was the added challenge of how to pass this on to foster mothers and ensure that they followed the advice given.

Was looking after so many babies just too ambitious at this time in our history?

When the Foundling Hospital was built, London was developing big water problems. Streets were awash with human and animal waste which ended up pouring into the Thames. Open cess pools added to the smell. The poor of London had little access to clean water other than the Thames, with water being taken out almost at the same point at which the sewage was going in. Since the first London Mayor came up with the idea in the fourteenth century, London even had toilets directly overhanging the Thames. No need to flush or clean as there was always another tide on the way to rinse it all out. The link between filthy water and disease had not been made, with bad air tending to get the blame rather than bad water. The result was that London's population suffered greatly from cholera in the early nineteenth century. Later that century a sewage system was built for the city which still directed sewage into the Thames, although further downstream. Clean drinking water from taps in homes came with the twentieth century. Drinking water and bathing water was necessarily restricted in the early days of the Foundling Hospital. Hygiene took a great leap forward when baths were introduced in 1815.

The Poor Law system was in place, as it had been for some years, but it was buckling under the strain of providing support for all those who needed it and the Foundling Hospital suffered enormously as a result, with babies brought into the hospital, often without the mother's consent, instead of remaining in their own parish and receiving local support.

If Thomas had had the urge to build a foundling hospital a century later, he would have had the benefit of a far greater knowledge of medicine, surgery and infections as well as better sanitation and a clean water supply. With the infrastructure around the hospital so under-developed in the 1700s, Thomas had a task that was almost too much for a large foundling hospital.

However, what Thomas Coram and the Foundling Hospital did manage to achieve was phenomenal given the undeveloped state of communication, transportation, medicine, childcare and sanitation.

Thousands of pounds were raised for a hospital while it was still only a concept. The mobilisation of hundreds of men of influence, power and wealth to form what must have been one of the largest and most influential bodies of men outside parliament using only paper petitions and shoe leather is an achievement which remains unmatched.

A Personal Legacy

'A man who, in spite of limitations and drawbacks, left his mark on the life of the eighteenth century.'

Compston, 1918

It could be argued that, on a personal level, Thomas did not reach his potential. He could have achieved so much more. At pinnacle times in his life, he reached a point where the relationship with those around him broke down to the extent that he walked away. How much more could he have achieved had he stayed? If he had not fallen out with his neighbours in Dighton, he could perhaps have become the biggest shipbuilder in Taunton, and a very rich man. If he had not fallen out with his fellow trustees on the Georgia project, he could have made his name as a man of the new colonies. If he had stayed on the General Committee of the Foundling Hospital, he may have been knighted for his work. Without reaching these levels, while he rubbed shoulders with the rich, successful and powerful men of his country, he failed to receive acknowledgement as being one of them until he died.

In Brunswick Square, amidst the wealth of Bloomsbury, is the statue of Thomas Coram carrying the legend 'Pioneer of the cause of child welfare'. I would argue that this description barely touches the surface of what he achieved, and little of it is to do with his pioneering child welfare.

An astonishing achievement was the acquisition of 56 acres of land which became subsumed into central London and enabled the governors to survive disaster and carry on taking in children for another 150 years. The governors were even able to buy back part of the land they sold and on this a new charity is based in Thomas's name. The money has enabled a twenty-first century charity, Coram, to offer support to thousands of children each year. Coram, despite its very historic roots, has a modern approach as a consortium of charities together championing children's rights and their welfare. It is a long way (and 300 years) from what Thomas envisaged his Foundling Hospital to be, but it continues what Thomas started – a belief that children should have the best start in life possible, no matter who they are and what their circumstances are. We may take that ideal for granted now, but it was revolutionary in Thomas's day.

But this legacy goes beyond the organisation itself. When Queen Caroline asked the Paris Foundling Hospital to report back on how they ran their organisation, the focus was very much on the complex record-keeping that they maintained. In 1740, when the London governors published their General Plan, it too focused on the details that were to be kept of each child in various registers. This focus on meticulous record-keeping and myriad registers detailing

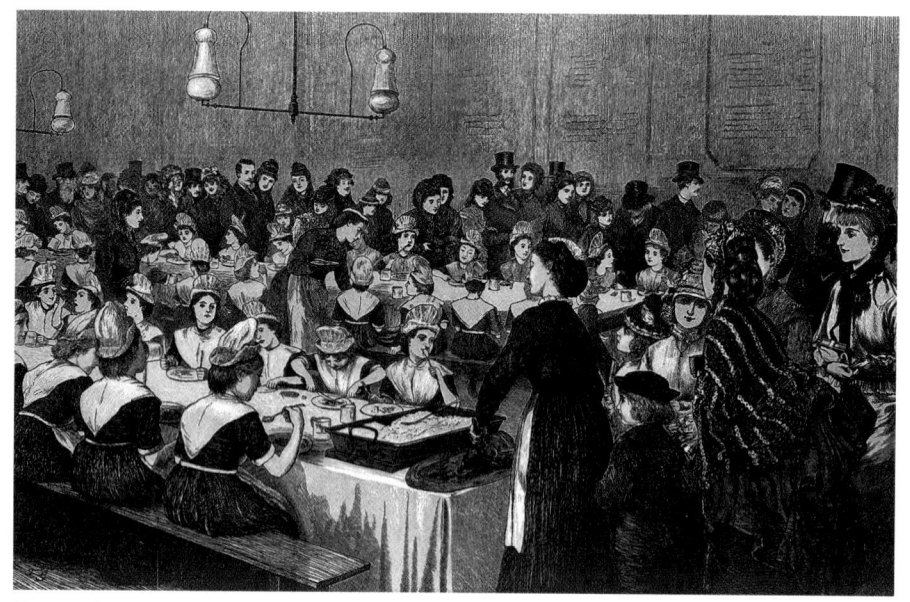

Even in the late nineteenth century, the Foundling Hospital was still able to draw crowds to the most mundane of hospital activities. Fashionable London comes to observe Sunday lunch at the Foundling Hospital. Wood engraving by J. Swain, 1872, after H.T. Green. (*Wellcome Collection*)

every life stage that each foundling reached, has resulted in an estimated eight tons of paper. This has been kept safely all this time and is currently housed on 800 linear feet of shelving by the London Metropolitan Archives. It is a vast archive consisting of over a thousand plans, committee reports, inspectors reports and the details of the thousands of foundlings who were taken in by the hospital. Paris has similarly impressive records of the Foundling Hospital there dating from 1639 to 1930.

The hospital archives give an unrivalled insight into the running of an institution but also an understanding of society through the centuries, particularly those people excluded from traditional histories – women, children and poor people. As researchers have pored over the details, it has given rise to fascinating studies and improved our understanding of society in immeasurable ways not just childcare. This is a period of history before modern national census-taking took place. The apothecary records give an insight into the understanding of health and medicine; the apprenticeship records tell us about work, work skills and business; the letters from country foster mothers tell of rural domestic life.

One unexpected outcome is that the archives have hugely impacted on researchers' knowledge of textiles in the second half of the eighteenth century. The small pieces of cloth left by mothers with their babies as tokens to help identify them have formed an archive of 7000 scraps of cloth representing an unprecedented snapshot of the array of fabrics worn by primarily poor women and their babies. The vast majority of scraps of fabric remain intact with patterns and colours still clear. Some are embroidered with stitching that remains in place after three hundred years, spelling out a child's name and perhaps a date. For the casual observer, the scraps tell a human story of a woman saying goodbye to her baby without giving up hope that she will see her child again. To the textile expert they tell a story about how textiles were made, dyed and patterned so many generations ago.

The Foundling Hospital Museum puts on public view many items from the archives including tokens that were left with babies, documents, scraps of fabrics, items from the hospital of the various sites, and places them in the context of Thomas's life, the history of the Foundling Hospital and how society as a whole has changed over the decades, particularly in London. The archives are not only for serious researchers but are, in this way, available for perusal by members of the public. This allows many people to learn about the hospital and what it meant at the time and the thousands of children who lived there. This has a particular resonance for those for whom the Foundling Hospital is a part of their own family history.

The third aspect of Thomas's legacy is far less tangible. When Thomas saw children abandoned on London dunghills, children were very much a disposable part of society. People saw little value in poor children, only a potential bill for their care by the local parish.

In the eighteenth century 'children were regarded as a necessary evil and except in times of alarming and grave illness were little considered. Evidence of neglect, cruelty and infanticide are so abundant that one is forced to believe that at times, children were not even considered'.[8]

Far from being valued, illegitimate children were seen as an evil to be hidden away or, at worst, destroyed along with their mothers. What Thomas did was to present to society a perspective that gave poor and illegitimate children a value. Given the right training, he theorised, these children could become useful members of society – they could fight for Britain in the seemingly endless European wars, or they could be trained to be effective workers in myriad jobs which needed good labourers. Girls could be domestic servants who were in short supply, particularly efficient, well-trained ones. He placed a financial and military value on the very lowest members of London society at a time when London and the Empire were growing hugely and needed people to support that growth.

More than this, the Foundling Hospital, with the spectacle of the reception and christenings of the foundlings, the art of Hogarth and his peers, the music of Handel, the writings of Dickens and Fielding, all came together to make the

Foundling Hospital a fashionable place to be. That hundreds of people squeezed into the chapel to hear music that was being played by Handel to raise money for, of all things, poor illegitimate children, was an incredible feat. The king of England signing a charter to establish a hospital for the lowest in society was unprecedented. That his son, the Prince of Wales, gave a pension to the man who championed poor people, was unheard of.

Thomas's quest of persuasion was a slow one, and the journey of accepting poor and illegitimate children as worthy of some investment continued to be a slow one long after Thomas had died. The Foundling Hospital represented a pocket of acceptance, a pocket which didn't falter, but nonetheless, stood largely alone for more than a century. Without the Foundling Hospital, however, and Thomas's impressive powers of persuasion and the fame and celebrity he managed to achieve for the cause of foundlings, the journey would have been so much slower and longer.

The Foundling Hospital was a shining example of hope, a glimmer of the value society should place on children, even if they were poor or illegitimate. The Foundling Hospital, filled with hundreds of aristocrats and royalty, all dressed in their finery clutching their precious tickets, to be a part of helping children who were the very lowest of society, is an astonishing achievement for a man who made boats.

Postscript: Elinor's story

Once they had taken John, Elinor had no choice but to leave the Foundling Hospital. She stood outside sobbing, holding onto a wall to keep herself standing. She had known she was taking John to the hospital to leave him there but, until the door closed behind her with her baby still inside, she had not thought how this would feel. The pain of leaving him felt like a physical tear in her flesh, pulling her apart from him. She was fighting to breathe as she sobbed but she didn't want to breathe, she didn't want to live.

She had no idea where to go. She staggered a short distance away and spent the night leaning against the wall of the hospital. She couldn't stop shivering in the cold, but it was too dark to find her way anywhere else.

Her crying did not stop for weeks but she came to train herself to cry only first thing in the morning and last thing at night. Those were the times, alone and in the dark, when she allowed herself to think about John. She had, with no other options, gone back to the house in Cavendish Square where she had worked before as a domestic. She had left when she feared her pregnant belly would be seen by the others and give her away. Going back, she had a story about looking after her sick mother to explain why she hadn't worked for so many weeks.

She was given her job back although everyone knew her story was just a story because the Master of the house was sweet on her. Mrs Baggs promised to tell the Master that she was back to take her job and she was as good as her word. The Master agreed Elinor could work there again. But he expected her to work through her fortnightly afternoons off to make up for the trouble she had caused by leaving.

It was just a few months before he raped her again. She was making up the fire in the library when he came in. Her second child, another boy, was born with no life in him. He never even cried. She couldn't take him to be buried as they would say it was her who killed him. She stitched his little body into her underskirt and walked with him for hours. She could feel him bumping against her legs as she moved. When it was dark and she found a place where there was no-one else, she ripped the stitches that held the fabric of her skirt around him and left him there. She fainted on the way just from the pain of seeing him lying there on his own.

When she knew that she was going to have a baby for a third time, the despair was overwhelming. She vowed that she would not go back to the house on Cavendish Square and would take whatever was to face her when her baby was again taken from her. It was a long walk and she arrived at the gates of the Foundling Hospital exhausted. This baby hadn't wanted to leave her, and it had taken all that she had to make him be born. She was still bleeding and sore now. When the time for reception came, she joined the queue with the other women. She told another woman in the queue in front of her about the wooden balls and, together, they tore a ribbon from her petticoat to give her daughter as a keepsake. Elinor had sewn a handkerchief this time. It was pressed into a perfect square like Grace's had been when Elinor left John here. She had added a small, stitched flower in the corner.

It was Elinor's turn. She picked the wooden ball from the bag. It was so black that she couldn't see it as she brought it out of the dark insides of the bag. It was like she was holding nothing.

The man grabbed the ball from her and shouted to the next woman to come forward. They were not taking Elinor's baby.

She could not return to the house on Cavendish Square. They could not see her baby. She walked the streets, sat in alleys, sang for pennies. Her baby died in her arms two days later, of the cold, of hunger, because the ball was black.

She went into the workhouse exhausted, weak from hunger and grief. The people there were kinder than they needed to be. They left her in peace as she died, and only found her baby's body wrapped in her shawls when they moved her out to bury her.

Notes

Prelude: Elinor's Story
1. Kentish Weekly Post. 12 March 1752.

Introduction
1. Photograph taken by Ceridwen and licensed for reuse under the Creative Commons Attribution-ShareAlike 2.0 license.
2. 'The custom of the common people's drinking great quantities of a most inflammatory and poisonous liquor certainly created an incredible devastation amongst the children of the poor.' Hanway, J., 1759, p.11.

Part I
1. Quote taken from *Oliver Twist*.
2. *Canterbury Journal*, 8 September 1731.
3. Royal Museums, Greenwich. rmg.co.uk.
4. Gerard I. and Root K. 2017.
5. *Caledonian Mercury*. 6 March 1721.
6. McMahon P. 2017.
7. Brownlow, J. 1865, p.1.
8. Muir, A.J. 2018.
9. Births in England and Wales: 2022 (refreshed populations). Census 2021.
10. *Kentish Gazette*, 19 May 1789.
11. Brownlow, J. 1847, p.183.
12. *Ipswich Journal*, 29 August 1795.
13. *Northampton Mercury*, 17 July 1790.
14. Muir, A.J. 2018.
15. Queen Caroline (at the command of). 1739.
16. *Kentish Weekly Post*, 10 March 1756.
17. Old Bailey online.
18. *Derby Mercury*, 1 December 1758.
19. Davenport, R.J. *et al.* 2013
20. ONS 2023 Child and infant mortality in England and Wales 2021
21. Gibson, K.L. 2018.
22. Brocklesby, R. 1751

Part II
1. Roberts, G. 1823.
2. The detailed research of Wagner, G. (2004) has discovered that there was a first son born before Thomas who did not live long.
3. Compston, H.F.B. 1918.

4. Tarbox, I. 1879, p.50.
  5. Old Colony Historical Society. 1879.
  6. Hill, H.A. 1892, p.134.
  7. Ibid., p.133.
  8. Hill, HA. 1892 p 138
  9. Ibid. p139
10. Hill, H.A. 1892, p.135.
11. Compston, H.F.B. 1918, p.33.
12. Emery, S.H. 1893, p.353.
13. Compston, HFB. 1918. p31
14. Emery, SH. 1893. p241
15. Ibid., p.255.

Part III
  1. Compston, H.F.B. 1918, p.68.
  2. Brocklesby, R. 1751.
  3. Compston, H.F.B. 1751.
  4. Oliver Twist (or the Parish Boys Progress, as it was initially known) was actually written when Dickens lived very close to the Foundling Hospital on Doughty Street. He was an astute observer of the poverty of London and the hardships of the city's residents and became a supporter of the Foundling Hospital itself. Later novels also described the experiences of foundlings, and *Little Dorrit*, for example, has a character who grew up in the hospital.
  5. Hanway, J. 1759, p.17.
  6. Dickens, C. 1853.
  7. Caledonian Mercury 15th November 1726
  8. Thomas, B. 1796 p 3
  9. Report of the Trustees, 1720.
10. *Caledonian Mercury*, 25 July 1721.
11. Rose, C. 1990.
12. Hanway, J. 1759, p.17.
13. For example, *Newcastle Courant*, 5 April 1729.
14. Hill, H.A. 1892, p.144.
15. Jefferson, T. 1774.
16. O'Shaughnessy, P. (Undated.)
17. Compston, HFB. 1918.
18. Compston, H.F.B., pp.90–91.
19. Hill, H.A. 1892, p.146.
20. Brownlow, J. 1865, p.17.
21. Hill, H.A. 1892, p.146.
22. *Newcastle Courant*, 19 June 1736.
23. *Newcastle Courant*, 6 September 1740.
24. Caledonian Mercury 30th January 1739
25. Compston, H.F.B. 1918, p.108.
26. Hill, H.A. 1892.
27. Brocklesby, R. 1751, p.21.
28. The full title of the General Plan, published in 1740, was 'The Report of the General Committee for directing, managing the Business, Affairs, Estate and Effects of the

Notes 209

Corporation of the Governors and Guardians of the Hospital for the Maintenance and Education of Exposed and Deserted Children Relating to the General Plan for executing the Purposes of the Royal Charter, establishing this Hospital'.

Part IV
1. Photograph by Elisa Rolle and licensed under the Creative Commons Attribution-Share Alike 4.0 International license.
2. Brownlow, J. 1847, p.166. Brownlow has suggested that the advertisement specified twenty children to be admitted. The hospital minutes state thirty children.
3. *Newcastle Courant*, 28 March 1741.
4. *Newcastle Courant*, 25 April 1741.
5. Fildes, V. 1988.
6. Obladen. 2023, p.136.
7. Sarúsa, C., Erdozáin, P. and Hernández. 2023.

Part V
1. Compston, HFB. 1918. p69
2. Compston, H.F.B. 1918, p.106.
3. Allin, DS. 2010.
4. Hilohello and Qq1122qq. Licensed under the Creative Commons Attributions-ShareAlike 4.0 Unported License.
5. Allin, D.S. 2010.
6. *Newcastle Courant*, 18 September 1742.
7. Allin, D.S. 2010.
8. Brownlow, J. 1847, p.7.
9. Brownlow, J. 1847, p.8.
10. *Ipswich Journal*, 5 May 1750.
11. Thomas, B. 1797, p.18.
12. 'The Foundling Hospital and the Royal Academy' in *Sydney Morning Herald*, 2 August 1860, p.8.
13. Ibid.
14. *Newcastle Courant*, 5 May 1750.
15. *Kentish Weekly Post*, 18 April 1752.
16. Lee, D. 2007, p.138.
17. Brocklesby, R. 1751.
18. Compston, HRB, 1918, p112
19. Brownlow, J 1865

Part VI
1. Dodsley, R. & J. 1761.
2. Bernard, T. 1796 p29
3. Dodsley, R. & J. 1761.
4. Allin, D. 2010, p.400.
5. Hilohello and Qq1122qq. Licensed under the Creative Commons Attributions-ShareAlike 4.0 Unported License.
6. 1757 Regulations of the hospital.
7. Hilohello and Qq1122qq. Licensed under the Creative Commons Attributions-ShareAlike 4.0 Unported License.

8. Cadogan, W. 1748.
9. Hilohello and Qq1122qq. Licensed under the Creative Commons Attributions-ShareAlike 4.0 Unported License.
10. *An Account of Several Workhouses*, Anon. 1732, p.iii .
11. Regulations of the hospital, 1757.
12. *Newcastle Courant*, 14 April 1744.
13. Bernard, T. 1796.
14. Brownlow, J. 1865, p.53.
15. Bernard, T. 1796.
16. Bernard T, 1796, p.40.

Part VII
1. Walford, E. 1878. He describes the words in Latin, *in amore hac sunt vitia*, engraved on a trinket.
2. Alllin, DS. 2010, p.401.
3. Allin, DS. 2010, p.400–401.
4. Brownlow, J. 1865, p.20.
5. A biggin was a child's skull cap which tied under the chin; a barrow was a long sleeveless flannel dress; a mantle was a sleeveless cloak; a pilch was a leather or woollen coat. 'Waiscoat' is the spelling given on the billet.

Part VIII
1. *Derby Mercury*, 12 October 1753.
2. *Aris's Birmingham Gazette*, 24 June 1754.
3. *Oxford Journal*, 6 July 1754.
4. *Aris's Birmingham Gazette*, 27 November 1752.
5 Bernard, T. 1796, p.276.
6. Allin, D.S. 2010, p.400.
7. Dickens, C. 1853.
8. Allin, D.S. 2010, p.400.
9. *Aris's Birmingham Gazette*, 7 May 1759.
10. Bernard, T. 1796, p.32.
11. Tuesday, October 11 1763.
12. Baines, *Directory of the West Riding*, 1822.
13. Bernard, T. 1796, p.37.
14. Allin, D.S. 2010, p.400.
15. Ibid.
16. Bernard, T. 1796, p.28.
17. Walford, E. 1878, p.358.
18. Wodsworth, W.D. 1876.
19. Obladen M., 2023, p.140.
20. Allin, D.S. 2010, p.400.
21. Allin, D.S. 2010, p.401.
22. Ibid.
23. Allin, D.S. 2010, p.401.
24. Hilohello and Qq1122qq. Licensed under the Creative Commons Attributions-ShareAlike 4.0 Unported License.
25. Allin, D.S. 2010, p.401.

26. His 1756 article was entitled 'An essay on tea: considered as pernicious to health, obstructing industry, and impoverishing the nation'

Part IX
1. Bloomsbury Project, University College London.
2. Compston, H.R.B. 1918.
3. Demographia.com.
4. Limbrick, G. 2014
5. Drawn from Limbrick, G. 2013.
6. Bloomsbury Project, University College London.
7. Limbrick, G, 2018.
8. Caulfield, E. 1930, p.481.

Bibliography

Aichroth, P., *A Brief History of Westminster Hospital.* (2018.)
Allin, D.S., *The Early Years of the Foundling Hospital 1739/41–1773.* Privately published. (2010.)
Anon., *An Account of Several Work-houses for Employing and Maintaining the Poor.* 2nd edition very much enlarged. (1732.)
Bernard, T., *An Account of the Hospital for the Maintenance and Education of exposed and deserted young Children.* Bernard is the assumed author; it was written anonymously. (1796.)
Bernard, T., *An Account of the Foundling Hospital, in London, for the maintenance and education of exposed and deserted young Children.* (1799.)
Boyston, A., 'William Watson's Use of Controlled Clinical experiments in 1767' in *Journal of the Royal Society of Medicine.* (June, 2014.)
Bright, J., *Fashioning the Foundlings – Education, Instruction and Apprenticeship at the London Foundling Hospital c.1741–1800.* MRes in Historical Research, University of London. (2017.)
Brocklesby, R., *Private Virtue and publick Spirit Display'd. In a succinct Essay on the Character of Capt. Thomas Coram.* (1751.)
Brownlow, J., *Chronicles of the Foundling Hospital including Memoirs of Captain Coram.* (1847.)
Brownlow, J., *The History and Objects of the Foundling Hospital with a memoir of the Founder.* (1865.)
Cadogan, W., *An Essay upon Nursing and the Management of Children from their birth to three years of age.* (1748.)
Caulfield, E., *The Infant Welfare Movement in the Eighteenth Century.* (1930.)
Compston, H.F.B., *Thomas Coram: Churchman, Empire builder and Philanthropist.* (1918.)
Cowie, L.C., 'Holy Thursday: The charity School movement in the eighteenth century' in *History Today,* vol. 27, issue 8. (1977.)
Davenport, R.J., Poulton J.P. and Black J., *Infant Mortality by social status in Georgian London: a test of the epidemiological integration model.* (2013.)
Dickens, C., *Foundling Hospital its internal management.* Household Words no. 56. (1853.)
Dodsley, R. and J., *London and Its Environs Described Containing an Account of Whatever is Most Remarkable for Grandeur, Elegance, Curiosity Or Use, in the City and in the Country Twenty Miles Round It. Comprehending Also Whatever is Most Material in the History and Antiquities of this Great Metropolis – Volume 2.* (1761.)
Emery, S.H., *History of Taunton, Massachusetts from its settlement to the present time.* (1893.)
Fildes, V., 'The English Wet-Nurse and her role in infant care 1538–1800' in *Medical History,* vol. 32. (1988.)
Foundling Hospital Governors, *Summary of the Royal Charter establishing an Hospital for the Maintenance and Education of Exposed and Deserted Children.* (1739.)
Foundling Hospital Governors, *The Royal Charter establishing an Hospital for the Maintenance and Education of Exposed and Deserted Children.* (1740.)
Foundling Hospital Governors, *The Report of the General Committee for directing, managing the Business, Affairs, Estate and Effects of the Corporation of the Governors and Guardians of the*

Hospital for the Maintenance and Education of Exposed and Deserted Children Relating to the General Plan for executing the Purposes of the Royal Charter, establishing this Hospital. (1740.)

Foundling Hospital Governors, *Regulations for Managing the Hospital for the Maintenance and Education of Exposed and Deserted Young Children.* (1752.)

Gerard I. and Root, K., *Convulsions Living with Dying: Everyday cultures of dying within family life in Britain 1900–50s.* AHRC Project, University of Leeds. (2017.)

Gibson, K.L., *Experiences of Illegitimacy in England, 1660–1834.* A thesis submitted in partial fulfilment of the requirements for the degree of Doctor of Philosophy. The University of Sheffield. (2018.)

Hanway, J., *A Candid Historical Account of the Hospital for the Reception of Exposed and Deserted Young Children representing the Present Plan of it as productive of many Evils, and not adapted to the Genius and Happiness of this Nation.* (1759.)

Hill, H.A., *Thomas Coram in Boston and Taunton.* (1892.)

Jefferson, T., *A Summary View of the Rights of British America.* (1774.)

Lee, D., 'Lost Girls, Lost Women: Foundlings in the Art and Poetry of William Blake' in *Essays in Romanticism*, vol. 15, number 1. (January 2007.)

Limbrick, G., *Deeds of Love: The Story of Josiah Mason's Orphanage and School.* WordWorks, Birmingham. (2013.)

Limbrick, G., *Leaving the Workhouse: the Story of Victorian Orphanages.* WordWorks, Birmingham. (2014.)

Limbrick, G., *Inside the Gates of Children's Cottage Homes.* WordWorks. Birmingham. (2018.)

McMahon P., *The Tippling Act and London's 300 Year Love of Gin.* Parliament, UK. (2017.)

Muir, A.J., 'Courtship, Sex and Poverty: Illegitimacy in Eighteenth-Century Wales' in *Social History* 2018; 43(1): pp.56–80. (2018.)

Obladen, M., 'Exposed and Abandoned. Origins of the Foundling Hospital' in *Neonatology*, 120: pp.134–141. (2023.)

Old Colony Historical Society, *Collections of the Old Colony Historical Society. Papers read before the Society during the year 1878.* (1879.)

O'Shaughnessy, P., 'How A Law About Hats Contributed to the American Revolution' in *Aspects of History*, 2021. (Undated.)

Pugh, G., *London's Forgotten Children.* The History Press. (2007).

Queen Caroline (at the command of), *An account of the foundation and government of the Hospital for Foundlings in Paris.* (1739.)

Roberts, G., *The History of Lyme Regis from the Earliest Periods to the Present Day.* (1823.)

Rose, C., 'London's Charity Schools 1690–1730' in *History Today*, vol. 40, issue 3. (1990.)

Sarúsa, C., Erdozáin, P. and Hernández, 'Nursing babies to fight poverty: wages of wet nurses of Spanish foundling hospitals in the 18th and 19th centuries' in *Revista de Historia Economica – Journal of Iberian and Latin American Economic History*, vol. 41, issue 2. (September 2023.)

Shutt, N.J.L., *Nobody's Child. The theme of illegitimacy in the novels of Charles Dickens, George Eliot and Wilkie Collins.* D Phil. University of York. (1990.)

Tarbox, I., 'The Pilgrims and Puritans or Plymouth and the Massachusetts Bay' in *Old Colony Historical Society.* (1879.)

Wagner, G., *Thomas Coram, Gent, 1668–1751.* The Boydell Press. (2004.)

Walford, E., *Old And New London*, vol. 5. (1878.)

White, J., *London in the eighteenth century. A great and monstrous thing.* The Bodley Head. (2012.)

Wodsworth, W.D., *A Brief History of the Ancient Foundling Hospital of Dublin, From the Year 1702. With some account of similar institutions abroad.* (1876.)

Index

Absconding 149–150
Ackworth branch hospital 169–173
Act of Supremacy 11
Addison, Joseph 39, 40
Adoption 93
Africa 24, 45
Albemarle, Countess of 48
American Revolution 55
Anglicanism 26, 27
Anne, Queen 39, 52
Apprenticeships 93, 150–152, 184, 185
Aylesbury branch hospital 169

Ballots 95, 108–109
Barnet branch hospital 169
Barnard, Anne Weldon 48, 56
Barnard, Sir Robert 56
Barnardo, Dr 42
Beauclerk, Lord Vere 66
Bedford, Duchess of 48
Bedford, Duke of 64, **65**
Bentinck, William 56
Bernard, Sir Thomas xix, 179–180, **190**
Bills of Mortality 5
Bloomsbury xvii, 65, 196
Boleyn, Anne 11
Bolton, Dowager Duchess of 48, 49–50
Bolton, Duchess of 48, 49
Bolton, Duke of 49, 87
Boston 27, 28, 29
Bow Street Runners 4
Boyle, Dorothy 48, 52
Boyle, Richard 52
Branch hospitals 169, 172–173
Bristol County Court 28
British Empire 3, 18, 22, 25, 33, 150
Brocklesby, Dr Richard xviii, 122–123
Brownlow, John xix
Brudenell, Elizabeth 48, 53
Brudenell, George 53

Burlington Countess of 48, 52
Burrell, Peter 66, 120
Burt, Abel 30, 31
Byron, Baroness Frances 48, **51**, 52, 71

Cadogan, Dr William 102–104, 136–137
Cadogan, Lord 50
Campbell, Alexander Hume 69
Cardigan, Countess of 48
Caroline, Queen 49, 50, 52, 53, 56, **57**, 58, 60, 61, 63, 69
Catherine of Aragon 10–11, **10**
Catholic Church 42, 94
Chapel 121, 124
Chapel xix, 110, 115, 131
Charity for Relieving the Sick and Needy 41
Charity schools 43, 82, 137–138
Charlemont, Lord 64
Charles I 26
Charles II 20, 21, 50, 52, 66
Charter 44, 58, 61, 62, 64
Chester branch hospital 172
Children's Act 1948 197
Christ's Hospital 43, 126
Church of England 11, 26
Coat of arms 71, 83
College of Physicians 79
Colonisation 15, 53, 55, 105
Compston, Reverend Herbert xx
Cook, James 66
Coram Fields xvi, 196
Coram, Eunice 29, 44, 47, 73–74
Coram, Thomas
  childhood 19–22
  in the New World 23–24
  marriage to Eunice 28
  quest to start the foundling hospital 32–67

removal from the General
 Committee 96–100
death 117–120
pension 119
funeral 120–122
statue xvi, 123
as captain 124
legacy 189–201
Cork Foundling Hospital 40, 70, 164
Corporation seal 68
Cottage homes 196–197
Court cases 28
Coxhaven 34–35
Cromwell, Thomas 10

Daily Committee 79
de Paul, Vincent 46, 75
Derby, Lord 60
Dickens, Charles 36–37, 167
Diet (in the Foundling Hospital) 102–104, 130–131, 132–134
Dighton 1, 27–30, 33, 68
Disabilities 146–148
Dissolution of the monasteries 11, 12
Domestic service 150
Dublin Foundling Hospital 40, 70, 149, 164, 175–177
Dung hills 38, 39, 43

Education 21–22, 27, 42, 137–140, 186, 195
Eyles, Sir Joseph 66

Fawthorpe, Joseph 121
Female Orphan Asylum 187–188
Fielding Henry 187
Fielding, John 187, 188
Finch, Frances 48, 52
Folkes, Martin **65**, 66, 69
Foundation stone 100, 106
Francke, Professor 115
Frederick, Prince of Wales 49, 58, 64, 115, 119, 120, 124
Fundraising 69, 71, 73

Gainsborough, Thomas 113
General Committee 67–69, 78–79, 83, 96–98

General Court 67, 78
General Plan 67, 69, 76–81
George I 13, 34, 40, 61
George II, King 55, 56, 58, 61, 233
George, Prince 52
Georgia 24, 99, 33, 55, 60
Gideon, Sampson xviii, 119, 120
Gin Craze 8–9
Governors 62, 64, 67, 69, 78–79, 101
Great Fire of London 2, 3, 36
Great Migration 25
Great Northern War 44–45
Great Ormond Street Hospital 106, 189
Great Plague 2, 5
Great Storm 2
Guy, Thomas 38–39, 45
Guy's Hospital 67

Hales, Frances 48, 52
Handel, George Frideric 52, 111, 114–117
Hanley, Sir Joseph 120
Hanover 34, 61
Hanway, Jonas xix, 43, 186, 188
Harley, Margaret Cavendish 48, 56
Harold, Countess of 48, 55
Harold, Earl of 56
Harvard University 27
Hastings, Selina 39
Hat Act 53–54, 55
Hathaway, John 28
Hatters' Company 54
Hatton Garden 69, 74, 82–86, 88, 106, 161
Heglioland 35
Hele, Juliana 48, 52
Henry VIII 10–11
Hertford, Countess of 48, 53
Hill, Hamilton Andrew xx
Hogarth, William 51, 70–73, 83, 111–113, **112**, 135, 164
Hospital for Incurables 38
Huntingdon, Countess of 48, 52

Illegitimacy 12, 13–14, 44, 50, 59, 111
Industrial Revolution 2
Infant mortality 5, 15, 100, 152–153, 160, 168, 171, 177, 178–179, 180
Infanticide Act 15
Inspectors 79, 92, 167

James II, 20
Jefferson, Thomas 55
Joddrell, Paul 121

King, Anne 48, 56
Knight, Elizabeth 48

Ladies of the Bedchamber 50, 52, 53, 56, 63
Lamb's Conduit Fields 44, 96, 106, 132, 180
le dames de charité 47
Leeds, Duchess of 48
Lennox, Anne 48, 52
Lennox, Charles 50, 56
Lennox, Sarah 48, 52
Lichfield, Countess of 48, 52
Literacy 83
Lyme Regis 19–21, 22, 23, 24, 119

Magdalen Hospital 188
Malthus, Thomas 95
Manchester, Duchess of 48, 50
Marine Society for Destitute Boys 186
Mason, Sir Josiah 21, 193–195
Massachusetts 1, 23, 24, 27, 55, 73, 117
Mayflower, The 26
Meals (in the Foundling Hospital) 102–104, 130–131, 132–134
Measles 102
Messiah (Handel's) 115
Mi'Kmaq nation 33
Military Company of Taunton 28, 29
Milner, John 106, 120
Monmouth, Duke of 20
Montagu, Isabella 48, 50
Montagu, Lady Mary Wortley 146
Montagu, William 50
Mortality 5, 15, 100, 152–153, 160, 168, 171, 177, 178–179, 180
Moses 68

Navy Office 16, 33, 36, **37**, 40, 73
Needham, Henrietta 48, 49–50, 52
Nemasket nation 26
New World 3, 16, 20, 21, 22, 25, 32, 33, 47, 53, 55
Nova Scotia 33, 60–61, 117

Ockham, Baroness 48, 56
Onslow, Baroness 48, 50
Onslow, The Hon Arthur 46, 62, **63**
Opiates 86
Orphanages 192–193
Osborne, Peregrine 52

Paris Foundling Hospital 47, 58, 75, 153
Parish church 6, 11
Paulet, Charles 49
Pepys, Samuel 36
Perry, Micajah 66
Petitioning 32, 36, 46, 60, 117
Physician 102, 146
Pierrepoint, Anne 48, 51
Plymouth Puritans 23, 24
Poor Law 11–12, 191
Poor Relief 11, 151, 170–171, 191–192
Portland, Duchess of 48, 56
Portland, Duke of 56
Pounds, John 42
Powlett, Nassau 50
President (of the Foundling Hospital) 64–65
Prince of Wales *see* Frederick, Prince of Wales
Puritanism 26, 27

Ragged schools 42
Receiving day xiii, 83–86
Record-keeping 75–76, 80–81, 154, 159, 202
Reynolds, Joshua 65, 113
Richmond, Duchess of 48
Rotherhithe 16, 17, 36, 38
Royal Academy of Arts 114
Royal Africa Company 24
Royal Society 7
Russell, Ann 48, 50, 64
Russell, John 64–65, **65**
Russell, Wriothesley 50

Salisbury, Earl of 96, 180
Seaflower, The 34–36, 39
Seething Lane 36
Sewerage 4
Seymour, Algernon 49
Seymour, Charles 49

Seymour, Charlotte 48, 49
Seymour, Elizabeth 53
Shipbuilding 20, 22, 25, 27, 28, 68
Shirley, Selina 48, 52
Shrewsbury branch hospital 169
Slave trade 3, 23, 24, 45
Smallpox 86, 131, 144, 145–146, 182
Somerset House 67
Somerset, Duchess of 48, 49
South Carolina 55
South Sea Company 38, 45, 61, 65, 112
Southwark 36–37
St Andrew's Charity school 82
St Andrew's Parish 150
St Thomas's Church 31
St Thomas's Hospital 7, 38
Staff 88–89

Tar Act 30, 32, 48, 119
Taunton, Massachusetts 1, 26–31, 99, 100
Tench, Francis 82
Tenterden, Lord 73
Thames, River 2, 4, 6, 17
Thynne, Frances 48, 52, 53
Tippling Act 9
Tokens 153–159
Torrington, Baron 51
Torrington, Dowager Baroness 48, 51
Treasurer (of the Foundling Hospital) 64, 67, 179
Treaty of Union 3

Trevor, Baroness 48
Trevor, Thomas 56
Trinity House 36
Tuberculosis 5, 102
Tufton, Isabella 50
Tufton, Mary 48, 55, 180
Typhus 5, 86, 186

Uniform (of the foundlings) 135–136

Vagabond Acts 11
Vaughan, Ann 48, 49
Vice-president (of the Foundling Hospital) 64, 65, 66

Wagner, Gillian xx
Walford, Edward 175
Walpole, Horace 33, 64
Walpole, Sir Robert 33, 45, 61, 62, **63**, 65
War of the Spanish Succession 44
Watson, Dr William 146, 178
Way, Lewis 67
Westerham branch hospital 172
Westminster Hospital 41, 105
Wet nursing 74, 91, 103–104, 105, 166
White, Taylor 69, 121
Wild, Jonathan 5
Winchilsea, Countess of 48, 52
Workhouses 128, 143, 191
Wren, Christopher 67

Dear Reader,

We hope you have enjoyed this book, but why not share your views on social media? You can also follow our pages to see more about our other products: facebook.com/penandswordbooks or follow us on X @penswordbooks

You can also view our products at www.pen-and-sword.co.uk (UK and ROW) or www.penandswordbooks.com (North America).

To keep up to date with our latest releases and online catalogues, please sign up to our newsletter at: www.pen-and-sword.co.uk/newsletter

If you would like a printed catalogue with our latest books, then please email: enquiries@pen-and-sword.co.uk or telephone: 01226 734555 (UK and ROW) or email: uspen-and-sword@casematepublishers.com or telephone: (610) 853-9131 (North America).

We respect your privacy and we will only use personal information to send you information about our products.

Thank you!